HISTORY OF THE INDIAN OCEAN

HISTORY OF THE INDIAN OCEAN

by

AUGUSTE TOUSSAINT

Translated by

JUNE GUICHARNAUD

The University of Chicago Press

Library of Congress Catalog Card Number: 65–20964
The University of Chicago Press, Chicago
Routledge & Kegan Paul Ltd.,
London, E.C.4, England

Translated from the French
HISTOIRE DE L'OCÉAN INDIEN
© *1961 Presses Universitaires de France*

English translation
© *1966 by The University of Chicago. All rights reserved*
Published 1966

Printed in Great Britain

Contents

CONTENTS

CONTENTS

CONTENTS

MAPS

Author's Preface
to the English Edition

IT is now nearly five years since this book was published for the first time in French, which is my mother tongue and the one in which I naturally prefer to write.

Since 1960 history has moved fast in the Indian Ocean area. I have expanded the chronology at the end to include the most significant happenings during these last five years, but I think it is too early yet to revise my views on the possibility of an Indian Ocean community. This is why I did not feel like rewriting the final pages and introducing a pessimistic note which China's aggression against India, the strained relations between Indonesia and Malaysia, and the Zanzibar affair might perhaps justify.

In the field of written history, too, things have kept moving and several recent publications have increased our knowledge of this part of the world. All those I could trace are listed in an addendum to the bibliography, but this, of course, lays no claim to exhaustiveness.

As will be seen, it includes, side by side with new contributions to oceanic history or to the history of countries in and around the Indian Ocean, new and revised editions of Indian Ocean 'classics'. This testifies to an increasing interest in this region, which is very gratifying.

Equally gratifying is the formation since 1960 of two international associations dedicated to the study of the past of the Indian Ocean.

The first international conference of South-East Asian historians took place in Singapore in January 1961. Its proceedings will be found in the 1961 issues of the *Journal of South-East Asian History*. The second one was held in August 1964 in Hong Kong and proved most fruitful.

The second meeting of the International Historical Association of the Indian Ocean—in which, as in the previous one, I took an active part—was held in Lourenço Marques in August 1962 in conjunction with the sixth session of the International Commission of Maritime History.

The proceedings of this joint gathering were published in a special issue of *Studia*, the organ of the Portuguese *Centro de Estudos Historicos Ultramarinos* in January 1963.

The present work being only a general outline, and no major fault having been found with it by historical critics, I saw no reason for making any substantial alterations to my original text for this English version.

What I felt bound to do was only to correct a few errors which were kindly brought to my notice by two eminent scholars, Professor C. Boxer, of the University of London, and Professor P. W. Coolhaas, of the University of Utrecht. Their help is gratefully acknowledged.

My greatest debt, however, is to Holden Furber and Elizabeth Chapin Furber of the University of Pennsylvania, who most kindly agreed to read this English version and made valuable suggestions. I am most grateful to Holden Furber for giving me the benefit of his knowledge of a region on which he is a well-known authority.

A. TOUSSAINT

Forest Side,
Mauritius.

Nächst dem Nordatlantischen Ozean hat kein Weltmeer auf die Entwicklung der menschlichen Kultur und Geschichte tiefere Einwirkungen ausgeübt als der Indische Ozean.

K. RODENBERG

I. A Neglected Ocean

IN the literature of oceans not much attention has been paid to the Indian Ocean—a fact easily ascertained by glancing through, for example, the bibliographical surveys published in the *American Neptune* since 1952 by Robert Greenhalgh Albion, Professor of Oceanic History at Harvard, the only university in the world, so far as I know, where this kind of history is taught. For oceanic history must not be confused with naval history, which, more often than not, is merely a chapter in maritime warfare. The former belongs rather to the realm which Braudel, in his magnificent study of the Mediterranean, suggests calling *geohistory*—that is, true retrospective human geography. Now that the character of this study has been made clear, we can go back to the Indian Ocean.

Of the few comprehensive works on the subject which so far exist—if we neglect the essays of Drygalski and Rodenberg, which are only short surveys, and Rogers' work, which is frankly bad—only some three books, all quite recent, are worth considering: those of Poujade (1946), Villiers (1952), and Auber (1954). Even so, the first is rather a study of naval archaeology than a general survey. Both Villiers, a sailor, and Auber, an orientalist, write very well, but neither of them is a historian. On geography, only one comprehensive work can be mentioned, that of Schott (1935). All these together would not take up much space in a library.

Such paucity is hardly an excuse for opinions such as the

following, found in a textbook purporting to be a serious work: 'the Mediterranean is the ocean of the past, the Atlantic the ocean of the present, and the Pacific, the ocean of the future.'[1] Not even a mention of the Indian Ocean!

Written history records nothing in the nature of seafaring expeditions earlier than the voyages of Egyptian sailors along the east coast of Africa at the beginning of the First Dynasty (c. 3000 B.C.). The Atlantic had scarcely begun to be explored when a seafarers' manual of the first century A.D. (the famous *Periplus of the Erythraean Sea*) described with extraordinary precision the world of the Indian Ocean.

Moreover, it was for the purpose of reaching the Indian Ocean and, beyond it, Asia and its treasures—not America, which was discovered only by chance—that Christopher Columbus undertook his famous journey. It was also in order to reach the Indian Ocean that Vasco da Gama and the Portuguese, choosing a more certain route than that taken by Columbus, launched out in the direction of the Cape of Good Hope.

It is undeniable that the Atlantic has had, since the formation of the United States—which means only since 1775— a preponderant place in history. Yet according to Toynbee, it was with da Gama's expedition that modern history really began. And contemporary or current history begins, in the opinion of many good historians, with an event that is closely concerned with the Indian Ocean: the opening of the Suez Canal.

As to the claim that the Pacific is the ocean of the future, nothing could be more debatable, for although the Pacific is indeed the youngest of the oceans, in the sense that it was the last to be explored, that fact alone affords no guarantee for its future. By similar reasoning, it might also just as well be affirmed, for example, that Europe is the continent of the past, America that of the present, and Australia that of the future.

The history of the Indian Ocean, in actual fact, is just beginning. We hope to show in this study that the events recorded up to the present provide merely the prelude to the main chapter, which has still to be written—an extraordinarily long prelude, since it has lasted almost five thousand years,

[1] O. W. Freeman (ed.), *Geography of the Pacific*, London, 1951, p. vii.

beginning with the Egyptian navigators of the First Dynasty. In the perspective of the history of recorded events, that is a long time; in the perspective of geohistory, it is a very short one.

2. THE ROLE OF THE ISLANDS

By what gateway shall we enter the Indian Ocean? What is the most favourable approach for considering it as a whole? Is the most usual route of entry, that by the Suez Canal, really the best? It puts us, no doubt, quickly in touch with the Arab world and leads us direct to India, but are the Red Sea and the Arabian Sea the best places from which to discover the ocean and, as it were, feel its heart-beat?

The Red Sea is a little world in itself, whose history is identified with that of the oldest civilisations of the globe, but still a world of rather limited horizons, and one that has always developed somewhat apart from the ocean. It is rather an extension of the Mediterranean than a gateway to the Indian Ocean. To cross the Arabian Sea from Aden to Bombay —a four days' voyage—is hardly enough to enable us really to feel the formidable breath of the monsoon in all its fullness, to appreciate the huge expanse of the Indian Ocean.

It is by the Cape route, da Gama's route, that the Indian Ocean should be approached, so that, like da Gama, we leave the coast of Africa in the neighbourhood of Mombasa and head straight for India. It is an unforgettable experience to sail out on the open sea near the Cape of Good Hope, either rounding it on a southern summer morning in clear weather, with a slack tide, or passing it on a midwinter night, tossed by the Cape rollers and lashed by the southwest wind. And it is by letting oneself be carried by the monsoon from Mombasa to Bombay or Colombo at any time between May and September that one can really appreciate all the power, all the grandeur of that seasonal event.

What is the best place from which to feel the ocean's life? Cape Comorin, at the tip of the Indian peninsula, or Colombo, or Galle on the island of Ceylon? In Ceylon we are almost at the very heart of the ocean. Here, surely, we hear its heart beating very close at hand. From Colombo to Galle—which for a long time was the principal port of Ceylon—the train skirts the sea for most of its journey, and the traveller, as from time to time he sees the outrigger canoes drawn up on the shore, finds himself imagining the many expeditions that must have left those shores to explore the ocean. In fact, such was not the case. The Sinhalese people never looked towards the sea, and the navigators whom history records were always foreigners. The outriggers are themselves of foreign origin, and it is not in Ceylon that we shall really comprehend the ocean's story. To grasp it fully, we must set sail for other, smaller islands.

About half-way between Ceylon and the eastern coast of Africa are three island groups with strange names: the Chagos group, the Séchelles group—which the English, for some obscure reason, insist on spelling Seychelles—and, much farther down, the Mascarene group. Though separated by hundreds of nautical miles and though there is still no generic name by which to refer to them, these three groups actually make up a distinct entity with common characteristics. The name of 'African Islands' often given them is not only too vague, since it covers also Madagascar, the Comoros, and other islands still closer to the African coast (Zanzibar, Pemba, Mafia, etc.), but is unsuitable in other ways, for these islands have nothing to do with Africa either historically or geographically. What is more, when we realise that their history has no relation to that of Asia or even of Madagascar, we must admit that we are dealing with an entity which is really *sui generis*.

What constitutes the striking uniqueness of this insular world is the fact that it is *'tout baigné des tendresses marines'* as the geographer Weulersse[2] so lyrically noted. Maritime stations from the very beginning, colonised in the seventeenth and eighteenth centuries to act as stepping-stones to the East, all these islands are truly born of the sea and for the sea. 'The sea, the warm and calm sea of the tropics', wrote Weulersse, 'is the brilliant backdrop against which the islands are seen.' It is here, to these islands, where maritime exploits have always been so important, that we must come to be initiated into the life of the Indian Ocean.

They have also the advantage of having kept almost all their special charm intact and of not turning to the traveller a face

[2] J. Weulersse, *L'Afrique noire*, Paris, 1951, p. 456.

made up with borrowed cosmetics, as is the case with most of the islands of the West Indies and the Pacific. Villiers rightly notes that in this respect that insular world is probably unique. The misfortune is that it is hardly known today. Villiers himself would seem to have seen only the Seychelles, whereas the most important group is that of the Mascarenes, one of which, Mauritius—the former Île de France—still bears the proud motto: *Stella clavisque maris Indici.*

Braudel has underlined the importance of islands in the history of the Mediterranean. Many of his comments would apply, point for point, to those of the Indian Ocean; and anyone who seeks to understand the history of that ocean should not neglect the islands—not only those quasi-continents that bear the names Australia, Madagascar, Sumatra, Java and Ceylon, but also, and perhaps especially, such tiny islands as the Mascarenes, the Seychelles, the Chagos, and even the Comoros, the Maldives, the Laccadives, the islands off the Arabian coast, and a few others.[3]

3. BOUNDARIES AND DIVISIONS

It may seem extraordinary that, after several centuries of exploration and scientific surveys, the boundaries of the oceans have not yet been satisfactorily determined, but such is the fact. Since Fleurieu first raised the question at the end of the eighteenth century, it has been discussed at many a learned congress, but no definitive decisions have yet been reached.

In 1879 it seemed that an important step towards a solution to the problem had been taken by Krummel. According to that geographer, there are in fact only three quite separate oceans: the Atlantic, the Pacific, and the Indian. He considered the Arctic and the Antarctic not as separate oceans but as mere extensions of these three. Krummel's point of view seemed for a time to demand recognition, but today it would seem that conjuring away the polar oceans is not so easy. At Bangalore,

---

[3] There is still no comprehensive work on the islands of the Indian Ocean comparable to O. L. Oliver, *The Pacific Islands*, Cambridge, Mass., Harvard University Press, 1951.

in 1951, a scientific society called the Pan-Indian Ocean Science Association was established to try to solve the problem with regard to the Indian Ocean, but its members have not yet managed to reach agreement.

There are still two opposing theses on the subject. One, starting from the work of Vallaux (1933), considers it as an ocean separated from the Antarctic, or Southern sea, by a line drawn at 35° south latitude. The other, based on the work of Schott (1935), includes the Southern sea in the Indian Ocean, whose southern limit would thus be the Antarctic continent. Nor has there been any agreement as to its eastern limits. Should the Timor and Arafura Seas, between Indonesia and Australia, be included in it? Some say Yes, others No.

Given the present state of confusion on the question, it is difficult to determine exactly the area of the Indian Ocean. Taking the estimates of Vallaux and Schott as a basis, we have, in the first case, an ocean of a mere 16,362,742 square miles; in the second, a *gross Ozean* of 30,095,723 square miles. One point, at any rate, is clear: even in its largest dimensions, the Indian Ocean is the smallest of the world's oceans, a little smaller than the Atlantic, and much smaller than the vast Pacific. But everything is relative, and compared with the Mediterranean, that inland sea on the scale of man, it appears gigantic.

One further point is evident from a comparison of the oceans: the Indian Ocean's symmetry. Whereas the Atlantic resembles an S-shaped corridor and the Pacific has roughly circular shape, the Indian Ocean calls to mind an inverted W, a vast gulf with two branches, one formed by the Arabian Sea, the other by the Bay of Bengal, separated by the head of the Indian peninsula and each covering an area almost equal to that of Europe.

These harmonious proportions make it possible to single out, in the Indian Ocean, at least four separate seas, which, moreover, have been identified since classical antiquity. Indeed, for the ancients the actual Indian Ocean (*Indikon pelagos*) was limited to the waters round the coast of India. The western part of the ocean, round Arabia and along the African coast to the island of Menouthias (the modern Pemba), was called the Erythraean Sea (*Erythraeum mare*) or Red Sea, with its two principal arms, the Persian Gulf and the Sinus Arabicus (today the Red Sea), not to mention the secondary subdivisions. The eastern part formed the Gulf of the Ganges, or simply the Great Gulf. The southernmost part of the ocean, which extended beyond a line drawn from Cape Delgado to the farthest shores of the Great Gulf, passing in the vicinity of Ceylon, was known as the *Mare Prasodum*, or Green Sea.

Of these four seas, the ancients had a good knowledge of only the first three—that is, only the northern half of the ocean. As for its southern half, formed by the *Mare Prasodum*, although the Arabs and Chinese pushed out into it hardly enough on a few occasions towards the end of the first millennium A.D., its history does not really begin until much later, with the voyage of da Gama in 1498.

From a historical point of view, therefore, the divisions of the ocean might be reduced to two: to the north of the equator an 'ancient' region well known to Mediterranean and Eastern sailors, and to the south a 'modern' region explored for barely five hundred years by European navigators from the Atlantic.

Yet we must be careful not to over-simplify by considering these two regions, as Auber does, as two distinct worlds, which he suggests calling the 'world of Cancer' and the 'world of Capricorn' respectively, opposing them one to the other. Such opposition is clearly prompted by the East-West dichotomy. But while the dichotomy cannot be denied today, we must at the same time remember that it is a recent phenomenon, going back little beyond the beginning of the nineteenth century.

Auber's thesis is acceptable only if it can be established that the world of Cancer and the world of Capricorn constitute two units, each possessing a solid entity forged by common traditions and ideas; and nothing is more open to doubt. Despite appearances, there is indeed reason to think, as we shall see later, that each of these two worlds is very divided, and that they interpenetrate to such a degree that it is difficult to draw a clear line between them.

We must also be on our guard against certain divisions of recent date conveyed in terms currently very much in fashion, such as 'Middle East' and 'South-east Asia', divisions based far more on strategic considerations than on historical and

7

geographical reality.[4] Without denying that the regions so designated possess today a certain social and political unity, such divisions can hardly be taken into account in a historical study; they are far too recent and artificial.

The only valid divisions in this connection are the natural ones based on the simplest elements that constitute the Indian Ocean. From whatever point of view this question be considered, these elements are four in number: first, the ocean itself; next, the African shore; third, the Asiatic shore extending to the East Indies; and finally, the islands scattered over the ocean's expanse, whose role has been indicated above.

Let it be said immediately that these 'simple' elements are in reality not so simple. We should introduce here, as Braudel did for the Mediterranean, the idea of 'confines', and show that the Levant on the one hand, and the Far East on the other, can also be considered part of the Indian Ocean. The truth is that in history there are no absolutely simple elements.

4. THE MONSOON

We do not propose at this stage to describe the regions of the Indian Ocean. We shall come back to them as we relate how they came into history. For the moment we shall keep to a few general ideas on the ocean itself, taken from the facts of physical geography.

And firstly its basically tropical character, which makes it free from fog, mist, drift ice, and other conditions apt to interfere with navigation.

The fact that it is open towards one pole only, whereas the Atlantic and Pacific are open from one pole to the other, gives it also a special pattern of wind, marked by the phenomenon of the monsoon, very favourable to navigation, or rather to a certain kind of navigation.

The word monsoon (Arabic *mausim*) in no way implies the idea of a wind storm. It originally meant 'market' or 'feast', and in India (whence the Europeans adopted it), 'season',

---

[4] For 'Middle East' see the introduction to W. B. Fisher, *The Middle East*, 3rd edn., London, 1956, and for 'South-east Asia', B. Harrison, *South-east Asia*, 2nd edn., London, 1955. While trying to justify the use of these terms, both writers admit that neither of them designates a natural entity.

the monsoon being an essentially seasonal phenomenon occurring at fixed periods. A description of its working would be out of place here, for this study is not meant to take the place of an oceanographic manual. We would mention only that there are two monsoons, the north-east or winter monsoon, which blows from India towards eastern Africa from October to April, and the south-west or summer monsoon, which blows in the opposite direction from June to September. The first is normally dry, the second rainy. The latter is always impatiently awaited in India, for it brings much-needed water.

Revealed for the first time, we are told—for nothing could be less certain—to Mediterranean navigators by a Greek of the first century B.C., the phenomenon of the monsoon was known much earlier to Eastern sailors, who based their plans for coming and going on its variations. The two monsoons are not equally favourable to navigation, and sailors used almost exclusively the winter one. It was also the monsoon that drove da Gama towards the coast of India, and during the age of sail it had a major influence on the movement of shipping in the ocean.

Though generally beneficent, the monsoon can bring about disaster. In India it sometimes unleashes fearful floods. And the reversal of monsoons, when one follows another, is often accompanied by violent cyclones in the Arabian Sea and in the Bay of Bengal.

In the region of the equator the Indian Ocean is regularly swept by other winds as well: the trades and the antitrades. The former, which blow to the north of the equator, are favourable winds, whence their name. The antitrades, which blow in the southern hemisphere, cause cyclones and storms, especially in the vicinity of Madagascar.

Despite its cyclones and storms, the Indian Ocean remains, in the opinion of sailors, the kindest of all the oceans, that on which ships have always been least buffeted by the elements. Furthermore, it is the only ocean still used in certain regions by rather fragile craft which would not hold out for long in the Atlantic or the Pacific. On the other hand, any wooden ship must reckon here with those tiny marine creatures which gnaw the hull and quickly transform it into a sieve, if the wood is not sufficiently resistant. In these seas oak, for example, is useless for

9

hulls. The only wood capable of resisting these terrible animalcules is teak, or 'stinking wood', which fortunately nature has provided in abundance in India, Burma, and a few other countries of the Indian Ocean.

5. THE MARE PRASODUM

Continuing the comparison with the other oceans, we may also note an absence in the Indian of very marked currents such as the Gulf Stream of the Atlantic and its counterpart in the Pacific. Yet the Indian Ocean is crossed from east to west by a south-equatorial current coming from the Pacific, which leaves the Timor Sea between Australia and Indonesia, ending up at the Mozambique Channel between east Africa and Madagascar. This current explains the presence in Madagascar of a race of Indonesian extraction, whose ancestors in olden times were driven by it towards the island. However, this extraordinary adventure is an exception, unique in the annals of the ocean. The great south-equatorial current never became a 'royal way', as Auber noted, and maritime trade was always carried on along the coasts, the sailors preferring to trust to the play of the winds, which they knew well, rather than to that of the waters, which they knew very little. Besides, nothing spurred them on to cross the ocean from one end to the other, since there was no large body of land to attract them, the central part of the *Mare Prasodum* being filled with insignificant atolls which, in addition, formed dangerous reefs. For navigators the true centre of the Indian Ocean has always been the country whence it takes its name—India, for more than 2000 years El Dorado of the ancient world,[5] before it became that of the Portuguese conquistadores and their modern successors.

Even after da Gama had opened the gateway of the Cape into the *Mare Prasodum*, about a century and a half elapsed before European navigators dared to cross the southernmost part of that sea. Australia, whose existence was not even suspected, except perhaps by the Chinese, was not really explored and colonised until the eighteenth century. Even today, very few

---

[5] El Dorado of the ancients, however, comprised the entire region today called South-east Asia, and it was in fact to the Malay Peninsula that they gave the name *Chryse* (the Golden).

sailors cross that part of the ocean, and it is only recently that air communcations have been established between South Africa and Australia, whereas all the countries situated north of the equator had already been linked by air for some time.[6]

Although the year 1498 marks a very important era in the history of the ocean and even in that of the world, one point must be emphasised: the discovery of the Cape route did not *immediately* influence, in any perceptible way, the movement of shipping in the Indian Ocean. For a long time navigation continued to take the peripheral routes it had followed for centuries. The maritime revolution—for as we shall see, it was indeed a real revolution—presaged by the opening of the Cape route did not come about until so much later that some writers tend to place the beginning of the modern era in the Indian Ocean as late as the nineteenth century—that is, three centuries after da Gama's discovery. It seems not unreasonable, then, to say that the history of the Indian Ocean is only just beginning.

These few basic facts having been indicated, are we sufficiently informed about the Indian Ocean and the elements that go to make up its main features? How can we make such a claim when so many questions have yet to be asked. If a Braudel, at the end of his monumental work on the Mediterranean—a work that took twenty years—admits that he is not yet satisfied, must not the imperfections and lacunae of this study indeed be evident! How can one help but be terrified at tackling so vast and complex a subject, were it not for the knowledge that history is made up of approximations, that only so can a subject be grasped, bit by bit, its distinctive features painstakingly brought out, and that, in Goethe's words, 'error exists to enhance the truth'.

---

[6] The first air crossings of a great expanse of sea in this region were made by Dutch KLM planes between Java and Mauritius (3,462 miles nonstop) in 1949. Thereafter, a regular service between Australia and Africa via the Cocos and Mauritius was inaugurated by Qantas Airways in 1952.

II. Punt and Ophir

THE beginnings of navigation most assuredly go back to protohistory, and it would seem impossible to say in what region of the globe the first skiffs appeared or in what shape they were fashioned. In this realm we shall be forever limited to conjecture. By the same token, to try to establish the role of such boats in the earliest manifestations of human navigation seems an extremely risky undertaking, belonging much more to ethnography than to history. So far very little is known of the migrations themselves; they still belong to a realm where hypotheses and myths abound. Yet we may mention, for curiosity's sake, the extraordinary bit of nonsense which a notary called Jules Hermann, whose hobby was archaeology, devoted to the origins of the Indian Ocean in two volumes entitled *Les Révélations du grand océan.*

Without going back as he did to the obscure ages of Lemuria, we shall simply begin our account of navigation in the Indian Ocean with the period about 2300 B.C., when in the Egypt of the Pharaohs there lived a certain coquette whose importance with regard to the subject under discussion was shown by Paul Herrmann (who has nothing in common with the Hermann already mentioned).

The archaeologists who opened the tomb of the lady in question found there, still intact, among other objects of feminine use, a small box of rouge which on chemical analysis was found to contain antimony. Now we know that the antimony mines in Iran, Asia Minor, and North Africa were not discovered or exploited until well after the lady's death. We also know that the only other region of Africa rich in antimony is situated on the east coast, near the mouth of the Zambesi; and we know that the Egyptians in very early times sent maritime expeditions to an ill-defined region called in their annals 'the land of Punt'. From this Paul Herrmann concludes that Punt is no other than the present Mozambique. Is he right? Most writers who have studied the question do not situate the mysterious country of Punt so far south as this, but rather on the Somali coast.

One thing is certain; voyages to Punt began very early and were very numerous. Maspero, who was the first to study them, traced them back only to the Eleventh Dynasty (2100–2000 B.C.), but Breasted, who came after him and whose authority is even greater, thought he could affirm that relations with Punt had existed since the First Dynasty, which began about 2900 B.C. Under the Fourth, Fifth, and Sixth Dynasties—that is, from 2650 to 2200—there were again several expeditions to Punt. The Egyptian annals even give quite precise figures about the products brought back by one of those expeditions sent by the Pharaoh Sahure (2958–2946). From the Seventh to the Tenth Dynasty (2200–2100) no mention is made of voyages to Punt, the Pharaohs then having been busy with land expeditions, but they began again under the Eleventh Dynasty (2100–2000), and are then mentioned continuously until the Twentieth (1200–1090).

2. THE BAS-RELIEFS OF DEIR EL-BAHARI

Two very different accounts of these voyages have survived. The first is a tale called 'The Story of the Shipwrecked Sailor', which somewhat recalls Sindbad the Sailor's adventures in the *Arabian Nights*. It tells of a sailor who had taken off for the country of Punt and was shipwrecked on an island which may have been Socotra. There he came upon an enormous serpent, which, after having made as if to devour him, ended by taking pity on him and furnished him with the means to return to Egypt with a rich cargo. The second account engraved in stone on the walls of the temple of Deir el-Bahari near Thebes, refers to an authentic expedition organised by queen Hatshepsut in 1493, in the Eighteenth Dynasty (1580–1350).

What is perhaps most interesting in the frescoes of Deir el-Bahari—which have been the object of many studies—is the portrayal of a procession in which we see the king and queen of Punt bringing their country's products to the leader of the expedition. The queen of Punt is shown as a steatopygous woman who might well be of Hottentot race. Paul Herrmann makes much of this detail, and sees it as a further proof of the fact that Punt was far lower down on the African coast than archaeologists in general locate it. But was the woman really of the Hottentot race?

What could have been the motive for the expeditions to Punt? The search for gold and incense, most certainly. The Pharaohs, those great builders, were always in search of gold to finance their gigantic works. As for incense, Egypt consumed enormous quantities of it in religious services, the preparation of mummies, and for medical purposes. It was therefore natural for the rulers of Egypt, after they had exhausted the gold mines of the eastern desert of Upper Egypt and had long bought incense at fabulous prices from the tribes of the Hadhramaut, to have been led to send for such products to far-off countries: the island of Socotra, Abyssinia, and even Mozambique.

The strongest objection that has been made with regard to these voyages is the following. As sailors accustomed to fresh water and the river navigation of the Nile, the Egyptians had only boats made of reeds, which were incapable of crossing great distances on the high seas. Villiers, himself a sailor, is absolutely categorical on the subject, and even goes so far as to think that the representations in the Deir el-Bahari frescoes are imaginary.

It is true that papyrus, originally the only material that the Egyptians possessed, would have provided only rather mediocre ships; but it is equally true that they procured wood at a very early period, first from the nearby peninsula of Sinai, whence they also got copper, then from the Phoenician coast (the present Syria), at Byblos, where they found cedar, an excellent wood which made the construction of sturdy ships possible.

The first expedition to Byblos to obtain wood dates back to

2640 B.C., under the Pharaoh Sneferu. Their relations with the Phoenicians and Cretans, the two great maritime peoples of the ancient Mediterranean, gave the Egyptians the benefit of very useful nautical experience. Finally, since navigation to Punt did not involve crossing the high seas, it did not call for especially large ships. Wooden vessels of about 100 feet long, with a displacement of from 80 to 85 metric tons and designed for propulsion by oars or sails, such as those portrayed on the walls of Deir el-Bahari, were well suited to coastal navigation, which meant moving forward by small stages.

It cannot, therefore, be said that the Egyptians practised only river navigation. Perhaps they lacked that wanderlust, that taste for adventure and exploration so characteristic of the Cretans and Phoenicians, but nothing could show their interest in maritime navigation more clearly than the Pharaohs' efforts to link the Red Sea to the Mediterranean by a canal, first attempted during the reign of queen Hatshepsut (1490–1475). Another effort was made in the seventh century by the Pharaoh Necho II, and the project was finally carried out by Darius, king of Persia, in the following century.

Egyptian navigation, however, had a purely utilitarian objective, and was in no way similar to voyages of exploration. It does not appear that the Egyptians ever tried, for example, to establish any regular contact by sea with the contemporary civilisations of Mesopotamia or of the Indus valley. Since the end of the prehistoric era there had certainly been an exchange of influence between the Egyptian civilisation and that of Sumer, but from the little we know about it even today, it would be impossible to say that any really important contacts existed.

In any case, we must unquestionably consider as legend the supposed conquest of the Arabian Sea by a fleet of four hundred ships equipped by the Pharaoh Sesostris (whose real name was Khakhepere Senusret II, and who ruled from 2115 to 2099 B.C.). Egypt was not really to enter into history until much later, during the Hellenistic period.

3. SUMERIANS AND SABAEANS

It may be presumed that the Sumerians, whose period of greatness lasted from 2850 to 1900 B.C.,[1] began to navigate the Persian Gulf almost at the same time that the Egyptians launched out into the Red Sea towards Punt. The first mention of Sumerian ships there occurs in the reign of Sargon I (2637–2582). We also know that his successor, Naram-Sin (2557–2520), sent maritime expeditions against a country called in Sumerian inscriptions sometimes Magan and sometimes Melukhkha. According to Sir Arnold Wilson, these names indicate the coast of Oman in eastern Arabia.

In the reign of Gudea (*c.* 2420) there is again some mention of produce brought back by ships that the king had sent to Magan, Melukhkha, Gubi, Niduk-Ki, and other countries whose names are not given, which might indicate that the ships in question went farther than the coast of Oman, but this is highly doubtful. We likewise know almost nothing of the vessels used for this early navigation, as the oldest portrayals of ships in the Mesopotamian region date only from the period of the Assyrian king Sennacherib (704–681).

Like the Nile Valley, the Tigris and Euphrates region is devoid of large trees. The boats that sailed on those rivers were basket boats or rafts on inflated skins, made of planks set edge to edge and animal skins, materials unsuitable for the construction of seagoing vessels. For coastal navigation in the Persian Gulf the Sumerians used a type of boat represented on a seal cylinder of the beginning of the third millennium. In profile it resembled a slightly flattened crescent; the bow and the stern rose up like gigantic horns, sometimes crumpled at the ends.

It is therefore hardly probable that there was a Sumerian fleet for trading round Arabia with the western countries by way of the Red Sea. It was not until later, when Assyria was at the height of its power under Sennacherib (704–681) and Ashurbanipal (668–626) that those sovereigns built up a fleet with the help of the Phoenicians.

Of the maritime activity of the actual inhabitants of Arabia during the Sumerian era we know absolutely nothing. Hourani,

---

[1] For Sumerian chronology we have followed Breasted, but his figures remain debatable.

who has exhaustively studied Arabian navigation from its very beginnings, has only this to say on the subject:

> in view of the flourishing condition of the Minaeans and Sabaeans in the first millennium, and in the light of what can be learned of their nautical activity in Hellenistic times, it is a sound conjecture that Arabs were playing some part in the sea-faring life of their times for many centuries before Alexander.[2]

Obviously, this tells us little.

The Minaean kingdom was in the western part of the Arabian peninsula, along the Red Sea, with Karna as its principal city. At first, from about 1200 to 650 B.C., the Minaeans co-existed with the Sabaeans, who inhabited the legendary kingdom of Sheba, in the south of Arabia, whose queen visited Solomon (1 Kings x). They exported incense by caravan at the same time as they brought in spices from India by way of the sea. Their capital was Marib. According to Hitti, their era runs from about 650 to 115 B.C. Their successors were the Himyarites, whose era of greatness began about 115 B.C. and lasted until A.D. 340. We shall hear of them again later.

4. THE DRAVIDIANS OF MOHENJO-DARO

What part did the Dravidians[3] of Mohenjo-Daro in the Indus valley play in early ocean navigation? This ancient Dravidian civilisation, which was at its height in about 2600 B.C., has caused much ink to flow. Some writers see it as the source of a so-called 'proto-Indo-Mediterranean culture'. Father Heras, the main champion of this thesis, goes so far as to say that it was a phenomenon of expansion towards the west comparable to the Indian expansion in the eastern region of the Indian Ocean during the first centuries A.D. This is not impossible, although agreement on Fr. Heras' thesis is far from unanimous, but there is nothing to indicate, in any case, that this expansion took the maritime route.[4]

---

[2] George F. Hourani, *Arab Seafaring in the Indian Ocean in Ancient and Early Medieval Times*, Princeton, 1951, p. 11.

[3] The word Dravidian should perhaps be in quotation marks, for archaeologists are not all agreed on the subject of the founders of the Mohenjo-Daro civilisation.

[4] Father H. Heras, S.J., who died recently, was the founder and director of the Indian Historical Research Institute at Saint Xavier's College, Bombay.

The origins of Indian navigation have been carefully studied by Kennedy and by an Indian scholar, Dr. Mookerji, in a work that was republished in Bombay in 1957. The early relations between ancient Indian and Sumer have also been the object of a recent study by another Indian scholar, Dr. Pandya. The works of these three writers make it clear that the first direct evidence of maritime relations between India and Mesopotamia goes back no further than the first millennium B.C.

Of all the evidence the most convincing is, to all appearances, that of the *Baveru-Jataka*, which mentions a maritime trade as existing in the sixth century B.C. between Bharukacha (today Broach), Surparaka (Suppara) on the coast of Gujarat, and Baveru (Babylon). Nineveh, the third capital of Assyria, is also mentioned in the *Puranas* as Shonitapur, along with the race of the Asuras (Assyrians) and their king, Asura-Bana (Ashurbanipal).

Kennedy's conclusions, as cited by Mookerji, are as follows:

> The evidence warrants us in the belief that maritime commerce between India and Babylon flourished in the 7th and 6th, but more especially in the 6th, centuries B.C. It was chiefly in the hands of Dravidians, although Aryans had a share in it; and as Indian traders settled afterwards in Arabia and on the east coast of Africa and as we find them settling at this very time on the coast of China, we cannot doubt that they had their settlements in Babylon also.[5]

But here we are back in the sixth century B.C., very far indeed from the civilisation of Mohenjo-Daro, which had then been long extinct.

From all that has been said, we may conclude that before the first millennium B.C., the only really noteworthy expeditions in the Indian Ocean were the Egyptians' voyages to Punt. It is clear that the ocean did not play a great part at the beginning of the first known civilisations, those of Egypt, Sumer, and Mohenjo-Daro, and that these three civilisations were above all continental in nature. It was the Phoenicians, a people foreign to the Indian Ocean, a people from the Mediterranean, who were to give, for the first time, some width of scope to the hitherto modest maritime exchanges between the principal countries of the ocean.

[5] R. K. Mookerji, *Indian Shipping*, Bombay, 1957, p. 62.

5. THE PHOENICIANS IN OPHIR

A mysterious people, the Phoenicians: 'With regard to the history of Phoenicia, European scholars are still in the same situation as they were with respect to the history of Egypt and Babylonia before the discovery of hieroglyphic and cuneiform inscriptions.'[6] This comment, made in 1925 by the Russian orientalist Barthold, is still valid, and the Phoenician mystery is yet unsolved.

On the activity of the Phoenicians in the Mediterranean the reader might profitably consult Poujade's study already mentioned. As long as the Cretan thalasocracy lasted (1750–1450 B.C.), the Phoenicians played a rather minor part. The decline of the Cretans, coinciding with that of the Hittites in Asia Minor, gave the Phoenicians a magnificent opportunity to take the lead in the eastern Mediterranean and soon after throughout the inland sea. Following the Cretans' example, they did not attempt conquest, but did in fact succeed in securing, by peaceful means, the command of the seas known at that time. Their success was all the more noteworthy in that Phoenicia was never a united state, but was made up of a group of cities and ports held together by rather loose ties: Byblos, Beirut, Sidon, Tyre, and Acre.

The Phoenicians' first appearance in the Indian Ocean is connected with the creation of the port of Ezion-geber at the head of the Gulf of 'Aqaba, on the Red Sea, by King Solomon (973–933 B.C.). The only other important port on the Red Sea at that time was Kosseir, on the Egyptian coast, where the vessels going to Punt set sail. Ezion-geber was a gateway to the 'India' of that time—that is, to the land of Punt. But a port was not enough; ships also were needed, and the Israelites, with no maritime tradition, were incapable of building them. Solomon had thus no alternative but to seek an alliance with Phoenicia.

Why did the Phoenicians agree to work for Solomon? No doubt because they intended to use his information about Punt —which he himself had obtained from Egypt—so as to trade there later on their own account. The fact is that they agreed

[6] V. Barthold, *La Découverte de l'Asie*, Paris, 1947, p. 54.

to build him a 'navy', and in 945 they took it to a region referred to in the Bible (1 Kings x) as Ophir, from which they brought back 'gold, and silver, ivory, and apes, and peacocks'.

The biblical tale speaks of Ophir and not of Punt, but, according to Paul Herrmann, both names designate the same region, which he situates on the coast of Mozambique. This is a hypothesis. Others identify Ophir with certain regions of Arabia, India, Ceylon, or Malaya. In all these hypotheses philology plays a great part, and although the method is not to be disdained, we must sometimes be on guard against the parallels it suggests. Suppara, on the coast of India, is as much like Ophir as Sofala, on the coast of Africa, to give but one example.

6. QUESTIONABLE EVIDENCE

Those who, with Herrmann, lean towards an African localisation of the biblical Ophir claim to have more than vague assonances to support their view. First is the presence, around the gold-bearing zone of Mozambique, at a place called Zimbabwe—today in Southern Rhodesia—of extraordinary ruins, which several archaeologists have agreed to consider as the work of Phoenicians. There was also the discovery at the beginning of this century, at Macequece in Mozambique, of a stone bearing mysterious signs, of which two at least correspond to Phoenician-type letters of the tenth century B.C. In the third place, there was the circumnavigation of Africa from east to west by Phoenicians in the seventh century B.C., recorded by Herodotus—an exploit which, if authentic, would indicate that they were then quite familiar with the east coast of Africa.

One of the latest works on Zimbabwe is that of Paver, who excellently summarises all the earlier works, starting with the German explorers Mauch and Merensky, the first to describe these extraordinary ruins. We learn from his book that after having been long considered definitive, the hypothesis of a Phoenician origin for Zimbabwe has been seriously challenged first by MacIver in 1906, and more recently by Miss Caton-Thompson in 1929. The former dates Zimbabwe from about the fourteenth century A.D., and the latter between the ninth and tenth centuries; both claim that it is of Bantu origin.

The method of atomic dating by carbon-14, applied in 1952 to a wooden lintel from a wall in Zimbabwe, poses a new riddle, for it established the date of the lintel as about the year A.D. 590. Now at that time the Bantu had not yet reached the region around Zimbabwe. But if the carbon-14 test demolishes the theory of Zimbabwe's Bantu origin, it likewise unquestionably overthrows that of its Phoenician origin; and those who are seeking to clear up the mystery of the ruins of Rhodesia are now turning towards Abyssinia.

The Macequece stone is obviously a document to be remembered, but even so we must be certain that the signs it bears are indeed Phoenician characters. But only two of these signs are really identifiable. In various parts of the world inscriptions have been found which have been taken to be Phoenician, though it would be impossible definitely to guarantee their authenticity. To keep to the Indian Ocean, there have recently been found on a rocky wall near Fianarantsoa, in Madagascar, signs which some believe to be Phoenician-type characters, though unfortunately they have greatly deteriorated. But an official geological report on these rock inscriptions states that they are simply due to erosion.

As for the circumnavigation of Africa, which, according to Herodotus, the Phoenicians accomplished about 600 B.C., in the reign of the Pharaoh Necho II—the same who had tried to cut a 'Suez Canal'—quite as many writers are disposed to contest as to accept it. The main arguments of both sides are well summarised in a few pages of Cary and Warmington's classic work on the explorers of antiquity. We shall therefore not consider them here, but will cite only a few arguments of two more recent writers, who have also taken up a stand on this question.

The first, Hourani, is absolutely against the event reported by Herodotus—who, it must be emphasised, asserted that he did not believe it himself. A circumnavigation of that kind, says Hourani, covering a distance of some 16,000 miles, would have been the longest sea voyage made before the fifteenth century A.D.; and if it had really taken place, it should have given the ancients definite information on the shape of Africa. But we know that they always believed that Africa was continued to the south by a southern continent completely enclosing the Indian Ocean.

The second, Paul Herrmann, whom we shall cite again, accepts Herodotus' account as true, and for the following reasons. Necho *knew* that the circumnavigation of Africa was possible, and he could only have obtained that knowledge from previous voyages to Punt-Ophir. If we take into account the current that is prevalent in the Mozambique channel, it is highly possible that had sailors entered that channel, situated directly south of the Zambesi, they would have been forced to return to the mouth of the Nile, by going round Africa. In organising the seventh-century periplus, Necho was thus doing no more than renewing a very ancient tradition. And the reason that the periplus passed almost unnoticed was that it had taken place too early for Necho's contemporaries to realise just how important it was. All this is very plausible; but is it true?

7. A WELL-KEPT SECRET

Whether or not they sailed round Africa, it is probable that the Phoenicians carried their navigation far into the Indian Ocean. Even those who think that Ophir should be placed on the coast of Africa rather than in Asia must agree that Phoenician maritime activity reached the Asian coast as well. Indeed, we learn from the Assyrian tablets, that King Sennacherib employed Phoenicians to build and man a war fleet, which he used to exterminate the dwellers along the Arabian coast of the Persian Gulf, who had rebelled against him. It would therefore seem probable that once the Phoenicians reached the Persian Gulf, they began to explore it as they explored the Red Sea, and that they no doubt finally made contact with the people of Gujarat, whence, as we have seen, a flow of trade had begun to be established with Mesopotamia in the sixth century B.C. It does not appear, however, that the Phoenicians ever tried to set up settlements along the coast of Gujarat; in any case, no trace of them has yet been found. On the other hand, Jews were deported to that coast by the Assyrian kings, probably on the fall of the kingdom of Israel in 555 B.C. Their descendants still live in that region of India, where they were known as *Bene-Israël*.

Phoenician navigation in the Indian Ocean continued from the tenth to the seventh century B.C., from the reign of King Solomon of Israel to that of the Egyptian king Necho II—that is, for four hundred years. Although we possess only scraps of information concerning those four hundred years of maritime activity, is it credible that so long a period, beginning with voyages to Punt-Ophir and ending gloriously, as it were, with so remarkable an exploit as the circumnavigation of Africa, was not marked by other voyages equally worthy of interest? And when we reflect on the passage in which Strabo calls the Phoenicians 'philosophers of the science of astronomy and arithmetic', how can we suppose that they had not, during those four centuries, observed the phenomenon of the monsoon and made use of it?

If on the other hand, such was the case—if, as many writers are inclined to believe, the Phoenicians really explored so many areas of the ocean—how is it that no trace of those explorations has survived? Should not this lack of evidence be seen rather as the proof of a systematic determination jealously to protect a monopoly? We know that later the Portuguese acted in precisely this way, keeping silent about their discoveries and even intentionally spreading false information. All that we know of the Phoenicians leads us to believe that the obscurity which now covers their maritime activities was deliberate.

But although students of ancient monuments remain almost silent on the subject of the Phoenicians, the same need not be said for naval archaeologists. Poujade, who examined the question from a technical point of view, thinks that the Phoenicians' great discovery in naval construction was a type of boat whose lower part was a dugout canoe hewn from large Lebanese cedars and its upper part a planking of boards increasing the height of the dugout. The existence of boats of this type was revealed to us by an Assyrian bas-relief from Sennacherib's palace in Kuyinjik, dating from the middle of the seventh century B.C. Boats of the same type have also been found in various regions of the Indian Ocean, especially in Ceylon, as well as in the Atlantic, in a region of Senegal which the Phoenicians also visited.

The other Phoenician boats were fairly similar to the vessels of Punt portrayed on the walls of the temple of Deir el-Bahari, with the difference that they were decked, were squatter, and used sails exclusively, whereas the Egyptian vessels were designed to permit the use of both oars and sails. Nor were the Phoenician ships quite as long, never exceeding 100 feet, with a width of 26 to 33 feet, and an 8-foot draught, and consequently of about 400 tons burden. They had only one sail, of some 360 square yards, and a crew of about thirty men. Save in a few particulars, this is a prefiguration of the Portuguese caravel of the fifteenth century.[7] Why then should the Phoenicians not have tried what the Portuguese themselves attempted with their caravels?

Clearly, all this proves nothing. The Phoenician mystery still remains insoluble, and it is with the Greeks, who came after the Phoenicians, that all the textbooks of historical geography persist in making geography itself begin, and will continue to do so until the day when a Phoenician sea-manual or some other such lucky find is discovered, thus perhaps causing the whole matter to be taken up afresh.

8. THE VOYAGE OF SCYLAX

Before we come to the Greeks, we must not overlook the Medes and the Persians, who flourished from about 500 to 330 B.C.—that is, between the fifth and the third centuries. Apropos of these peoples, whom the classical tradition, based on Greek sources, called barbarians, it must be recalled that Herodotus himself reacted against that tradition. For a truer idea of them, we may go to Ghirshman's remarkable work on Iranian civilisation.

The Persians, descended from a branch of the Aryan people settled on the central plateau of Iran, were originally under Assyrian domination. They threw off the yoke in 550, under a leader named Cyrus, who after having crushed the Assyrian power, soon replaced it by a Persian empire which was to stretch from the Indus to the Mediterranean, from the Caucasus to the shores of the Indian Ocean. Cambyses, his son (530–521 B.C.), extended his conquests to Egypt, which had been declining since 674 and had also fallen under the Assyrian yoke.

[7] For a comparison between the Phoenician and Egyptian ships, see J. de La Varende, *La Navigation sentimentale*, Paris, 1952, pp. 42–44.

Darius I (521–485), who succeeded him, gave the Persian empire its definitive structure, which was to subsist until its collapse under the blows of Alexander the Great in the year 331 B.C.

If we compare the Persian *imperium* to the Assyrian *imperium* which had preceded it and to those of the Arabs and the Turks which were to follow it, we must agree that it was still the best— or at any rate, the least bad—of the three. Under Persian dominion, Western Asia for the first time experienced peace and prosperity and reached an unprecedented degree of development. The Persians, too, gave the world the first great monotheistic religion apart from that of the Jews, based on the teachings of a prophet and derived from reasoning clear— religion in remarkable contrast with the rather crude animism of the other peoples of that time, Oriental and Mediterranean, the Greeks included.

From the point of view of maritime history, the interest of the Persian *imperium* lies in the fact that it aimed at exploiting sea as well as land routes, to ensure communication between the Orient and the Occident. Situated as it was between the East and the West, the Persian realm must indeed have appeared to its masters as the possible centre of a universal empire. Hence their attempt to subjugate the eastern Mediterranean and, along with it, Greece. The failure of this attempt at Salamis, far from turning the Persians away from the sea, was on the contrary to incite them to seek compensation on the ocean.

A mountain people, ignorant of things maritime, the Persians, like the Assyrians, had necessarily to appeal first to the Phoenicians, who served them faithfully on the sea as they had served Sennacherib, and then to the Greeks themselves. And it was to a Greek sailor, not to a Phoenician, that Darius I entrusted the direction of the first great Persian maritime expedition about 510 B.C.

The object of that expedition, undertaken by Darius after his conquest of the Indus valley, was to establish a maritime link betwen India and Egypt. The Greek who directed it, named Scylax, was the first European to sail in the Indian Ocean. Why did Darius go to a Greek rather than to a Phoenician? Herodotus, to whom we owe the story, does not tell us. He gives only concise details about the voyage of Scylax, whose own report is no longer in existence. Setting sail from Kaspapyrus (probably Kasyapapura) on the Indus, Scylax, after two-and-a-half years, arrived at Arsinoë, in the Gulf of Suez, where Darius, who had taken the land route, was awaiting him.

The length of the voyage, especially if we take into account the fact that the Persian Gulf was not explored, indicates that it was carried out in small stages and without haste. Scylax must therefore have had plenty of time to inquire about the places he reached and the customs of the inhabitants of the southern coast of Arabia. But the information he brought back contributed little to a wider knowledge of Arabia. Nor did his report result in the conquest of that country; indeed, to ward off such a possibility, the Arabs offered to pay Darius a certain amount of incense yearly, a tribute with which Darius had to be content.

On the other hand, the success of the Indus-Red Sea voyage persuaded Darius to take up Necho II's plan again, and to restore the canal that connected the Nile with the Gulf of Suez. This undertaking was meant to make Egypt, and no longer Mesopotamia, the main line of communcation between the Mediterranean and the Indian Ocean. The plan had some measure of success, for a hieroglyphic inscription found in Suez and dating from the reign of Darius attests that ships were then going from Egypt to Persia by way of the south of Arabia.

The use of money as a means of exchange, which became general under Darius, also made commercial operations easier. The use of money would seem to have begun with the Sumerians, but owing to the incessant wars that raged in Mesopotamia up to the arrival of the Persians, it did not spread until the epoch of the Achaemenids. Commercial activity under those kings is attested by the quantity of coins bearing their effigies that have been found in India.

Ghirshman says that during the sixth and fifth centuries B.C. the volume of Eastern trade reached unprecedented proportions. He also emphasises that this trade was far less in luxury items, as it had been hitherto, than in articles of daily use. But this would seem to apply, above all, to exchanges by land. Exchanges by sea would not seem to have been much intensified or to have changed greatly in nature. The Persians themselves had little share in these exchanges, which were almost entirely in the hands of Phoenician or Arab sailors. All the same, it is important to stress the establishment of a maritime link between India and the Red Sea under the Achaemenids, even if that link lasted but a short time.

III. The Erythraean Sea

After Darius, Alexander was the first to conceive the brilliant plan of making international economic routes the basis for a universal empire by organising them around urban centres. In a few years 70 Alexandrias were created. The great routes of central Asia were, from then on, established for the future. But the main artery of the empire was the sea, and along its coasts the great centres were to take shape.[1]

So Pirenne sums up, in a few lines, the maritime plans of Alexander the Great; and they could not have been expressed more felicitously.

Of the 'Alexandrias' set up in India, from Alexander's conquest of the Punjab to his death (329–323 B.C.), we shall mention only the most important: that on the ocean shore, near the modern Karachi; Alexandria Urachosiorum, the modern Kandaher in Afghanistan; Alexandria on the Indus, at the junction of that river and the Akesines; and Patala, on the Indus delta. Patala was to remain the most important port of north-west India long after the Greeks had left the country. Alexandria on the Indus likewise survived for a long time after Alexander's soldiers had departed, and even became the centre of a curious Greco-Bactrian kingdom.

As for the maritime expeditions organised by Alexander, we may mention first of all that of Nearchus. Its story is told in

---

[1] J. Pirenne, *Les Grands Courants de l'histoire universelle*, Paris, 1944, I, 201.

Arrian's *Indica*; there is also a good account of it in Sir Arnold Wilson's work on the Persian Gulf. Leaving the mouth of the Indus in November 326, with an imposing fleet constructed in India—estimated by Arrian at about eight hundred vessels—Nearchus reached Diridotis, on the Persian Gulf, in February 325. It is the first exploration of that gulf of which we have an account. Indeed, we remember that Scylax, during his own periplus, never entered it.

From that first expedition Alexander went on to three others in the same region. The first, led by Archias, reached Bahrein; the second, under Androsthenes, went a little farther; and the third, led by Hiero, reached Cape Musandam. At the same time, he had ship parts constructed in Phoenicia, which were then to be taken to Babylon for assembly, so that Nearchus might undertake a new voyage from the Persian Gulf to the Red Sea, along the Arabian coast. But just as Nearchus was about to set sail, death put an end to Alexander's plans.

Barthold has pointed out that, while notably extending the Greeks' geographical horizon, Alexander's campaigns did not have the results that might have been expected. We find in Greek literature no description of the regions crossed by the great conqueror comparable to those of Herodotus and Xenophon. On the Greco-Bactrian kingdom the Greek sources are hardly more informative. Nor did Alexander's campaigns result in any greater knowledge of the languages, literature, or history of the East. So much is true, but on the other hand—and here the results were important—the knowledge gathered during Alexander's conquests and later codified in Alexandria was not without influence on the subsequent works of such geographers as Strabo, Pliny, and Ptolemy.

Poujade notes two other results of the Greek influence in the Eastern seas, one of which relates to naval construction. The first is a type of image of 'Buddha-Apollo' which, after having overrun all India, went on by way of the Ganges valley and across Burma into the pagodas of Siam and Cambodia, and later found its way even to China, Korea, and Japan; the second is a type of long boat which is found on the routes taken by the Buddha image, and so constantly that we cannot but be struck by the similarities of various native boats now

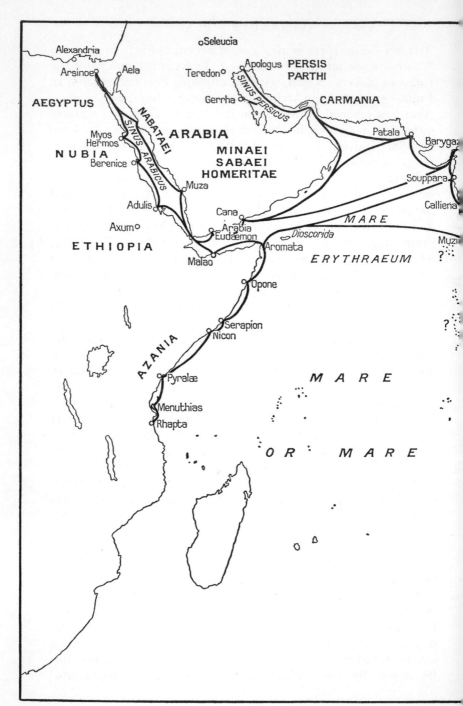

Alexandria

Arsinoe

Aela

Seleucia

Teredon

Apologus · PERSIS
PARTHI

SINUS PERSICUS

Gerrha

CARMANIA

AEGYPTUS

NABATAEI

ARABIA

Patala

Barygaz

Myos
Hermos

SINUS ARABICUS

**MINAEI
SABAEI
HOMERITAE**

NUBIA

Berenice

Souppara

Calliena

Muza

Cana

M A R E

Adulis

Arabia
Eudæmon

Dioscorida

Muzi

Axum

Aromata

E R Y T H R A E U M

?

ETHIOPIA

Malao

Opone

M A R E

Serapion
Nicon

?

A Z A N I A

Pyralæ

M A R E

Menuthias

Rhapta

O R   M A R E

ᴏ ᐃ

HAN
EMPIRE

Tamralipti
Sada
Dosarene   *SINUS*
GANGETICUS
ANDHRAS
Temala
Mosalia
Kattigara?
Poduca
CHRYSE
TAPROBANE

R A S O D U M

B S C U R U M

ECO-ROMAN PERIOD. PRINCIPAL ROUTES

scattered around India, Burma, and Malaya, to the long boats of classical Greece. Everything considered, therefore, the Greek conquerors' meteoric passage through the East was not to be without significance for the history of the Indian Ocean.

2. THE SELEUCIDS AND THE PTOLEMIES

After Alexander's death, his lieutenants divided up his empire among themselves and thus broke its unity. One took Western Asia, including Iran, and founded the dynasty of the Seleucids; another took Egypt, where he founded that of the Ptolemies. The former controlled the Persian Gulf, the latter the Red Sea, which thus became rival trade routes during the Hellenistic period. But they were trade routes of very unequal importance, since the Seleucids, for their part, never managed to establish any regular trade by sea between the Persian Gulf and India, as Alexander had dreamed.

After Seleucus Nicator had concluded a treaty with the Indian king Chandragupta in 302 B.C., it would seem that his subjects made a few sea voyages to India in order to procure spices; but the attacks on them by the unsubjugated peoples of the Persian Gulf, especially the inhabitants of Gerrah, quickly discouraged such attempts. Ghirshman says that the Seleucids had to keep a fleet in the gulf to protect navigation, and Pliny reports at least two punitive expeditions against Gerrha, one undertaken by Antiochus III in the year 205 and the other by Antiochus IV in 165.

The Seleucids very soon found themselves also at grips with the Parthians, an Iranian people who had come from the shores of the Caspian Sea. After Antiochus IV's death (164 B.C.), they ended by overcoming the Seleucid kingdom. They were to dominate Western Asia, and especially Iran, until A.D. 228, setting up a veritable 'Parthian Wall' between the East and the West, which even the Romans never managed to break through.

The Ptolemies were luckier, and their sovereignty in Egypt lasted longer, up to the Roman conquest of that country in A.D. 30—that is, for almost three centuries in all. During those three centuries the Greco-Egyptians systematically explored what they called the Erythraean Sea, which, as we have said, included not only today's Red Sea but the Arabian Sea also. During that period, Alexandria in Egypt became both the most important emporium of Eastern trade and a great centre of geographical science.

The first Ptolemy (Ptolemy I Soter, who ruled from 305 to 285 B.C.) had the Red Sea explored by a navigator called Philo, who in fact pushed out far along the coast of Africa. His successor, Ptolemy II Philadelphus (285–246), created a large port at Arsinoë (Suez) and reopened the 'Suez Canal', which had got sanded up. To relink Alexandria with the Red Sea, he built a second port called Berenice, whence goods were dispatched by land to an emporium called Koptos, on the Nile, and from there transported by river to Alexandria. As the journey from Berenice to Koptos took too long (eleven to twelve days), a third port called Myos Hormos was established about 180 miles higher up, and the trip shortened by five days. Ptolemy Philadelphus also had the coast of Yemen explored, as well as the Somali coast. Ptolemy III Euergetes (246–221), who succeeded him, had the explorations continued and built the port of Adulis (today Massawa) on the Red Sea.

In the second century B.C. the navigations of the Greco-Egyptians reached their height with the voyages of Eudoxus of Cyzicus, reported by Strabo. This Eudoxus had earned himself a certain reputation as a geographer in the reign of Ptolemy VII Euergetes II (146–117) and had first been employed by that king to explore the Nile. One day when he was in Alexandria, the coastguards of the Red Sea brought there a foreigner whom they had found in a disabled ship, half dead from hunger and thirst. When he could make himself understood, the stranger informed Eudoxus that he came from India, and offered to guide him there. The king procured a ship and a cargo, with which they did in fact make their way to India. There Eudoxus exchanged his cargo for goods even more precious. This took place in 119 B.C.

Five years later, Eudoxus made a second trip to India, but on the way back he was driven by a storm on to the African coast, well below Cape Guardafui. There he made a sensational find: a prow in the shape of a horse, which the natives told him had come from a boat from the West. Brought to Alexandria, the prow was recognised by sailors as part of a vessel from Cadiz, which had sailed for distant lands and never returned. Eudoxus then decided to attempt to circumnavigate Africa himself, leaving from Cadiz. The attempt failed, but it is worth recording, for it shows the courage of the Greek navigators of that time.

Eudoxus of Cyzicus would seem to have been the first navigator after Scylax—and consequently the second Greek—to work out a direct maritime communication between India and Egypt. But while Scylax's voyage did not lead to others, Eudoxus soon found imitators, for the demand for exotic goods among other factors led the Greco-Egyptians increasingly into voyages in search of trade. The decadence of the Ptolemies did not stop these explorations, and when the Romans arrived in Egypt, direct communcation by sea with India was already established.

Before leaving the Ptolemies, we must mention the efforts these rulers made to develop navigational and astronomical science in Alexandria. Of the works then written on the subject, two deserve particular attention: the treatise on geography by Eratosthenes, who was director of the famous library of Alexandria from 240 to 196 B.C., and a description of the Erythraean Sea by Agatharchides, Ptolemy VIII Soter II's tutor (117–81 B.C.). This work ranks among the first written documents on the history of the ocean, and gives precise indications as to the sea trade between Egypt and India. The trade was carried on in two stages: the Indian merchants from Potana (Patala) brought their cargoes to Aden and Muza (Mocha) on the Arabian coast, where the merchants from Egypt came to fetch them and brought their own. Note that Agatharchides wrote before the voyages of Eudoxus.

3. THE ROMAN ERA

The Roman conquest of Egypt (30 B.C.) only gave new stimulus to direct maritime relations with India, and it is really at this point that we enter into the era of the great commercial expeditions, for those of Eudoxus and his imitators were, despite everything, merely the voyages of adventurers.

In this connection an important question must be raised at

the very beginning. Should this era—which lasted until about the end of Marcus Aurelius' reign (A.D. 161–180)—be called 'Roman', and should we speak, as several writers have done, of a Roman trade in the Indian Ocean? The question is rather a complex one.

If we take into account the fact that without the Roman push in the East, and the 'Roman peace' that followed, this trade would not have been organised, such a point of view is justifiable. Consider, on the other hand, that the Romans themselves had practically no share in that trade and that they hardly ever put in an appearance in the Indian Ocean. How, then, can we argue in favour of a Roman 'presence' there? This question was recently the subject of a rather lively contro-versy in the *American Neptune*, between R. L. Bowen, who says Yes, and C. Quigley, who says No.[2] We are led to agree with the latter, more especially as the most important document on this period that we possess, the famous *Periplus of the Erythraean Sea*, is the work of a Greco-Egyptian, not a Roman.

If it is necessary to characterise this period in the history of the Indian Ocean, the name 'golden age', given it by certain writers, seems still the most suitable. Perhaps 'age of gold' is even more appropriate, for the main element of the trade of the period was in fact that beautiful Roman gold coin, the aureus, the dollar of that day. Extraordinary quantities of this coin, according to Pliny, were despatched from Rome to India, as Rome had almost nothing else to offer the Indians in return for their products.

An anecdote likewise reported by Pliny clearly shows the prestige in which the Roman aureus was held by the Eastern peoples. A Roman merchant—probably, in fact, a Roman subject—and a Persian merchant landed together on the island of Ceylon and were received by the king of that country. The Persian spoke glibly about his own country and, to use a slang expression, boosted it. The Roman said nothing, but handed the king a magnificent aureus, asking him to compare it with the Persian drachma, made of silver and of a rather crude im-pression. The Sinhalese king was, of course, quick to make his choice between the two coins.

One other point. According to Barthold, it was during the

[2] See the *American Neptune*, XVII (1957), 262–91, and XVIII (1958), 25–28.

Roman era that for the first time the idea of the *Orient* as a world apart, opposed to the Greco-Roman and, in general, the European world, came into being. With that meaning the words *oriental* and *Orient* appear for the first time in the works of Latin writers (for example, *res orientales* in Pompeius Trogus, *Oriens* in Tacitus). Barthold is probably right, but even so it must be pointed out that this idea of the Orient was still very vague. Where exactly the Orient began and ended for the Romans would be difficult to say; also, what exactly did this idea of the Orient imply?

4. THE PERIPLUS OF THE ERYTHRAEAN SEA

For the movement of shipping in the Indian Ocean during the Roman era, the main sources are Strabo, who wrote under Augustus (29 B.C.–A.D. 14), Pliny the Elder, who wrote under Nero and Vespasian (A.D. 54–79), the unknown author of the *Periplus* (first century A.D.), and Ptolemy, whose *Geographia* dates from the second century A.D. All four were what may be called serious writers, and their works have been the subject of several studies by Rawlinson, Charlesworth, Warmington, Gérini, Filliozat, Berthelot, and Schoff, to mention only the most important.

But any elucidation of the nature and scope of commercial activities in the Indian Ocean during the Roman era is to be had, above all, from archaeology and numismatics, as the recent works of Jouveau-Dubreuil and Sir Mortimer Wheeler have clearly proved. The discovery of a 'Roman' trading station (Ptolemy's *Podouca*) at Arikamédou, near Pondichéry, gives us more information on this subject than all the texts; and one must have actually visited this site and have handled, in the small museum of Pondichéry, the vestiges of the Roman era—the intaglios, carnelian seals, coins, and pottery found on the banks of the Ariancoupan River, where the natives, digging around in the mud, still from time to time unearth fascinating fragments; one must have heard direct from the mouths of his collaborators how that extraordinary man Jouveau-Dubreuil discovered the site of Arikamédou; one must have seen and heard all this if one is really to understand the history of the exchanges between India and the Roman Empire in the first centuries of the Christian era, and if the accounts in the 'classics' of the Indian Ocean are really to make sense.[3]

Foremost among these 'classics' is naturally the *Periplus*, the work not of an armchair geographer, but of a man who really went to sea. It is therefore from this work, which exists in several good critical editions, that we take the following account.

Navigation in the Indian Ocean followed two quite separate routes, depending on whether it went towards the south—that is, in the direction of the ancient land of Punt—or towards the east, to the Indies proper. We will begin by describing the former.

One set sail from the Egyptian coast, either from Arsinoë, Myos Hormos, or Berenice. Of these three ports, Myos Hormos seems to have been the most important. Passing down towards the south, one came on the Somali coast first to Adulis, and then, going along the coast to Cape Guardafui, Avalites (Zeila), Malao (Berbera), Mundus (Bander Hais) Mosyllum (Ras Hantara), and finally Cape Guardafui itself, then known as Cape Aromata, because all the previously cited 'trading posts' exported mostly aromatic products—gums, myrrh, and incense.

To the south of Guardafui there were two more harbours: Pano (Ras Binna) and Opone (Ras Hafun)—which shows a resemblance to Punt—and then one went along the coast of Azania, arid and devoid of ports but provided with a few anchorages, notably Sarapion and Nicon (both rather difficult to identify). Finally, one arrived at the Pyralaae islands (Patta, Manda, and Lamu) and at the island of Menuthias, which must be Pemba or Zanzibar. 'Two days' sail beyond lies the very last market-town of the continent of Azania, which is called Rhapta (probably Quiloa); which has its name from the sewed boats (*rhaptôn ploiariôn*).'[4] This was the terminal point beyond

---

[3] To the discovery of Jouveau-Dubreuil must be added that of the site of Oc-Eo by another French archaeologist, Louis Malleret. Situated on the maritime fringe of the Mekong delta, bordering on the Gulf of Thailand, Oc-Eo appears as an ancient commercial and industrial centre, which had maintained extensive navigational relations, by direct route or through intermediaries, with the shores of the Gulf of Thailand, the Malay Peninsula, India and Indonesia, Iran, and certainly the Mediterranean. On Oc-Eo, see L. Malleret's recent work, *l'Archéologie du delta du Mékong*, Paris, Publications de l'Ecole française d'Extrême-Orient, 1959.

[4] W. H. Schoff, (ed.), *The Periplus of the Erythraean Sea* (London, 1912), p. 28. The custom of sewing the planks of the ships was current in the entire western part of the Indian Ocean until the 15th century. The use of nails did not become general until after the arrival of the Europeans. See Hourani, *op. cit.*, pp. 89–97.

which 'the unexplored ocean curves around toward the west'.

In proceeding towards India, the first port encountered on descending the Red Sea was Muza (Mocha), on the Arabian coast. Then one arrived at Ocelis, which Strabo and Pliny called Acila (Cella). It was rather a watering place for ships than a port.

Past the strait of Bab el Mandeb, which is not named in the *Periplus*, one came to the important port of Aden, then called Eudaemon Arabia, or Arabia Felix. The name, explains the *Periplus*, came from the fact that it had long been the junction where merchants from Egypt and India met. From Aden, one followed the coast of Hadhramaut to Cana (Hisn Ghorab), not far from the present port of Mukalla. From there, those whose destination was the south of India rounded Socotra and took to the high seas, while the others went along the coast of the country of incense toward the north. On this journey they reached, in succession, beyond Cape Syagrus (Ras Fartak), the port of Moscha (Khor Reiri), then the port of Oman in the Persian Gulf, and at the head of the gulf, at the mouth of the Euphrates, the port of Apologos (Obollah).

The first port to be touched on the coast of India was Barbaricum (probably Bahardipur) at the mouth of the Indus, the next was Barygaza (Broach). Descending the Malabar coast, one again came upon a half-dozen secondary harbours before arriving at Muziris (Cranganore), another important port.

Continuing his voyage, the navigator rounded Cape Comorin and hugged the Coromandel coast, whose main ports were Camara, at the mouth of the Cauvery, on the present site of Karikal; Poduca (near Pondichéry); and Sopatma (Madras). Still higher, on the eastern coast of India, he came upon Mosalia (Masulipatam), Dosarene (Orissa), and finally reached the mouth of the Ganges, where his journey ended.

The descriptions in the *Periplus* are completed by those of Ptolemy, who wrote fifty years later. The first port mentioned by Ptolemy after Masulipatam is Palura, at the beginning of the gulf of the Ganges and a little to the north. It is from this port that ships left for the Far East. Crossing the Bay of Bengal, they arrived at Sada, situated on the coast of Burma, facing

Cheduba island—probably the modern port of Sandoway. From Sada they went to Temala, near Cape Negrais; the journey thence to a port called Zaba, on the Gulf of Thailand, not far from the Kang Kao river, took twenty days, and the distance between Zaba and Kattigara (perhaps Oc-Eo) was about the same.

But after having described the coast of Indo-China, Ptolemy went completely astray. For him the Chinese coast bent towards the south, joining a southern continent connecting it to Africa, thus making the Indian Ocean a completely closed sea. That is why he placed Kattigara, the last Asian port known to the Romans, on what he considered to be the eastern shore of the Indian Ocean, just facing Rhapta on the coast of Africa. As we have seen, the *Periplus* was better informed as to the true direction of the coast of Africa beyond Rhapta. Unfortunately, Ptolemy's mistake was to prevail, and for a long time.

5. A SPLENDID AND TRIFLING TRADE

It is clear from the *Periplus* that in the first century A.D. Mediterranean navigators had explored a good part of the Indian Ocean but only along its periphery. The African shore was well known up to the vicinity of Quiloa, and the Asian shore up to the mouth of the Ganges, but the greater part of the ocean remained still unconquered. The *Mare Prasodum* continued to be a *mare obscurum*, an enormous vacuum, which the imaginations of sailors peopled with a thousand monsters and a thousand dangers. Ceylon, although situated very near India, was little known and seldom visited, and the *Periplus* does no more than briefly allude to it; the Malay Archipelago, Madagascar, the Mascarenes, and Australia were still *terrae incognitae*.

Even after the discovery of the monsoon, Western sailors were not really masters of the open sea. It is difficult to say exactly how long it would have then taken to cross it from north to south and from east to west, for the indications of the *Periplus* are clearly inadequate in this regard, but a crossing in both directions must surely be reckoned in terms of months. The discovery of the monsoon reduced to a certain extent the ocean's 'dimensions', but not so very much, especially in that the discovery was not made suddenly but in successive stages—

four in number, according to Warmington. Therefore, traffic on the ocean must not be seen as having been transformed between one day and the next by some sensational event.

The truly sensational element of this discovery was that it increased the movement of shipping in one direction only: west to east. Why did it not attract the people of India towards Egypt and the West to the same degree that it urged the subjects of Rome towards India and the East? Is the explanation to be sought in a difference in mentality—the dynamism of the one, the inertia of the other—or rather in the fact that India, rich in products of every kind, needed nothing from the Mediterranean world?

Be that as it may, everything goes to show that the West had nothing to offer the East in exchange for its products other than metallic currency, an enormous quantity of which was thus absorbed by trade with India. 'Not a year passed', wrote Pliny in this regard, 'in which India did not take fifty million sesterces away from Rome.' Over a period of more than two hundred years that makes quite a large total.

What did Rome receive in return? If we consider only the articles mentioned in the *Periplus*, we could draw up an imposing list of products which then made up the substance of Eastern trade—nothing, however, similar to what today we call 'raw materials' but, on the contrary, almost uniquely luxury items: spices, perfumes, silks, muslins, tortoise-shell, ivory, pearls, precious stones, unguents, dyes, and other rare products, all bearing strange-sounding names, so that Gibbon, the historian of Roman decadence, described this trade as 'splendid and trifling'. Splendid, certainly; trifling, indeed. But after all, are not trifles the very spice of life? Yet van Leur, the author of an illuminating study of Eastern trade in antiquity, while agreeing with Gibbon, does emphasise the fact that this trade did not consist exclusively in high-quality products, but that it also dealt in at least some raw materials intended to supply certain places of manufacture and what he calls 'the ergasterium [workshop] industry.'

In any case, the volume of trade was never very high; the cargoes were modest—although there was an increase in the burthen of vessels after the discovery of the monsoon—and in no way comparable to the freight of modern times or even of the sixteenth century. Besides, if we want to get a precise idea of 'Roman' trade in the Indian Ocean during the first centuries of the Christian era, we must not lose sight of the fact that the ancient economy was very different from ours.

6. AXUM AND BYZANTIUM

What significance did Roman intervention in the East, from the reign of Augustus (29 B.C.–A.D. 14) to that of Marcus Aurelius (161–180), have for oceanic history? It is obvious that by encouraging and developing sea trade, the Roman Empire diverted to its own channels the enormous revenue which the Parthians derived from trade by land. Although Rome did not succeed in overthrowing the Parthians, she did, in this way, deal them an indirect blow and seriously weaken them.

She also weakened the maritime peoples of Arabia, the Nabataeans, Sabaeans, and Himyarites, whose role as intermediaries put them in a position to control, as it were, the markets and movement of shipping in the time of the Ptolemies. Rome was not satisfied merely to take away that control through the play of competition and a real policing of the Erythraean Sea; she also launched expeditions against them, some of which were successful, as with Trajan's raid on the country of the Nabataeans in the year 105.

By thus weakening the maritime peoples of Arabia, Rome indirectly favoured the rise of their rivals in Abyssinia and the founding of that kingdom, with Axum as its capital—whence the name Axumite kingdom—and with Adulis (today Massawa) on the Red Sea as its main port. Subsequently the Axumite kingdom was to play an important part in the Indian Ocean, and it was to Adulis that the subjects of Rome came to procure Eastern products when, on the decline of Roman power, they could no longer obtain them directly from India.[5]

It is possible that if the Romans had been able to maintain sufficient pressure in Western Asia and had managed to create there a greater Rome, they would have established themselves

[5] For a detailed history of the Axumite kingdom, see Dillmann, *Geschichte des Axumitischen Reichs*, Berlin, 1880. Among the more recent works, see A. Jones, *A History of Ethiopia*, Oxford, 1955, and J. Doresse, *L'Empire du Prêtre Jean*, Paris, 1957.

permanently in the Indian Ocean and history might well have been different. Islam might perhaps never have come into the picture. But the Indian Ocean was a pretty large mouthful for a people who already had to control the Mediterranean, North Africa, Asia Minor, and a good part of Europe, and who, into the bargain, were not really oriented towards the sea.

In India itself, despite the creation of a trading factory in the region of Pondichéry and perhaps another at Muziris, on the Malabar coast, the influence of Rome was scarcely felt.

Yet nothing exemplifies Roman audacity more clearly than the creation of those settlements, which some like to regard as anticipations of the sixteenth-century Portuguese trading factories, or than the attempt, in the year 160, to make contact both by sea and by land with China, the Rome of the Far East; an attempt all the more remarkable in that it took place not at the height but rather during the decline of Roman power. For this very reason it was doomed to failure, and the route to India really did stop at India.

Poujade notes:

> Had it been otherwise, the Chinese and the Western civilisations would have met and mingled earlier and the face of the world would have been changed. But the Parthians had been able to prevent any intercommunication by land route; and events in the Mediterranean prevented any communication by sea. The liaison did not come about until later, by land, and thanks to the Venetians.[6]

On reflection, it was perhaps not logical that Rome should become the centre of commercial exchanges between East and West; logically, that role would seem to belong rightfully to a city better situated geographically. This is obviously one of the reasons that decided the emperor Constantine in the year 324 to dispossess Rome to the benefit of Constantinople. As Byzantium, this city was to play a very prominent role indeed in the history of Eastern trade, until its conquest by the Turks in the fifteenth century, but all historians agree that the maritime activity of the Byzantines in the Indian Ocean always fell short of that of the Romans.

[6] J. Poujade, *La Route des Indes et ses navires*, Paris, 1946, pp. 84–85.

Under Constantine (324–337) and his successors, there was a resumption of trade in the Erythraean Sea, again with a view to procuring luxury goods, for which the Byzantines were as mad as the Romans. But they never pushed all the way to India, and merely bought Indian products from the Axumites who themselves went to India for them. They also often went to enemies of the Axumites, the Himyarites of southern Arabia, and even signed commercial treaties with them. Adulis and Aden thus became true Byzantine markets. But the maritime power that really replaced Rome in the Indian Ocean was not Byzantium but Iran, as we shall see in the next chapter.

IV. From the Sassanids to the Caliphs

THE decline of Roman power coincided with two events that were of great iportance to the history of the Indian Ocean. The first was a renaissance of the Iranians, who under Sassanid leadership recaptured their country from the Parthians in the year 228. Under the Sassanids, Iran soon regained the ascendancy she had once held in the time of the Achaemenids in the western region of the ocean, and that ascendancy was to last until the Arab conquest of Iran in the seventh century. The second was an expansion of the Dravidians of southern India towards the countries of South-east Asia, leading to the formation of several Hinduised maritime states in the eastern region of the Indian Ocean, where, at the same moment, the presence of the Chinese began for the first time to be felt.

In this chapter we shall first speak of the Iranians and the Arabs; of the two chapters that follow, one will be devoted to the Dravidians, the other to the Chinese. We must keep it in mind, however, that the maritime activities of all these peoples took place not successively but almost all at the same time, and that the order in which they are here described, does not strictly correspond to their order of importance.

I. THE SASSANID PERIOD

As we have seen, the Mediterranean traders did not suddenly disappear from the Indian Ocean at the end of the reign of Marcus Aurelius.

44

The Iranians had thus at first to reckon with these competitors, as well as with the Axumites of Ethiopia. The latter were far more serious rivals, for they had managed not only to make Adulis the centre of an important maritime trade in direct communication with the ports of western India and the island of Ceylon, but were also aiming at extending their dominion over the Himyarites of southern Arabia. In 529 an Axumite force of 70,000 men invaded Arabia by way of Aden and subjugated Yemen for over half a century.

But the Iranians finally retaliated. In 570 they drove the Axumites out of Arabia and established their own dominion there. Earlier, they had succeeded in evicting the Axumite merchants from the island of Ceylon. According to the historian Procopius, about the year 530 these merchants were unable to obtain enough silk from Ceylon to supply the Byzantines. In order to produce silk, Byzantium had therefore to bring in silkworms secretly from China by the overland route.

At the end of the sixth century, the Iranians were so far in command of the Erythraean Sea that Khosrau I (531–579) was able to send out an expedition against Ceylon, which suggests the existence of a powerful fleet. That naval expedition, however, was unique in Iran's history under the Sassanids—in fact, in all of Iran's history—so that it in no way implies a real thalassocracy.

But one thing is certain: at the apex of Sassanid power, in the fifth and sixth centuries, trade in the Erythracan Sea was completely in the hands of the Iranians and centred mainly in the region of the Persian Gulf, whereas activity in the Red Sea fell off.

Our main sources regarding this trade in Byzantine literature are the historian Procopius (c. 500–c. 565) and the traveller Cosmas (fl. c. 519), whose real name was Constantine of Antioch. In modern literature the recent works of Christensen, Ghirshman, and Hourani must be mentioned. The last, in particular, has excellently summarised all that we so far know about Iranian commerce. He finds that it had three main centres: Apologos (Obollah), on the Persian Gulf; Barygaza (Broach), on the west coast of India; and finally, the island of Ceylon, which would seem just then to have become a depot where Iranian merchants met their colleagues who had come from the Far East. Contacts between Iran and China by sea seem to have been quite rare. According to Hourani, it is probable that ships from Apologos reached China before Islam; it is less probable, though possible, he adds, that Chinese vessels had also entered the Persian Gulf.[1]

With India, on the other hand, there had been regular and frequent exchanges. They are described in the *Topography* of Cosmas Indicopleustes (meaning 'traveller in the Indies'), which dwells particularly on the pepper trade along the Malabar Coast, and also speaks at length about the island of Ceylon. India was then experiencing a real golden age under the Gupta dynasty (4th to 6th centuries), which encouraged literature and the arts. Moreover, Iran's contribution to this Indian renaissance was not negligible.

Iran's influence was also shown in a religious development, Manichaeism, which strongly influenced Indian Buddhism. Manichaeism spread even farther, to Turkestan, China, and even to the West, where Levantine trade brought it to several Mediterranean countries, including France.

Cradle of Manichaeism, the Iran of the Sassanids was also a refuge for the Nestorian Church, whose doctrines were condemned by the Third General Council at Ephesus (431). Thanks to the commercial expansion of its adopted country, that church was to experience extraordinary good fortune in the East, where the Portuguese, on entering the Indian Ocean in the sixteenth century, found it established in various Asian countries.[2]

The Sassanid civilisation represents the culminating point of Iran's millenary history. From an economic point of view it is especially notable for the creating of an institution which has ever since played a leading part in the history of commerce: the bank. Although banks perhaps existed in a rudimentary state before the Sassanids, they owe their legal existence, as it were, to them. Few people are aware of the fact, brought out

---

[1] Christensen, who is more affirmative on this point, enumerates the products bought by the Chinese in Iran: the famous Iranian make-up for eyebrows, which was very costly; Babylonian rugs; natural and artificial precious stones from Syria and Egypt, and the fabrics woven in those countries; and finally, narcotics from West Asia.

[2] On the Nestorian Church in the East, see especially A. R. Vine, *The Nestorian Churches: A Concise History of Nestorian Christianity in Asia*, London, 1937.

by Ghirshman, that the word *cheque* and the French word *avaliser* (to endorse) were taken from the Persian language.

Yet the Sassanid economic system can be criticised for its excessive control and for the institution of state monopolies, especially with regard to the silk industry. Such state interference restricted to a certain extent the freedom of exchange and was a hindrance to commerce. Consequently, if we compare the Sassanid trade in the Erythraean Sea with that of the Roman era which preceded it, we find that it did not represent a more developed stage, save for the generalised use of the bill of exchange. It was still what Gibbon called a 'splendid and trifling' trade, dealing primarily with luxury items, which were in great demand for the Iranian court and aristocracy. The economic value of this trade is in no way comparable to its cultural importance.

2. ARAB EXPANSION

How a civilisation as remarkable as that of Iran under the Sassanids let itself be so easily crushed by the Arabs, and how the Arabs themselves were transformed into world conquerors by Islam, is here irrelevant. The fact is that with the advent of Islam in the seventh century, the Arab tide unexpectedly rose and broke over Western Asia and North Africa, to cover in less than seventy years a wider expanse than that of the Roman Empire.

This sudden expansion was the work of Arabs of the north— that is, of the desert—and not the maritime tribes of the south descended from the Sabaeans and Himyarites, who, as we have seen, had managed to control for a time the markets of the Red Sea in the Hellenistic as well as in the Roman era. Under the Sassanids, however, the commercial activity of the southern Arabs had been insignificant, for first the Axumite and then the Persian conquest had had a considerable effect on the life of such ports as Mocha and Aden.

Also, at the very beginnings of Islam, one of the first caliphs (Omar I, a cousin of Mohammed, who ruled from 654 to 664) imposed a judicial interdict on any maritime undertaking— an interdict not lifted for thirty years.

It was natural that the first leaders of Islam, in fear of dispersing too widely the already scattered forces they had so rapidly acquired, should refuse to give their approval to plans for expeditions to distant lands. It was also natural that they should prefer to attack the Byzantine Empire and that of the Sassanids, which they could easily reach by land, rather than become involved in a struggle on the sea against the Axumites or the Indians.

Iran was conquered within a few years, and became a province of the Ommiads whose capital was at Damascus, in Syria, from 661 to 749. When they were overthrown by their rivals, the Abbassids, the seat of the caliphate was removed to Baghdad on the Tigris, which for five centuries was to remain the great capital of Islam in the countries of the Indian Ocean, until its conquest by the Mongols in the thirteenth century. Its port was Basra, which soon supplanted Apologos (Obollah) and continued to be the main port of the Persian Gulf until the eighteenth century. Under the Abbassids, the port of Masqat (Muscat), on the Arabian side of the gulf, and that of Siraf, on the Iranian side, also attained importance.

At almost the same time that they conquered Iran, the Arabs also subjugated Egypt. Having thus become masters of the countries of the Red Sea and the Persian Gulf, they re-established the unity of Alexander's former empire which, as we have seen, had been divided up between his successors. Under their dominion, the two arms of the Erythraean Sea were no longer rival routes, but on the contrary became seaways leading to the same goal: India and its riches.

In the relations between Islam and India there is good reason to distinguish between military operations on the one hand and commercial operations on the other. The military conquest of India, begun early in the eighth century and not brought to a close until the end of the sixteenth, was a long series of land operations on a limited scale, in which the sea played no part. The conquest had no influence on the organisation of Indian trade, in which the Moslem conquerors never had any part.

Thus the maritime trade between the Moslem countries and India continued in much the same way as before. The most frequented coast of the peninsula was that of Malabar, while Barygaza and Cranganore (the ancient Muziris), already important centres at the time of the *Periplus*, were still the main ports. Dhabol, Calicut, and Quilon, to mention only a few, were also very active.[3] The most eagerly sought products were still luxury items: spices, silks, precious stones, and so on. Teak was also in great demand for the construction of houses and ships. In exchange for these products, the Moslem merchants brought linen, cotton, and woollen fabrics; carpets; objects of wrought iron; coral; silver; and horses.

In the ninth century, according to the Arab historian Baladhuri, there were, if not real colonies, at least notable settlements of Moslem merchants on the Malabar coast and in several cities on the seacoast as far north as the Indus. There was also at that time a large colony of Moslems in Ceylon, which the Arabs called Serendip, or Island of Rubies. The Maldive and Laccadive Islands, known to the Arabs as Robaihat, also received them as immigrants.

At about the same period we find a flow of trade becoming established, for the first time, between the countries of the western Mediterranean and India, initiated by Jewish merchants whose curious itinerary is described by the Arab geographer Ibn Khurdadhbih (844–848).

> These merchants (he wrote) speak Persian, Roman [Greek and Latin], Arabic, and the Frankish, Spanish, and Slav languages. They travel from West to East and from East to West, sometimes by land, sometimes by sea. From the West they bring back eunuchs, female slaves, boys, silk, furs, and spices. They sail from the country of the Franks, on the Western Sea, and head towards Farama [near the ruins of ancient Pelusium]; there they load their goods on the backs of beasts of burden and take the land route to Qulzum [Suez], a five days' journey, at a distance of 20 parasangs. They set sail on the Eastern Sea [the Red Sea] and make their way from Qulzum to Al Jar and Jidda; thence they go to Sind, India, and China. On their return they load up with musk, aloes, camphor, cinnamon, and other products of the Eastern countries, and come back to Qulzum, and then to Farama, where they again set sail on the Western Sea. Some head for Constantinople to sell their goods; others make their way to the country of the Franks.[4]

[3] On the relations between the Arabs and the western coast of India, see S. M. H. Nainar, *Arab Geographers' Knowledge of Southern India*, Madras, 1942.
[4] Quoted by M. Devic, *Les Merveilles de l'Inde*, Paris, 1878, p. xxi.

These European Jews were apparently the only inhabitants of the Mediterranean region to trade in the Indian Ocean during the period of Arab ascendancy. The Venetians and Genoese did not arrive there until much later.

Recently Professor Goitein, of the University of Jerusalem, found in the *Geniza* (a kind of repository for archives) of an old Cairo synagogue highly important documents regarding the trade of the Jews between the Mediterranean and the Indian Ocean during the eleventh and twelfth centuries. They are business letters which, by some providential chance, have escaped the ravages of time. Professor Goitein has given a brief general idea of them in a few articles in scholarly journals, and he is at present working on a critical edition of the documents.[5]

3. THE MOSLEMS IN THE FAR EAST

Moslem navigation in the west-east direction did not stop at India; it extended to distant China and to Indonesia. The 'route to China', opened up at the end of the seventh century, and used until the end of the ninth, is of very special interest. It was described in detail in an Arab nautical guidebook entitled *Silsilat-al-Tawarikh*, written in the year 851 by a traveller called Suleiman. After the *Periplus of the Erythraean Sea*, this is the first guide to navigation in the Indian Ocean that we possess. It was also the source for all the Arab travellers who wrote after Suleiman.

From the Persian Gulf, the vessels on their way to the Far East first went direct to Quilon, on the Malabar coast. From there they rounded the island of Ceylon and set sail from the Nicobar Islands, where they took on fresh provisions. They then called at Kalah Bar (probably Kedah) on the Malay coast, whence some sailed on towards Sumatra and Java, and others headed for China. The latter went through the Strait of Malacca, known to the Arabs by its Malay name, Salaht—that is, 'strait'—and stopped first at Tiuman island, then at the ports of the Champa kingdom (Annam), then at Luqin (Hanoi),

[5] See S. D. Goitein, 'From the Mediterranean to India. Documents on the Trade to India, South Arabia and East Africa from the Eleventh and Twelfth Centuries,' *Speculum*, XIX (1954), 181–97; and 'The Cairo Geniza as a Source for the History of Muslim Civilization,' *Studia Islamica*, III (1955), 75–91.

the last stop before reaching Kanfu (Canton), in southern China, the terminal point of the journey.

From Basra or Siraf the voyage took about six months, counting the stopovers: they left from the Persian Gulf at the beginning of winter, spent the summer at Canton, and came back with the monsoon of the following winter, making in all an expedition of a year and a half.

Hourani dates the first unquestionable Moslem expedition to Canton in the year 671. Less than a century later, in 758, the Arab colony was large enough to attack the port, which led to its being closed to foreign trade. Reopened in 792, Canton continued to be steadily visited by the Moslems until 878. In that year a frightful massacre put an end to the Moslem settlement. Subsequently, the Arab merchants merely met the Chinese merchants at the port of Kalah Bar in Malaya.

The Jews, however, though they had also suffered from the massacre of 878, continued to send expeditions to China in the tenth century and even later. As we have seen, they set out from the ports of Yemen to reach the Far East. Now in the tenth century, with the decline of the Abassids in Iran and the rise of the Fatimids in Egypt (Cairo was founded in 972), the centre of Islam in the Indian Ocean shifted from the Persian Gulf to the Red Sea. According to Hourani, it is therefore probable that Jidda and Aden had by then supplanted Basra and Siraf as the main ports for sailing to China.

4. THE MOSLEMS IN AFRICA

The relations between the Islamic countries and the east coast of Africa were very different in nature. For once, the determining factor was not the attraction of profitable trade but the desire to escape religious or political persecution. In the seventh century the inhabitants of Oman, in revolt against the Caliph Abdul Malik (685–705), were forced to flee to the African coast, where they settled in the vicinity of Patta. In 739, following a new conflict, the vanquished, whom the chronicles refer to as Emozeides (followers of Zaïd), also set off for Africa, where they settled on the Benadir coast.

Two centuries later, about the year 917, other 'political

refugees', from a region in Arabia or Iran referred to as Al Hasa, came to the Benadir coast. These newcomers are said to have developed the ports of Mogadiscio (Mogadishu) and Brava, where there is a considerable Arab population even to-day. Finally, in 975, a certain Hasan ibn Ali, son of a sultan in Shiraz, Iran, and perhaps a sultan himself, left his country for unknown reasons, with a fleet of seven ships and a great number of 'colonists', and settled in Mombasa, Pemba, and Quiloa. One of the vessels went as far as the island of Johanna in the Comoros, a name derived from the Arabic *Komr*.

With the arrival of Hasan ibn Ali, the colonisation—for it was indeed a true colonisation—of the African coast entered on an imperialistic phase, as it were. The ancient land of Punt, from the Somali region to Sofala, then became known as the country of the Zanj—a word the Arabs used to designate the natives. The name is to be recognised in modern times in the island of Zanzibar, actually a corrupt form of *Zanjebar*.

Moslem navigation along the coast of Africa does not seem to have gone beyond Sofala. The region today referred to as South Africa remained unknown to the Arabs, and there is no proof that the dhows ever tried to enter the Atlantic by rounding the Cape of Good Hope.

At the farthest point of the African world known to the Moslems, Arab tales mention a land called Waqwaq. According to Ferrand, this name can refer only to Madagascar, though that island was better known to the Arabs as Qanbalu.

Indeed, from the Comoros, the colonists of the country of the Zanj did not take long to reach Madgascar and the Mascarene islands, which on fifteenth-century Arab maps are referred to as Dina Arobi, Dina Moraze, and Dina Margabim, curious names on whose meaning geographers have not been able to agree.[6]

The works of Ferrand and the recent excavations carried out under the sponsorship of the Institut de la Recherche Scientifique of Madagascar give us fairly reliable information on the Moslem settlements in that island. From all we know, we can conclude that Madagascar was only very slightly Islamised, although the Antaimoros of the south-eastern coast still use Arabic script and possess a corrupt version of the Koran, known

[6] These names are also found on several European maps of the first decade of the sixteenth century.

as the *Shoura-bé*. In the Comoros, on the other hand, Islamisation was complete. As for the Mascarenes, nothing has been found up to now to indicate that the Moslems ever settled there; besides, the Mascarenes were then desert islands and had nothing to satisfy their greed.

5. THE SETTLEMENT OF MADAGASCAR

Here we must digress somewhat and go into the origin of the settlement of Madagascar, a subject which is still shrouded in mystery. Most of the theories put forward on this matter assume that there were one or several Indonesian migrations across the Indian Ocean at dates not yet precisely determined. How can we explain the fact that these migrations did not stop at the Mascarenes, which happened to be on the way?

The most ingenious theory would appear to be that of the American ethnologist Ralph Linton (1943), and can be summed up as follows. The aborigines of Madagascar were no doubt Negritos who date back to prehistory. During the first centuries of the Christian era, a stream of emigrants from Indonesia crossed the Indian Ocean, reached the Somali coast, and from there, a few generations later and mixed with Africans, made their way to Madagascar. Much later, probably about the tenth century, new Indonesian emigrants headed for Somaliland, but this time they did not stay for long and almost immediately went on to Madagascar, where they formed the tribe of the Merina, who are today called Hovas. But how are we to know whether or not Linton was right?[7]

Auber, who tackled the problem as a linguist, came to very original conclusions as to the relationship of Malagasy to the other Malayo-Polynesian languages and even to Chinese, tending to confirm von Heine-Geldern's theories about the Malayan migrations from China to Indonesia, and from there towards Madagascar on the one hand and the Pacific islands on the other. But this tells us little of the motives for such migrations and of the nature of the relations between Madagascar and Indonesia.

[7] To Linton's theory we must now oppose the more recent one of Marie-Claude Chamla (in *Recherches anthropologiques sur l'origine des Malgaches*, Paris, 1958), of which I did not learn until after this book was written.

One thing is quite certain: when the Moslems came into contact with Madagascar, the inhabitants of that country engaged in no maritime activity whatever. On this fact we have the testimony of Idrisi, who wrote in the twelfth century:

> The people of Madagascar have no boats for crossing the sea. Boats come to their country from Oman and elsehwere. These continue on towards the islands of Djavago [today, Java] which are part of the Indian archipelago. Foreign sailors exchange their goods for those of the Malagasy. The people of Djavaga come in large ships and export the goods of the Malagasy, because they speak the same language.[8]

There is also no doubt that in Madagascar at that time no civilisation existed comparable to that of Shrivajaya, which, as we shall see later, reached its height in Sumatra between the tenth and twelfth centuries.

Until the eighteenth century, the Hovas themselves were divided up into small principalities and had not as yet extended their dominion over the entire country. It was not until around 1794 that they were united by Andrianampoinimerina (the Coveted One of Imerina) and that Antananarivo became the capital of the Hova country. He was also responsible for giving the Hova people the laws that governed them until 1895. His successors continued his work in the nineteenth century with the help of several European advisers. As we see, the beginnings of civilisation in Madagascar are of fairly recent date.

6. GEOGRAPHERS AND SAILORS

We know that Islam gave rise to a very brilliant civilisation, in which geographical science held an honoured place. Arab geographers were numerous, and their works, after having been long forgotten, were given new importance during the last century by the researches of Langlès, Reinaud, De Goeje, and a few others. In the twentieth century they were again the subject of some excellent studies, among which Ferrand's and Sauvaget's deserve special mention.[9]

[8] Quoted by P. Herrmann, *L'Homme à la découverte du monde*, trans. R. Jouan and M. Roth, Paris, 1952, p. 467.
[9] Arab nautical and geographical texts were not always studied in detail. That is why Sauvaget undertook, shortly before his death, a new annotated translation of *Le Voyage du marchand Soleiman* and *L'Adjaib al Hind*.

An enumeration of those geographers, with their mile-long names and the even longer titles of their works, would be of no use whatever to the reader. Moreover, those who actually visited the places they described must be distinguished from those who merely got their tales from others. Among the former, those especially worthy of mention are Suleiman (851) the author of a remarkable guidebook, of whom we have already spoken; Masudi (c. 950); Idrisi (c. 1150); and, most famous of them all, Ibn Battuta (c. 1350), who was the traveller *par excellence*, the Arab Ulysses, curious, learned, courageous, and artistic. Among the compilers, the only works worth mentioning are those of Ibn Khurdadhbih (c. 850), Ibn Hawqal (c. 975), and the curious collection of Ibn Shahriyar entitled *Ajaib al Hind*, or *The Wonders of India*, which dates back to about 960.[10]

Were this list to be even more limited, the book we would recommend to those who would like to consult at least one Arab source on the Indian Ocean is perhaps the *Ajaib al Hind*, for really everything can be found in it, and that everything takes up very few pages, whereas the tales of Ibn Battuta, although of a higher standard, are far longer.

A last Arab source on the Indian Ocean is the famous tale of Sindbad the Sailor's travels in the *Arabian Nights*. Although the work has no scientific pretensions, it should not be neglected. How, indeed, could it be omitted when it is a veritable 'classic' and has given most people their ideas on the Arab activities in that ocean? False ideas, unfortunately, for it would be impossible to judge Arab sailors from the hero of the *Arabian Nights* or, for that matter, even from authentic characters such as Masudi, Idrisi and Ibn Battuta, who were literate men of another class, far different from the class of merchants and seafarers. This fact is emphasised by van Leur, who writes:

> The achievement of Islam in the fields of literary and human-
> istic culture had as such no direct relationship to the complex
> of social-economic organisation, let alone any influence on it.
> It was too much bound to tradition for that; the social distance
> between the learned and the merchants and tradesmen was too

[10] Translated into French by M. Devic and published in 1878 as *Les Merveilles de l'Inde*. There is an English translation by P. Quennell (1926) and a new French translation by Sauvaget in *Mémorial Jean Sauvaget* (Damascus, 1954).

great and the nature of learning too scholastic. This should be kept in mind in considering Moslem achievements in the fields of geography and nautical science; those achievements never had a decisive influence on the level of organisation of trade and shipping.[11]

These comments of van Leur, which are supported by facts, should be compared with Poujade's—also based on facts—on 'the routine the sailors so loved', recalling that during that period sailor and merchant were practically one and the same.

On the whole, therefore, the seven centuries of Arab ascendancy, or more precisely, Moslem ascendancy which is quite different, following on that of the Romans and the Iranians in the Erythraean Sea, would not seem to have brought about much change in the physiognomy of the ocean.

The Arabs doubtless went farther than their predecessors along the two great oceanic routes, that from west to east along the Asiatic shore and that from north to south along the African coast. Yet on close inspection, the sphere of Arab maritime activity was hardly more extensive than that of the Romans. It is the zone where today the dhows still sail, and it forms roughly the triangle Djibouti, Colombo, Zanzibar, and the Comoros. The Arabs named it the Sea of Lar, while they called the eastern region of the Indian Ocean the Sea of Harkand. They would seem to have had no single name for the ocean as a whole.

A true picture of their activity in the Indian Ocean from the seventh to the fourteenth century can probably best be found in the 'dhow harbours' of Mombasa, or in Makalla, on the Hadhramaut coast, or even at Moroni, the largest of the Comoro Islands. The picture is one of very moderate activity, if we compare it to that of modern times. Nowhere is the contrast between ancient and modern more striking than at Mombasa, or even at Aden, when in either port one goes from the region of the modern wharves, buzzing with intense life, to the part reserved for the dhows (Dhow Harbour in Mombasa; Maalla in Aden), where everything goes on at a much slower pace.

We must beware, in any case, of pictures that the *Arabian Nights* might call up, or even the map of the Indian Ocean (according to Idrisi), which would give the impression of a

[11] J. C. van Leur, *Indonesian Trade and Society*, The Hague, 1955, p. 74.

kind of *mare arabicum* somewhat similar to a long corridor most effectively linking Asia and Africa, whereas in fact vast tracts were still unknown to Arab navigators, and as we have just noted, their sphere of activity went little beyond the western region of the ocean.

We must also beware of the expression 'Arab thalassocracy', even though it is used by such distinguished historians as Toynbee and Pirenne. If it means only that the Arabs, or rather the Moslems, controlled all the ports and markets of the Erythraean Sea, well and good; but if the word implies the existence of a real sea-power, then the term is incorrect, for before Turkey, no Islamic country, whether in the Mediterranean or in the Indian Ocean, ever possessed any naval force other than small fleets of corsairs. The best proof of this is that the Arabs were quite incapable of holding their own against the Portuguese in the Indian Ocean during the sixteenth century, and had to call upon the Turkish navy.

Moreover, how can one speak of Arab 'thalassocracy' when it is undeniable that in the Moslem world the main lines of communication were land routes and not sea routes! Toynbee made a special point of this, and showed that the substitution of the ocean for the steppe at the end of the fifteenth century was a 'technological revolution' of vast significance.

7. THE ARAB SAIL

What then was there special or *sui generis* about the Arab ascendancy in the Indian Ocean? In the first place, the Arab dinar replaced the Roman aureus and the Persian dirhem. In the tenth century the dinar was the only coin commonly used throughout the Indian Ocean; Auber reports that Egyptian Fatimid specimens have been found even in Madagascar.

In the second place, Moslem merchants introduced into the countries of the Indian Ocean certain tropical plants (rice, coffee, sugar cane) and Chinese inventions such as gunpowder, paper, the compass, the saddle, and stirrups. It was also they who introduced the Chinese to the use of the astrolabe.

On the other hand, they have the sad reputation of having transported to all the countries of the Indian Ocean and even as far as China innumerable cargoes of slaves, brought mainly from the east coast of Africa, where that trade was to prosper until the end of the nineteenth century. Of course, the slave trade, like piracy, had existed in the Indian Ocean from time immemorial, but it was the Arabs who gave it its final form, and became, as it were, specialiscs in it. Although slavery in their countries was of a nature very different from the 'colonial' slavery of modern times, the systematic exploitation of Africans often provoked sharp reactions, in particular, the terrible rebellion of Zenj slaves in Basra during the ninth century.

From a cultural point of view, the spread of Islam through several countries of the Indian Ocean is a fact to be remembered. Yet it was not accompanied by artistic manifestations like those which accompanied the spread of Hinduism in Indonesia, as we shall see later. We are speaking, obviously, of the Islam carried by sea, by the sailors and merchants, and not of the Moslem conquests on the Asian continent, which had remarkable results with regard to art. It would be vain, in the part of the African coast 'colonised' by the Arabs, to seek out works of art comparable to those of the great Mogul period in India or even to the temples of Angkor and Borobudur.

It is true that recent excavations have brought to light, on the coast of East Africa, very remarkable Arab ruins, at Gedi and at Kilwa Kiswani. There is an important text on Kilwa, the *Sinet el Kilawia*, or Chronicles of Kilwa, which reports the peregrinations of Hasan ibn Ali; unfortunately nothing of it remains today but a résumé in the British Museum. An English archaeologist, Kirkman, devoted a very beautiful book to Gedi in 1852; Sir Arthur Conan Doyle's son became enthusiastic over the remains found in Kilwa Kiswani; but all this is still very far from great art. There is no doubt that Gedi, which can be reached in about two hours from Mombasa, makes a lasting impression on the visitor, especially if he happens to wander through that dead city at nightfall, but it cannot be compared with, for example, the enchantment of the Taj Mahal.

It was primarily in the nautical realm that the Arab left his mark on the Erythraean Sea, and even started a new technique. The triangular sail known today in the Mediterranean as the 'Latin sail' or lateen is not Latin at all; it was the

Arabs who introduced it into the Mediterranean. Originally it was a fore-and-aft sail of trapezoid shape, often with so small a base that from a distance it appeared to be triangular. It is still used on all Arab boats. Before the Arab sail, Europeans were familiar only with the square sail, of inferior aerodynamic efficiency but easier to handle in bad weather. The Egyptians and Phoenicians, also, were familiar only with the square sail.

Poujade, who gives these details, explains that with the same surface, that is, with a mast of a given height, the boat rigged with an Arab sail can set a course closer to the wind and cover it more quickly than a boat with square sails. It is therefore not surprising that the Arab sail rapidly replaced the square sail as soon as it was introduced into the Mediterranean.

According to Poujade, however, the Arabs did not invent this form of sail, which would seem to have come originally from western India, but merely perfected it. Moreover, the Arab sail is suitable only for certain kinds of navigation, and the sailors of the Atlantic never wholly adopted it; the rig of da Gama's and Columbus's caravels consisted mainly of square sails, with only a small lateen aft.

V. Greater India

I. THE COLONISER

INDIA, situated at the central point of the ocean that washes its coast on three sides, seemed destined very early for a maritime future. Yet nothing of the kind happened, and despite its privileged position, the country was not to play a part in maritime activities until fairly late in its history. In a scholarly work which has already been cited, Dr. Mookerji collected a great amount of evidence to establish the contrary, but his evidence, mainly artistic and literary, is hardly convincing. Other writers do not share his view, and one of them (Basham) wrote on the subject: 'Certain over-enthusiastic Indian scholars have perhaps made too much of the achievement of ancient Indian seafarers, which cannot compare with those of the Vikings, or of some other early maritime peoples.'[1]

There is no doubt that a very active coastal trade existed at certain points on the Indian coast, namely, in the region of Gujarat and the south of the peninsula, in quite early times, but the existence of 'liners' capable of transporting a thousand passengers, recorded in the ancient literature of India, is much more doubtful.

That Indian merchants had been in Egypt and even as far as Rome during the Hellenistic and Roman periods is also well established, but, as we have already emphasised, and it is a fact on which all the evidence concurs, their number was infinitesimal compared to that of the foreign merchants who at that time

[1] A. L. Basham, *The Wonder that was India*, London, 1954, p. 226.

frequently visited the ports of India. Actually, India has every reason to be thankful, since, as Mookerji very rightly commented, she had no need to launch out on the conquest of distant Americas to obtain a supply of metallic currency, and she thus escaped the vicissitudes of the exploiting peoples who were forced to go out and seek their fortune far from their own lands.

But although she was not a conquering maritime power, she nonetheless moved into the countries of the Indian Ocean. In fact, long before she was colonised herself, she gave proof of a very remarkable colonising activity, which long remained unknown until a French orientalist, Coedès, revealed it to the world, a short time back, in a work which none of those interested in oceanic history should fail to read.

A 'colonizing activity', we have called it, but we must add that the word 'colonizing' is not meant in the popular sense; or perhaps we should say that, on the contrary, it was true colonisation. Is not peaceful penetration, both economic and cultural, and occurring with the full consent of those colonised, for whom it proves beneficial and lasting in its effects, is not this, in fact, real colonisation?

2. FIRST CONTACTS WITH THE MALAY ARCHIPELAGO

According to Coedès, the geographical area involved in this Indian colonisation included the region called in French *Insulinde*, the Malay Archipelago (exclusive of the Philippines) and Indochina, along with the Malay Peninsula and Burma. Assam, which is simply an extension of India and Bengal is not included; nor are Tongking and North Annam, whose history developed outside the sphere of Hindu influence.

'The natural wealth and geographical situation of the region so defined,' adds Coedès,

> give it an all-important place. After having been, at about the beginning of the Christian era, the country of gold toward which the Hindu navigators steered their course, Indochina and, more especially, the Malay Archipelago became for the Arabs and the Europeans, a few centuries later, the country of spices, camphor, and aromatic woods, before establishing itself,

as it has recently done, as one of the most important pro-
ducers of rubber, tin, and oil. Furthermore, the position of the
Peninsula and the Sunda Islands makes them an obligatory point
of call for navigators making their way from the West and from
India to China, and vice versa; whence their importance for
maritime trade.[2]

The relations between India and the Malay and Indonesian
region began, in fact, long before the opening of the Christian
era. Hall traces them back to prehistory, and stresses the fact
that Indian navigators were not the only ones to cross the Bay of
Bengal, but that the inhabitants of Malaya and of the Malay
Archipelago had also made their way to India at a very early
time. This opinion is shared by van Leur, who gives a highly
original explanation of the Indian expansion, very different
from that of Coedès. We shall come back to it. For the moment,
we would recall only that the Malays have always been a
maritime people, to whom very distant migrations are attributed. We have seen that they had been unique in using the
south equatorial current, which crosses the Indian Ocean from
east to west, in order to reach Madagascar.

These first contacts across the Bay of Bengal were at the
beginning of little importance on either side. Colonising activity
did not start until the Christian era, and stretched over two
periods, of which the first, a period of gradual infiltration and
consolidation, lasted from the first to the sixth centuries, and the
second, one of development and ever-increasing fruition, from
the seventh to the tenth centuries.

3. CENTRES OF EXPANSION

The main centre of Indian expansion was the Tamil or
Dravidian region in the south of India. Chased from the north
of the peninsula by the Aryans, the Dravidians went all the
way down to the south, where the existence has been established
of three particularly flourishing Dravidian maritime kingdoms
at the beginning of the Christian era: those of the Chera, of the
Pandya, and of the Chola. The first controlled the entire
south-west coast of the peninsula, from Calicut to Cape

[2] G. Coedès, Les États hindouisés d'Indochine et d'Indonésie, Paris, 1948, pp. 1–2.

Comorin; it dealt primarily in the pepper trade, and its main ports were Muziris (Cranganore) and Nelkynda (Kottayam). The second occupied the district of Madura and Tinnevelly, and controlled the pearl fisheries on the Gulf of Mannar. The third stretched along the Coromandel coast, from Valiyar to Nellore and the Penner river. It was well known for the manufacture of muslin; its capital was Argam (Uraiyur; today Trichinopoly) and its main outlet was Kaviripaddinam (the Camara of the *Periplus*) at the mouth of the Cauvery. The secondary ports of Poduca and Sopatma, also mentioned in the *Periplus*, were also very active.

Of these three kingdoms the most important was the Chola kingdom, which controlled the Bay of Bengal. During the period of Roman commercial activity, it was to its ports that merchants from Egypt came to get their supplies, and as we have seen, they set up a kind of trading station at Poduca.

The points of departure and the routes of Hindu expansion in what is called 'outer' or 'Greater India' are not very well known. Cœdès, after an examination of the various testimonies, concludes that all the eastern ports of the peninsula contributed, but that the south, that is, the Tamil country, had the greatest share in it. Mookerji, for his part, mentions facts showing that the ancient kingdom of Kalinga, on the coast of Orissa, a kingdom 'whose early history nobody knows or cares to know', played a dominant part in the development, and that it led mostly to colonisation in Burma. Mookerji also mentions Bengal and Gujarat among the regions that sent colonists to the Malay Archipelago.

As for the causes that determined such expansion and led to the formation of true 'Hinduised states' in the region in question, it would seem doubtful today, after the light van Leur's work has shed on the problem, whether they were of a purely material order. In any case, it is hardly probable that the search for gold was the main cause of the rise in Indian maritime activity, especially if we take into account the mediocre gold-bearing capacity of Greater India.

According to van Leur, it is also highly improbable that the agents of colonisation of Greater India were tradesmen and sailors. That explanation, he says, has no historical value. In his opinion the planting of Indian culture in the Malay

Archipelago was due to the initiative of the Indonesian ruling classes, and the mercantile class took no part at all in it. In fact, we are to suppose a definite invitation on the part of the Indonesians, and those who issued the invitation were not tradesmen but priests, Brahmans. This would seem to have been the case not only in Indonesia but also in Ceylon and in Indo-China:

> The Indian priesthood was called eastwards, certainly because of its wide renown, for the magical, sacral legitimation of dynastic interests and the domestication of subjects, and probably for the organisation of the ruler's territory into a state. Alongside the priesthood, Indian artifice came to the royal courts, and the architectural activity of the rulers and the official religious activities of those overseas states alike show the unmistakable imprint of Indian civilisation. . . .[3]

The religion's regulations forbidding orthodox Hindus to associate with foreigners were not respected in the circumstances, for we have testimony showing that the Brahman immigrants married the natives.

The Indian influence expressed itself in a transformation of local customs in the form of institutions and works which have survived the erosion of time. The most striking are the monuments built in all these countries, first by Indian architects, then by the pupils they had trained on the spot, which testify both to Indian and to local genius. The temples of Angkor in Cambodia and of Borobudur in Java are among the most famous of these.

4. THE MAIN STAGES

We can do no more here than give a summary, and a most incomplete one, of the stages in the creation of Greater India; for the reader in search of further information, we would recommend Cœdès' remarkable work.

First stage: the founding, in the first century, of Funan, the predecessor of Cambodia, in the lower Mekong basin. In the second century Funan extended all the way to the Malay Peninsula and seems to have constituted a kind of empire or federation of small Hinduised states, whose ruler was called 'king of the mountain'. It was to last until the middle of the

[3] Van Leur, *op. cit.*, pp. 103–4.

second century, when it was then replaced by the kingdom of the Khmer or Kambuja.

Second stage: in the first century, Indian settlement in Malaya, mainly at Kedah on the Merbok river, soon to be called Langkasuka. The Indian colonies in Malaya, at first autonomous, gradually came under the control of the maritime state of Shrivijaya, in Sumatra.

Third stage: the creation in the fourth century (?) and the rapid expansion up to the end of the seventh of the Sumatran kingdom of Shrivijaya, with Palembang as its capital. Almost simultaneously there appeared in Java a state called Kalinga, made up of elements from an earlier Kalinga, on the coast of Orissa.

Fourth stage: the appearance, in the eighth century, in central Java, of a Buddhist dynasty which suddenly succeeded a Saivaite ruler descended from the Kalinga, revived the imperial title 'king of the mountain' (*Sailendra*, whence the name of Sailendra given the leaders of this dynasty), covered the country with great Buddhist monuments (Borobudur among others), and seems to have exercised a kind of hegemony in the seas of the Malay Archipelago, extending all the way to Cambodia. The Sailendra also dominated the kingdom of Shrivijaya.

Fifth stage: in the year 802 the Khmer freed themselves from the suzerainty of the Javanese Sailendra and formed the kingdom of Angkor, which for four centuries was one of the ruling powers of Greater India. The Sailendra were losing their influence in Java, where the rulers of the ancient Saivaite dynasty, who had retreated to the eastern part of the island, were gaining a new foothold. On the other hand, in Shrivijaya the Sailendra were holding their own and strengthening their power.

Sixth stage: the tenth century marked the height of the maritime power of Shrivijaya, which, because of its geographical position, controlled the straits. It also marked the height of the Angkor civilisation and that of the Chola in southern India, who were soon to intervene militarily in the Malay Archipelago. At the beginning of the eleventh century a powerful Chola fleet raided Shrivijaya, which was attacked soon after by the Javanese of Kadiri. Although weakened, the kingdom of

Shrivijaya held its own against both the Chola and the Javanese of Kadiri. The Chola had finally to give up the struggle at the end of the eleventh century, having derived no benefit from the many episodes of a maritime adventure that lasted almost a century.

Seventh stage: the twelfth century was marked by two important events: the decline of the Angkor civilisation and the penetration of Indian cultural influence into Burma, through Ceylon; Sinhalese Buddhism was brought to Burma, and from there was to spread to the Indo-Chinese peninsula.

Eighth stage: in the thirteenth century the maritime power of Shrivijaya was still great enough for one of its rulers, Chandrabhanu, to undertake with success two great expeditions, involving hundreds of vessels and thousands of men, against the island of Ceylon. At the same time, in Java, the advent of the kingdom of Singhasari, which succeeded that of Kadiri in 1222, marked the beginning of the recession of Hindu influence, confronted by the revival of the submerged Indonesian culture.

Ninth stage: in the fourteenth century Shrivijaya began definitively to decline. The maritime power in the Malay Archipelago then passed to a new Javanese kingdom, formed in 1293, called Madjapahit, which held its own until 1389. The second half of the fourteenth century witnessed also the final collapse of the Angkor civilisation. The Hindu period of Greater India was how nearing its end.

5. THE CONTRIBUTION OF HINDUISM

Before turning to the fifteenth century and showing how Hinduism had then to give way to Islam in Greater India, we must first try to take stock of the Indian colonisation in that region and identify its basic characteristics.

As we have already said, this was not colonisation in the sense generally given to the word, that is, the colonies so formed were never political dependencies of India, but merely cultural colonies. But the expression 'cultural colonies' must itself be defined somewhat more clearly. How much of this colonisation, for example, was actually due to Hinduism? How can we explain, in particular, the creation of masterpieces

66

such as the temples of Angkor and Borobudur, which, it must be emphasised, have no equals in India itself?

On this point the English writers (Hall, Harrison, etc.), who studied the problem after Coedès, have reproached the latter for neglecting, in speaking of 'Hinduised' states, certain aspects of this very complex problem and for giving too much credit to Hinduism. They point out, with justification, that Buddhism played a most important part in this cultural phenomenon and that it even survived Hinduism in most of the regions concerned.

Van Leur, for his part, stresses, at least with regard to Indonesia, the primary importance of the native substratum, which he refuses to call primitive. The Indonesian social and political organisation, he says, existed in all its fullness and force before the Indians ever came.

Moreover, during the whole period that we have just reviewed, the region designated as 'Greater India' was also subject to Chinese influence. So as not to weigh down this account with still more oriental names, we have made no mention of the activity of the Chinese in this region, but we shall see in the following chapter that it was not negligible.

To what conclusion, then, can we come? The study of the history of Greater India has only just begun, and it is obvious that much still remains to be written on the matter. A few years ago, a society was formed in India with precisely this study as its object. To one of its outstanding members, Dr. Nilakanta Sastri, of the University of Madras, we owe, among other works, a very good history of the south of India.

It would thus seem that, given the present state of the question, nothing definitive can be said. But is there anything definitive in history? And from all the past, present, and future studies of this question, will anything ever be established save that the remarkable civilisation of Greater India is the result not of one sole factor but of several, about which generations and generations of scholars will wrangle *ad infinitum*?[4]

[4] On this question, see also the works of the sociologist Quaritch Wales, especially his last book *Prehistory and Religion in South-East Asia*, London, 1957, in which the author, reverting to theses he had already proposed in his earlier works, explicitly states his ideas on the reciprocal contribution of the Indian and the native elements. See also Coedès' discussion of Quaritch Wales' ideas in the *Journal asiatique* for 1957.

6. THE ISLAMIC CONQUEST

While the expansion of the Hindu maritime kingdoms of the south and the east gave rise to a Greater India, a considerable part of India itself fell into the hands of the Moslems. Less than a century after its appearance in Arabia, Islam penetrated India as far as Multan on the Indus, after having conquered Afghanistan and Baluchistan. The very strong reaction of the rulers south-east of the Indus, and the great expanse of desert east of that river, stopped the Moslem push for three centuries, but it began again at the end of the tenth. In the thirteenth century the foreign conquerors, with Delhi as their capital, held the entire north of India, from the mouths of the Ganges to those of the Indus, and to the south as far as Gwalior.

Then it was the turn of south India, but there the Moslems were to meet with fierce resistance. After the decline of the Chola in the thirteenth century, the controlling influence in the Tamil country went to a new dynasty, which had set up its capital in the year 1336 on the banks of the Tungabhadra, giving it the ambitious, but soon to be justified, name of Vijayanagar (The City of Victory), and it was not until the sixteenth century, in 1566, that the forces of that heroic kingdom were crushed in the battle of Talikot. Vijayanagar was taken, sacked, and burned; its inhabitants killed or taken into slavery. The long resistance of the Tamils thus kept the Moslem wave from reaching Great India; but Islam managed to penetrate it in another way.

We have seen that the region of Gujarat, in north-west India, had taken part in the movement of Indian expansion in the Malay Archipelago. The relations between that region and the island of Java would seem to date back to the seventh century. After the Moslem conquest and the Islamisation of Gujarat, they continued, and subsequently developed so much that the Gujarat merchants soon became serious competitors with the Tamil merchants in Indonesia.

In the thirteenth century there was already one large Moslem colony at Perlak, in northern Sumatra; from there Islam spread to the other principalities of the island and won over Malacca, in the Malay Peninsula, in the fourteenth century. The entire

Malay Archipelago was then under the dominion of the kingdom of Madjapahit, and the propagation of Islam was effective in gradually alienating the leaders of the coastal regions from their allegiance to that kingdom. In the fifteenth century the Islamisation of the Malay Archipelago was an accomplished fact, more than twenty states having by then adopted as their official religion the faith of Mohammed. Naturally, in the sixteenth century the fall of Vijayanagar in India only hastened the process.

The decline of Hinduism in Greater India cannot be explained solely by the fact that the Hindu religion, reformed in these distant kingdoms, had finally resumed its character of exclusivity, had lost all popular support, and was, in a sense, fossilised. There is no doubt that Hinduism, in its special aspect as a royal cult, which it had taken on in Greater India, was an essentially aristocratic religion, without influence on the masses. But that does not suffice to explain why it was so quickly replaced by Islam.

The following is what van Leur has to say on this point. A mercantile aristocracy, which sprang up on the Malay Archipelago from the development of the maritime trade, would seem to have used Islam as a political weapon against both the Tamil merchants and the central authority of Madjapahit. Later, the opposition to the Portuguese, after they had taken Malacca in 1511, served only to reinforce Islam's position in that region.

Van Leur also points out that the propagation of Islam in the Malay Archipelago was by no means cultural in nature, for its agents were not learned men but simple merchants with little education. Also, according to him, Islam brought no new economic system to Indonesia. Besides, as we shall see further on, Chinese influence remained predominant in commercial matters in that region even after its Islamisation. Nor was customary law much influenced by Koranic law.

7. INDIA AND CHINA

The maritime activity of the Indians in the eastern part of the ocean was not limited to the Malay Archipelago, but extended also to the Far East. Mookerji devotes an entire chapter of his book to his country's relations with China. He begins by citing the opinion of Professor Lacouperie (an author whose works are a little out of date), who traces these relations back to the year 600 B.C. At that date Hindus from the eastern coast of the peninsula were said to have founded a colony called Lang-ga (*cf.* Lanka, the Indian name for Ceylon), on the Gulf of Kiao-chao. The colonists of Lang-ga are supposed to have retreated to Cambodia at a much later period.

Mookerji himself merely places the first maritime contacts between India and China during the first century of the Christian era, basing his view on Chinese annals and Indian texts. He also calls attention to several journeys to China made by Buddhist monks from India and Ceylon, as early as the year 398, that is, before the first known voyages of Chinese Buddhists to India. The main port for these sailings to China was Tam-ralipti, at the mouth of the Ganges, which was also a great Buddhist centre. Ptolemy mentions it, and several Chinese travellers have given descriptions of it also.

The voyages to China were particularly numerous in the sixth century. In 526 a famous Indian Buddhist named Bodhidharma made his way to Canton and there created a genuine missionary centre. The enterprise met with such success that in Lo-Yang there were soon more than three thousand Indian monks and ten thousand families of the same race who devoted themselves to proselytism in China.

All this is of more particular interest as we know, in another connection, that Chinese navigators themselves did not visit the Malay region until the fifth century and did not venture out into the seas of India, Persia, and Arabia until the sixth.

8. INDIA AND AFRICA

The Indians were apparently not satisfied to sail the sea to the east and west of the peninsula. They are said to have pushed out very far along the east coast of Africa as well.

In a curious study on the origins of Zimbabwe, a Dutch writer, Van Oordt, tries to establish it as a fact that the Dravidians sent expeditions to the region of Mozambique at a very early epoch, which he unfortunately does not specify. Unfortunately also, the 'proofs' he gives are based on nothing more than similarity of names. According to him, the words Zambesi and Zimbabwe are of Indian origin; but who can prove it?

There also exists, among a tribe in Mozambique, a tradition relating to the existence in that territory, in very olden times, of a dark-skinned, long-haired alien race reputed to have come from the Malabar coast. How comes it, then, that it has completely disappeared, leaving no trace?

Finally, the Swahili of East Africa have retained a memory of foreigners called Wadebuli, who are supposed to have come formerly by sea in vessels 'made of palm leaves'. The name Wadebuli might be derived from Dhabol, a port on the west coast of India often mentioned by Arab geographers. As for the palm leaves, they were apparently shelters covered with these leaves and placed on the decks of the boats. Such shelters are still frequently used on oriental ships.

Villiers, who closely studied the Indian *kotias*, especially in the region of Gujarat, is inclined to believe that boats of this kind were perfectly able to make long voyages to the African coast. The *kotias*, he says, are much sturdier than the dhows and the Arab *baggalas*, and the Gujarat region has always been renowned for its shipbuilding. Even today there are still, in that area, a large number of sailing boats which carry on regular traffic with Calcutta, Malacca, Basra, Aden and Zanzibar.[5] These comments remind us of descriptions of Indian boats found in the works of Arab geographers and in the accounts of European travellers in the Indian Ocean. They may also be compared with the portrayals of boats on the walls of the sanctuaries of Borobudur in Java, as well as with Poujade's conclusions as to the origin of the fore-and-aft sail in the Indian Ocean, cited in the preceding chapter.

According to Poujade, this type of sail originated in the region of western India, whence its use spread towards east and west at the beginning of our era. In the east it moved down the Malay Peninsula and between the seventh and ninth centuries was introduced into Java, where the Indian boats sculptured on the temple of Borobudur all have fore-and-aft

[5] In his work on the Indian Ocean (p. 97), Villiers stresses the importance of such traffic and cities on this subject K. B. Vaidya, *The Sailing Vessel Traffic on the West Coast of India and its Failure*, Bombay, 1945.

sails. From the Malay Archipelago, the fore-and-aft sail reached Indo-China; as it was perfected, and its efficiency increased, its shape changed to that of the sail on the Annamese sea-going boats or the boats on the Indian waters, whereas in its early rectangular shape it continued to spread along the coasts, towards Siam on the one hand and China on the other.

In the Malay Archipelago the Indian influence on native shipbuilding was to be radical. In fact, before the arrival of the Indians, the natives of that region had probably not been familiar with anything other than the catamaran.

Finally, in the western part of the Indian Ocean, in the region of the Erythraean Sea, the fore-and-aft sail, transformed, as we have seen, by the Arabs, gave rise to the triangular sail of the dhows, incorrectly called the 'Latin' or lateen sail.

9. THE INDIAN NAVY

Having discussed the Indians' maritime proceedings, we have still to consider briefly their naval activities. India seems to have been the first country of the Indian Ocean to possess real battle-fleets. The Maurya emperor Chandragupta, who ruled from 321 to 297 B.C., had even at that time, an actual Board of Admiralty, with a Superintendent of Ships at its head. There is a curious description of that organisation in Kautilya's *Arthasastra*, a Sanskrit work of the period, and Mookerji gives an interesting analysis of it in his book.

Unfortunately we know very little about the Tamil navy. But as Dr. Nilakanta Sastri points out, the conquest of Reva-tidvipa and Puri, on the west coast of India, by the Chalukya of Badami (543–753), the conquest of Ceylon by the Pallava, the Pandya, and the Chola (574–1173), and above all, the great Chola expedition against the kingdom of Shrivijaya in 1025, could not have been carried out without an efficient naval organisation. Moreover, the maritime trade, especially of southern India, must have required, from the very beginning, the setting up of means of protection against pirates.

This point of view, however, is not shared by another Indian historian, Mahalingam, who in a more recent work assures us that everything written about the Tamil navy is greatly exaggerated. He finds it doubtful whether even the Chola at the height of their power had real naval forces, and thinks that what they probably used were merely merchant ships equipped for war.

On Indian naval activities during the period of Moslem domination, especially in the reign of the Mogul emperor Akbar (1562–1605), we are better informed, thanks to the *Ayeen-i-Akbari*, or Chronicle of the Reign of Akbar, cited by Mookerji.

It has already been pointed out that the Moslem conquest had almost no influence on the country's maritime and commercial activity. From a naval point of view the same does not hold good. The creation of a naval organisation, similar to Chandragupta's but larger, must be dated from the reign of Akbar. The functions of that organisation were (1) to control shipbuilding; (2) to ensure the recruitment of crews; (3) to survey the ships and the coasts; and (4) to collect customs duties. The imperial fleet (*Nowwara*), when first created by Akbar, included no less than 3,000 vessels; this number was later reduced to 768. The main body of the fleet was concentrated at Dacca, on the Bay of Bengal, but there were large contingents on the coast of Gujarat.

After Akbar's death, those naval forces were strengthened by his successors. They did not succeed in standing up to the European vessels in the Indian Ocean, but, as we shall see later, their role was not entirely negligible.

VI. The Role of the Chinese

I. ITS BEGINNINGS

ALTHOUGH China is not a country of the Indian Ocean, her history is nevertheless very closely tied up with it. In fact, as we shall see, that ocean might well have become a Chinese lake.

Ancient Chinese voyages have been studied by Ferrand, Duyvendak, Hirth, Pelliot, Rockhill, Yule, and a few others. In the light of their work, three distinct phases of maritime activity can be traced. The first, a period of beginnings, stretched from about 1200 B.C. to about the end of the seventh century A.D. The second lasted from the seventh century to the year 1127, that is, to the end of the Sung dynasty: it was a period of very active expansion. The third lasted from 1127 to 1433, and marked the height of the maritime activity of the Chinese in the Indian Ocean, after which they suddenly returned home, literally turning their backs on the sea.

It was apparently about the year 1200 B.C., at the mouth of the Yang-tze Kiang, that their first rather hesitant attempts at navigation were carried out, but not until much later, in the fourth century B.C., did they venture out on to the high seas. In the third century they went as far as Japan; in the second they reached Tongking, which they soon conquered. At the beginning of the first century B.C. a ruler of the Han dynasty sent an embassy by sea to Conjeveram (Kenchipuram), the Pallava capital, on the Coromandel coast. The embassy travelled on Indian boats, but it was not long before the Chinese junks set out for India in their turn.

74

From the first century of the Christian era, trade relations with India became increasingly frequent. Yet the voyages to India made by the Chinese were far less numerous than those the Indians made to China. In any case, they did not go beyond the Coromandel coast.

In his work on Arab navigation, Hourani, after carefully considering all the evidence relating to the presence of Chinese ships in the Persian Gulf under the Sassanids, rejects it and concludes that before the Ming dynasty (beginning in 1368), Chinese navigation in the Indian Ocean went no farther than the port of Quilon on the Malabar coast. Yet before the seventh century, that is, before the end of that period of beginnings, several Chinese Buddhist monks had crossed all India on a pilgrimage to the sanctuaries of the Buddha, making a great part of their journey by sea. We shall speak further of these pilgrimages, which are of particular interest because of the accounts of them that were published. Moreover, before the seventh century, the Chinese had sent out several maritime expeditions against Indo-China. In the year 407, for example, a Chinese fleet laid waste the coast of Champa.

2. THE SUNG PERIOD

In the seventh century, according to Ferrand, the Chinese were among the most daring navigators of the eastern region of the Indian Ocean. They were already in possession of ships capable of transporting six to seven hundred people.[1] Their naval forces were also appreciable. In 605 a Chinese fleet victoriously beat off an attack by the Cham on Tongking; in 606 another fleet laid waste the island of Formosa; in 643, 658, and 660, other Chinese fleets, including as many as five hundred units, attacked Korea. The eighth and ninth centuries were also marked by several naval battles on the coast of Tongking against the Cham and their allies.

In the meantime, as we have seen in a previous chapter, Moslem, Mazdean, Jewish, and Christian merchants had settled

[1] Yet according to Pierre Paris, the seagoing junk probably did not exist until the ninth century, although it surely did from the twelfth onward ('Quelques dates pour une histoire de la jonque chinoise,' *Bull. Ec. franç. Ext.*—Orient, XLI, 1952, pp. 267–78).

in Canton, where they engaged in very active trading, so active in fact that it was soon necessary to set up a special office in that port to control foreign trade. The sack of Canton by the Arabs in 758 brought it to an end.

Reopened to foreign trade in 792, Canton was the scene of a new and even more frightful drama a century later (878), when rebel forces, rising against the then ruling dynasty (the Tang), massacred, in a fit of xenophobia, all the merchants of the Indian Ocean who were then set up in trade there. There followed great decline of commercial activity, which did not recover until the Sung dynasty (960–1127) came into power. The Sung again reopened China to foreigners. In 998 the customs were again working, and evidence from the twelfth century describes a situation rather similar to that of the ninth.

Special navigation inspection was initiated in the principal ports: Canton, Chuanchow, Hangchow, and Ningpo. Of all these ports Canton remained the most important until the twelfth century; it was then replaced by Chuanchow (or Tsinkiang), which Marco Polo was to make famous as Zayton. In the twelfth century Hangchow likewise developed in an unprecedented way. Marco Polo described it under the name of Quinsai (Kinsay).

The period of the Sung was also notable for considerable progress in shipbuilding and for the use of the compass, which began about the end of the eleventh century. It did not, however, immediately revolutionise the art of navigation, and for a long time sailors continued to put their trust instead in the sun and the stars.

3. KUBLAI KHAN

Duyvendak dates China's orientation towards the Indian Ocean and the beginning of its maritime predominance in the Malay Archipelago and the region of the Bay of Bengal from the time of the Southern Sung (1127–1279).

In a Chinese work entitled *Chu-Fan-Chi*, or the Chronicle of Foreign Nations, written in 1225 by Chau-ju-Kua, an inspector of maritime trade at Tsinkiang, we find numerous references to that maritime activity; but although the collection gives us reasonably good information on the trade of foreigners with

China, it shows that the geographical knowledge of the Chinese themselves was somewhat inaccurate.

For Chau-ju-Kua the West was almost exclusively the Islamic world. The Indian Ocean to the west of Ceylon and the Mediterranean were for him the 'eastern sea' and the 'western sea' of the *Ta'shi* (Arabs):

> Beyond the eastern sea of the Arabs, at the west are the Arab countries. Their territories are extremely vast and their kingdoms too numerous to be listed. Beyond the western sea of the Arabs there is Mu-lan-pi [Spain] and a thousand other kingdoms, and at the extreme west is the region where the sun sets and of which we know nothing.[2]

During the period in which Chau-ju Kua wrote, the Yuan dynasty (1279–1368) had replaced that of the Southern Sung. It was rendered famous by Kublai Khan, of whom Marco Polo paints a fascinating portrait.

The Mongol conqueror was not to have as good fortune by sea as by land. In 1281 he launched a formidable armada against Japan, but without success; in 1282 and 1287 he was beaten on the sea by the Cham and the Annamese; in 1292 another powerful fleet sent out from Canton against the kingdom of Kadiri in Java had to turn back after an indecisive battle.

These defeats did not, however, keep him from considerably fostering Chinese trade in the Indian Ocean. Between Zayton (Tsinkiang), Ceylon, Quilon on the Malabar coast, and Ormuz on the Persian Gulf, regular maritime 'lines' soon entered into competition with the Arab 'lines'. Numerous Chinese merchants settled in various ports of the Indian coast, namely, Kaviripaddinam, Quilon, Cail, and Calicut. The Chinese ships had then become the largest (they could transport up to a thousand persons) and best equipped in the Indian Ocean. On all this maritime activity we have the testimony of Marco Polo, who in 1291, by order of Kublai Khan, accompanied a Mongol princess as far as Iran by sea.

There were also, during this period, a great number of Chinese ships in the ports of the Malay Archipelago and

---

[2] Quoted in L.-H. Parias, *Histoire universelle des explorations*, Paris, 1955, I, 240.

77

Malaya. The attack in 1292 against Madjapahit did not break off the relations between China and the Javanese kingdom, which until the fifteenth century remained a great maritime power.

In the fourteenth century, fifty years after Marco Polo, Ibn Battuta marvelled, in his turn, at the maritime activity of the Chinese, and he chose to make his way from India to China by junk.

4. CHENG-HO'S EXPEDITIONS

In 1368 the Ming dynasty succeeded that of the Yuan. Continuing Kublai Khan's policies, but with greater success, it managed for some time to dominate the Indian Ocean. As soon as the first emperor of the dynasty ascended the throne, delegates extraordinary were sent to all the countries of the eastern region of the ocean to demand that tribute be paid to the new emperor.

As this new kind of ambassador was more or less welcomed, the request was repeated in a more peremptory way by sending out large naval expeditions under the command of Cheng-Ho, a great eunuch of the imperial palace. There were seven such expeditions in all, between the years 1405 and 1431. The first (1405–07) comprised 63 vessels and 27,870 men. Its main objectives were Java, Ceylon, and Calicut, and it was completely successful. On the return route, a flotilla of Sumatran pirates tried to block its way in the Palembang waters, but was totally annihilated. The objectives of the second (1407–09) were also the Malay Archipelago and the ports on the Malabar Coast, and its importance was secondary.

The third (1409–11) was made up of 48 vessels and 30,000 men; it visited much the same countries, and met with no resistance except in Ceylon; in the struggle that ensued, the Sinhalese forces were destroyed, the king of the country and his courtiers taken prisoners and brought to China, and until 1439 Ceylon had to pay an annual tribute to the victors.

The fourth expedition (1413–15) pressed on further than the three that preceded, going as far as the Maldive Islands and the port of Ormuz on the Persian Gulf. This was the first time that Chinese naval forces ventured beyond India.

During the fifth (1417–19), sixth (1421–22), and seventh (1431–33) expeditions, Cheng Ho went still farther, reaching Aden in Arabia, and several ports on the east coast of Africa, Mogadiscio, Brava, and Malindi. More than thirty ports in the Indian Ocean thus received a visit from Chinese sailors, and everywhere all that they asked was eagerly granted, either for fear of retaliation or from ignorance of the real motives of their visit.

These military expeditions, unique in the annals of the Indian Ocean before the arrival of the Portuguese, were to be short-lived. Pirenne expresses his opinion of them thus: 'There is no point in conquering the seas with naval squadrons if they are not preceded or followed by merchants. The Chinese had no bent for foreign navigation. They did not take advantage of the distant routes opened to them by the warships of the Ming emperors.'[3]

The fact is that China suddenly threw in the sponge when she had everything necessary to secure the command of the Indian Ocean; excellent ships, the compass, and gunpowder. Whether the Ming emperors had been too ambitious, whether the Chinese did not really, after all, have a seagoing temperament, or whether the ruling classes were opposed to costly and useless overseas conquests, whatever the reason, the Chinese navy departed from the Indian Ocean in the middle of the fifteenth century, never to return. It was a curious phenomenon, a real enigma.

In this connection, Grousset asks the following question: 'What would the destiny of Asia have been if European navigators, approaching the Indies and Malaya, had found a Chinese thalassocracy established there?'[4] Thousands of conjectures are possible, but history is not built up of conjectures. The Chinese never managed to establish a real thalassocracy in the Indian Ocean any more than the Arabs and the Indians had done. It was the European navigators from the other side of Africa, guided by the compass known to the Chinese, and equipped with arms invented by the Chinese, who were to accomplish at the end of the fifteenth century what the Ming had barely projected fifty years before.

[3] J. Pirenne, *Les Grands Courants de l'histoire universelle*, Paris, 1950, III, 320.
[4] R. Grousset, *Histoire de la Chine*, Paris, 1942, p. 318.

79

5. BUDDHIST PILGRIMS

One of the most important results, perhaps the most important, of Cheng-Ho's expeditions was the compilation of a volume of maps and nautical instructions known as the *Wu Pei Chih*, which did not see the light until 1621. Yet it has proved less important in the literature of the Indian Ocean than the peaceful journeys of the Chinese Buddhists alluded to above. Indeed, the accounts of these voyages have been published time and time again, and are numbered among the classics of the ocean. Their translation into several European languages has ensured them a large public, whereas the *Wu Pei Chih* is known only to a limited number of scholars.

The first, Chi-tao-an, made his way from China to India at the beginning of the fourth century. Unfortunately, his account is lost, and all we know of it are some extracts published by his disciples.

After him came Fa-hsien (Fa-hian), who left China in 399, and, after crossing central China and the Gobi Desert on foot, reached the north of India and went as far as the port of Tamralipti, on the Bengal coast. There he boarded a merchant ship which in fourteen days took him to Ceylon. After spending two years in Ceylon collecting Buddhist texts, he made his way by sea to Java. The voyage took ninety days and almost ended in tragedy. From Java he returned to China by sea after another eventful journey, bringing back with him a real harvest of documents on Buddhism. Abel Rémusat made an excellent French translation of the account of his peregrinations entitled *Foe-Koue-Ki* (Fo-kwo-ki).

A hundred years after Fa-hsien, two other Buddhist pilgrims, Hwei-sang and Sung-yun, also went to India to gain information about the life and works of the Buddha. The account of their adventures is better known than Fa-hsien's; it has been translated into German by Neumann.

Then came Hiuen-tsang, whose travel diary, called *Si-yu-ki*, is far longer and more detailed than those of his predecessors. He travelled through India and the outskirts of Iran from 628 to 645. In 638 he arrived, as did Fa-hsien, at Tamralipti and wanted to take a ship from there to Ceylon. News of civil war on the island made him give up this plan; but although he did not travel by sea, his account is nonetheless of interest with regard to the history of the Indian Ocean, for he gives a very vidid description of the port of Tamralipti, which was then an important emporium. He also gives very useful information on the state of Iran at the end of the Sassanid regime and on the Hinduised states of Indo-China. Hiuen-tsang has been translated into French by Stanislas Julien.[5]

Shortly after him, another Buddhist monk, named I-tsing, journeyed, in turn, through the eastern region of the Indian Ocean from 671 to 695. Unlike Hiuen-tsang, he travelled by sea a great deal, taking the sea route there and back. On his way he stopped at Sumatra and Malaya, before reaching India at Tamralipti. He left two accounts of his voyages, one of which has been translated into French by Chavannes.

Finally, to conclude the series of Chinese pilgrimages to India, Khi-nie's must be mentioned. Khi-nie left China in 964, with three hundred monks, and remained absent from his country for twelve years. Unfortunately none of his writings remains, save for fragments which Stanislas Julien has translated into French.

Although originally Buddhism was propagated in China by the Indians, eventually it was the Chinese who went out in search of it to India. And the Chinese Buddhist voyages between the fourth and tenth centuries should be seen against the background of that 'quest', unique in the history of religion.

We also discover from these voyages that the relations regularly established between India and China starting in the fourth century A.D. involved not only commercial but cultural exchanges. This can be compared to India's cultural expansion in Malaya and in the Malay Peninsula, described in a previous chapter. Finally, those voyages provide evidence of the existence of a very intense religious life in India at a time which corresponds approximately to the Middle Ages in Europe.

[5] (For the English translation by S. Beal, see below, Bibliography, p. 257—Tr.)

6. THE CHINESE JUNK

Although it did not manage to conquer the Indian Ocean under the Ming, and although its sailing range did not extend beyond the eastern region of the ocean, the Chinese junk deserves special mention. Its remarkable characteristics, pointed out by all European travellers since Marco Polo, have recently been studied once more by Poujade, who considers it one of the most successful types of ship. Its characteristics are: the fore-and-aft sail made of rush or rattan and reinforced by bamboo cross-battens; a hull lower and narrower at the bow than at the stern; a hold with watertight compartments; and a stern rudder.

In the opinion of all sailors, the battened sail is the best type of sail ever invented; it is of an aerodynamic perfection not yet reached by any of the European racing sails; it is also highly superior to the Arabs' lateen; and it makes it possible to tack in a headwind with remarkable ease. Poujade considers it an authentic product of the Chinese genius, since no other people of the Far East, neither the Malays, nor the Annamese, nor the Siamese, nor the Cambodians, nor the Japanese, batten their sails.

As to the originality of the Chinese hulls, low at the bow and raised at the stern, with great width astern of the middle, we quote Poujade at length:

> At the two extremities of the route to the Indies, two families of seafaring men have, it would seem, observed nature and interpreted it differently. In the West the men who wanted to perfect the form of their boats thought it best to give them the shape of fish; in the East they preferred the shape of the aquatic birds that swim on the water. The Chinese were to be the better observers; we already know that their sails are superior; perhaps there too they copied the wings of birds and their bamboos represent the feathering . . . a swan or a duck navigates like a boat, on the surface where two fluids separate on the surface disturbed by waves; fish and bird, on the contrary, move about in a homogeneous medium; they are both stronger in front than at the back; they have what may be called a 'torpedo' shape. But if we carefully observe the shape of a duck's body, we shall see that it is narrower in front than behind. This is the best shape

to give a boat; the Chinese suspected as much, but the Europeans never noticed it. It took thousands of years for the two conceptions to meet. During the last century an American schooner, built in general accordance with the shape of the junks, came to England to race in the regatta around the Isle of Wight against an English schooner of the same size. The *America*'s advantage was enormous; its speed was so great that there was no question about the reasons for its success. The experience proved that the Chinese were right. It led to an immediate revolution in the European navies; all the great builders changed their shapes, and experiments in tanks, more scientific than direct observation at sea, confirmed forever the established results. Today everyone admits that a good hull of a sailing ship must have its largest part (its midships frame) situated from 3 to 8 per cent astern of the middle on the waterline.[6]

Still, the good qualities of the Chinese ships should not be exaggerated. In spite of Marco Polo's great wonder at the junks on which he travelled from China to the Persian Gulf, junks with four masts, nine sails, and a crew of 250 men each, that imposing fleet nevertheless took almost two years to make the trip (three months from China to Java, and eighteen to cross the Indian Ocean), and almost 600 people died during the journey.

We might even wonder whether the Chinese junk despite its unquestionable nautical qualities, was really superior to the Arab dhow. In any case the Arabs, who were very familiar with the junks, the word *djunk* itself is Arabic, never adopted the battened sail or any other characteristic of the Chinese ships. Nor did the sailors of the Malay Archipelago, who were familiar with the Chinese sail, ever adopt it either.

7. THE CHINESE INFLUENCE

What was, then, on the whole, the scope of Chinese influence in the part of the Indian Ocean where there was Chinese maritime activity? Rather limited, we must admit.

In his work already cited, Coedès stresses the radical difference between the methods of colonisation followed by the Chinese and those followed by the Hindus. The latter have

[6] J. Poujade, *La Route des Indes et ses navires*, Paris, 1946, pp. 210–12.

already been described, and can be summed up in the two words: peaceful penetration. The Chinese, for their part, proceeded by conquest and annexation: the soldiers occupied the country, and every country so conquered was forced to adopt the institutions, customs, religions, language, and script of the Chinese. Also, although China had exercised a more or less effective political supervision over the many countries of South-east Asia for long centuries, her civilisation never really took root anywhere but in Tongking, a military conquest.

It is also important, in this connection, to note China's constant attitude of contempt for the peoples of the Indian Ocean, all of whom she considered indiscriminately as 'barbarians'. The word occurs frequently in the writings of the Chinese; that is how Chau-ju Kua, in the *Chu-Fan-Chi*, describes all the foreigners who traded in China; and Cheng-Ho's expeditions, entrusted with the task of making Ming suzerainty recognised everywhere, are also very significant. Besides, that frightful superiority complex of long duration was to be the ruin of the Chinese when later they had to deal with Europeans.

But alongside colonisation by military conquest, there was also peaceful infiltration, later accelerated by the importation of Chinese coolies into various countries of the Indian Ocean.

The interdictions imposed by the Ming emperors when they decided to change their policy of overseas expansion did not prevent a great number of Chinese from emigrating to Indo-China, Malaya, and Indonesia, as well as to regions of the Pacific, where they ended by establishing a kind of Greater China. In the seventeenth century that Greater China was even to produce a very remarkable man, the pirate Koxinga, who won fame from 1646 to 1662 for the struggle he waged by sea against the Manchu governors of the lower Yangtze, the Chukiang, Fukien, and the region of Canton, and who ended his career as 'king' of the island of Formosa.

'His endeavour,' writes Grousset,

> is of the greatest interest to the historian, for it was the first revelation of a fact that was up to that point quite unforeseen: the maritime and colonial vocation of the Chinese people. Indeed, Koxinga's adventure opened the era of the great emigration of the sons of Han, who today, from Cholon to

Singapore, from Batavia to Manila and the Hawaiian islands, cover all the coasts of the southern seas: a tremendous fact, whose remote consequences cannot as yet be evaluated.[7]

The civil war that followed the conquest of southern China by the Manchus at the end of the seventeenth century gave rise to a fairly intense Chinese emigration towards Indonesia. At the beginning of the eighteenth century there were no less than 100,000 Chinese in the island of Java alone, almost 80,000 of whom were in the region of Batavia, a fact which rapidly posed a problem for the Dutch in that city. The problem was, alas, resolved by bloodshed. In 1740 the Chinese of Batavia were the victims of one of those attacks of xenophobia of which they themselves had so often given an example in their history. Chinese expansion in South-east Asia nevertheless continued, with the result that today there are more Chinese in Singapore, for example, than there are Malays.[8]

Turning from the cultural and social levels to the economic, can we say that Chinese economy showed any progress over that of the Iranians, the Arabs, or the Indians? Reading the enthusiastic descriptions of the Chinese commercial system written by Marco Polo and Ibn Battuta, we are at first tempted to believe that it did; in point of fact, the descriptions of both travellers are based merely on appearances.

Van Leur, to cite him yet again, discovered nothing in thirteenth-century Chinese society to indicate the existence of an even slightly developed capitalism or of a mercantile bourgeoisie, despite a rather advanced organisation of finance; for the Chinese had come to make use not only of the bank and the bill of exchange but even of paper currency. They did have commercial companies, shipping concerns, and 'factories' of a sort in foreign countries, but nothing at all similar to the European trading companies of the seventeenth century; on the other hand, State control of all commercial activity was absolute.

As for the goods involved in the Far East trade, they were practically the same as those of the Erythracan Sea trade, and

[7] R. Grousset, *op. cit.*, p. 334.
[8] In 1954, out of a population of 1,167,682, there were in the colony of Singapore 893,004 Chinese and only 143,685 Malays, the rest being made up of Indians, Eurasians, and Europeans (*Colony of Singapore Annual Report*, 1954).

van Leur concludes that Gibbon's description may be applied just as well to Chinese trade as to that of the Romans, the Iranians, and the Arabs. A better type of naval construction means nothing in this respect, for it was the result of military far more than of commercial factors. Besides, despite the nautical qualities of the Chinese ships, they took, as we have seen, almost the same amount of time to cross the Indian Ocean as did ships in the Roman era.

VII. Quest for the Orient

I. A MERCANTILE REPUBLIC

Now that we have reviewed the activity of the Eastern peoples in the Indian Ocean from the fall of the Roman Empire to the end of the fifteenth century, we must turn back and briefly show the relations between the ocean and the Mediterranean world during that period, which corresponds roughly to the Middle Ages in Europe. The term Middle Ages cannot be applied to the Indian Ocean itself, for actually, as we have seen in previous chapters, the characteristics of the maritime and commercial relations of the two great regions of the ocean, the eastern and the western, remained almost the same as they had been in early times. Moreover, the history of Asia has little in common with that of Europe during that period. No comparison, especially as regards economic matters, can be made between the two continents.

When Constantinople took the lead over Rome, the Sassanids in Iran were in control of the land and sea routes leading, through central Asia and the Persian Gulf, to the Indies and the Far East. Since they held Egypt, the Byzantines were able to escape subjection to them, and through the Axumites of Abyssinia, remained in contact with India.

By occupying Egypt, Islam deprived Byzantium of the Red Sea route. In order to make contact again with India and China, the Byzantines then turned towards southern Russia and the region of the Caspian Sea. At the same time, having defeated the Arabs on the sea in the eastern region of the

Mediterranean and having held on to a few provinces in the Adriatic, they kept up communications with the West through the port of Venice, which had dominated the Adriatic since the tenth century.

In the eleventh century the Turkish invasions cut the lines of communication with Asia through the Caspian Sea. Forced to confront the Turks on land, the Byzantines had also to neglect their fleet and to entrust the policing of the Adriatic to the Venetians. Thus Venice, subsequently taking advantage of the decline of the Byzantine Empire and expanding at its expense, gradually captured the trade in the Levant. The development was furthered by the Crusades, for through them Venice gained entry into Syria, where she actively helped to establish the Latin Kingdom of Jerusalem.

By the twelfth century the Venetians were in possession of an entire quarter in Constantinople and had also settled in Tyre, in Syria, once the capital of the Phoenicians whom they succeeded, as it were, after a lapse of over two thousand years. Having no scruples about trading with the Moslems, despite papal interdictions, they even penetrated as far as Aleppo and Damascus, as well as Baghdad, where they concluded a commercial treaty with the caliph.

When at the end of the twelfth century the sultanate of Egypt eclipsed the caliphate of Baghdad, the Venetians managed to obtain special privileges in that country, then the centre of the Moslem world, making it possible for them soon to have a powerful colony in Alexandria, administered by a consul in the name of the republic of Venice. Continuing to defy the papal interdicts, they furnished Egypt, in exchange for the spices and other Eastern products they went there to procure, with goods that were expressly prohibited, arms, munitions, iron, timber, and even slaves. Rome, however, finally grew angry; in 1323 Venice had to give in and forbid her nationals for a while to trade with the Moslems. She then seriously thought of gaining access to the great markets of central Asia and the Far East by means of other routes.

2. THE SEARCH FOR PRESTER JOHN

Since the Byzantine monk Cosmas, who had gone all the way to the Indies in the sixth century and had returned with a fascinating account of his journey, no European had tried to explore and describe the world of the East until rather unexpected news incited others to imitate Cosmas.

About the year 1150 a rumour spread through Europe that somewhere in Asia there existed a powerful Christian ruler by the name of Prester John (*Presbyter Johannes*), whose kingdom was called Kara Kitai. In a Europe which cut a rather poor figure beside the Moslem Colossus, this mysterious 'priest-king' rapidly became a symbol of hope. In 1177 Pope Alexander III sent his own physician out in search of him; the envoy never returned, but the failure of that first attempt did not destroy the myth of Prester John, and we shall see how he was sought for now in Asia, now in Africa, until the end of the fifteenth century.

Another event played a considerable part in the resumption of European voyages to the Orient: the Mongol invasions. Although enemies of Islam, the Mongols did not seem hostile to Christianity; in fact, it was said that there were a great number of Christians among them. Pope Innocent IV, successor to Alexander III, thought seriously of converting them. He dispatched several missionaries, at least two of whom—John of Piano Carpini and William of Rubruck—although they did not succeed in converting the Mongols, brought back extremely useful information about Asia. That information was all the more precious since the only account Europe then possessed of the countries bordering the Indian Ocean was a work written in 1160 by a Jew from Tudela in Spanish Navarre, called Rabbi Benjamin. Interesting for the details it contains on Jewish settlements in various Asian countries, especially Persia and India, this work is unfortunately filled with inaccuracies, suggesting that the writer had not himself visited the countries he described.

Almost at the same time as the missionary Rubruck, two Venetian merchants named Maffeo and Nicolo Polo took, in their turn, the route followed by the Mongol camps. Their journey, which led them all the way to the Court of the Great Khan, lasted fifteen years, from 1254 to 1269. In 1271 they set out again on a new voyage which was to last twenty-four years, taking with them Nicolo's son, a very young man by the name of Marco. They also had with them a few Dominican friars, one of whom, William of Tripoli, wrote a report of the journey. Yet it was not his account, but rather that of the young Marco, that was to go down to posterity.

The Book of Marco Polo is too well known and his adventures have been too often described for there to be any need to go into them here. When the book came out in 1298, Europe discovered a really new world, a new world in which the Indian Ocean held a rather important place; for unlike Rabbi Benjamin, Carpini, and Rubruck, Marco Polo had travelled not only by land but also by sea. About the year 1288, while in the service of the emperor of China, he had been sent on a mission to the Indian seas, and during his voyage he visited Indo-China, Malaya, Indonesia, Ceylon, and much of the coast of India. All these countries are described in detail in his work.

He also took the sea route for his return to Europe. Having left Zayton with a fleet of thirteen vessels that was taking to Iran the fiancée of the Khan of that country, he reached Ormuz, on the Persian Gulf, after a voyage of two years, stopping en route at the main ports of the Malay Archipelago. From Ormuz he made his way to Trebizond and thence to Constantinople, from which he returned to Venice.

Although he had not visited Arabia, he gives a good description of Aden and other ports on the Arab coast. He was badly informed about the coast of Africa and speaks only of Abyssinia and Zanzibar. He mentions also 'an island of Madeigascar or Mogaleiso' whence some geographers have inferred that he knew of Madagascar, which, in fact he did not.

On the whole, however, Malte Brun is right in calling him 'the Humboldt of the thirteenth century' and in seeing him as the creator of the modern geography of the Indian Ocean, for his descriptions show a real advance over those of the Arab geographers.

3. MARCO POLO'S FOOTSTEPS

Two very different kinds of travellers were not long in following in the Polo brothers' footsteps in the countries of the Indian Ocean: missionaries in quest of the mysterious Prester John and of souls to convert to Christianity, and merchants searching for the riches of the Orient. In regard to the former, there are three names to remember: Montecorvino, Odoric of Pordenone, and Marignolli. Of the latter, Pegolotti and Conti in particular must be mentioned. It is notable that they were all Italians.

John of Montecorvino was a Franciscan whom Pope Nicholas V sent out to preach Christianity in the East in 1288. He was the first Westerner to go from Europe to China by sea. He was also the first incumbent of the see of Peiping (Peking), created in 1314.

Odoric of Pordenone left in 1317, also by sea. Taking a ship at Ormuz, he set sail for the Malabar coast and Ceylon, and continued thence to Sumatra by way of the Nicobar Islands. He then went to Java, Champa, and finally China. In 1330 he returned to Italy by land. His account complements Marco Polo's on a number of points, but unfortunately contains many fanciful details. John of Marignolli's itinerary was the reverse. In 1339 he made his way to China by land, but for his return in 1347 he took the sea route by China, India, and the Persian Gulf.

The merchant Francisco Balducci Pegolotti travelled in Asia about the year 1335. He then published a handbook on trade, entitled *La pratica della mercatura*, in which he describes the route taken by European merchants going from Tana, on the Sea of Azov, to Peiping. It is clear from the book that commercial expeditions to Asia had become fairly common in the fourteenth century and were not considered at all out of the ordinary. Pegolotti himself, however, never travelled beyond the Near East, and got his information mainly from Genoese merchants.

Nicolo Conti, a native of Venice, as was Marco Polo, had one advantage over him: he was a real scholar. Having learned Arabic in Damascus, he went on to the Persian Gulf and there took the sea route to India by way of Ormuz. In Calicut he then learned Persian. In addition to several places on the Indian sub-continent, he visited Ceylon, Sumatra, and other islands of the Malay Archipelago, as well as part of Indo-China. He returned by way of Aden and Egypt, though that particular route was forbidden to Europeans. His voyage lasted forty years, from 1404 to 1444, and his account of it is an important contribution to European knowledge of the Indian Ocean.

4. GENOA AND VENICE

The Venetians were not the only Italians to trade with the East. In the twelfth century, when Venetian ambitions became clear, the Byzantine emperors, in order to check them, guaranteed commercial privileges to the cities of Pisa and Genoa. There was soon fierce competition between Genoa and Venice, leading to a long struggle between the two cities which was not to end until 1381. On his return from the East, Marco Polo was captured by the Genoese during a naval battle between them and the Venetians, and it was in the Genoa prisons that he wrote his famous account of his travels.

Although the Genoese merchants who travelled in the East left no accounts comparable with those of the Venetians Marco Polo and Nicolo Conti, it would seem that their activities were even more important than those of their rivals. In the fourteenth century we find Genoese established in several countries of the Indian Ocean, especially in Iran and India. They were also in China, where they even enjoyed some degree of influence. We shall also see later the part they took in the first expeditions in the Atlantic, which resulted in the discovery of the Cape route at the end of the fifteenth century. And, needless to say, Christopher Columbus was a Genoese.

The struggle in which Genoa and Venice were engaged until the end of the fourteenth century considerably weakened both cities, but whereas after 1381 Genoa, a prey to internal revolutions, was on the road to decline, Venice recovered fairly rapidly and reconquered her supremacy in the eastern Mediterranean. In the beginning of the fifteenth century her commercial prosperity was at its height. We have a significant document on this subject: statistics contained in the treatise of the Doge Mocenigo (1423), and quoted by Diehl in his history of Venice.

What finally led to Venice's ruin was, first of all, the conquest of Constantinople by the Turks in 1453, and then the arrival of the Portuguese in the Indian Ocean in 1498. But the effect of these two events was not immediate, and was felt only in the course of time.

Thanks to a compromise treaty concluded with the Turks after 1453, the Venetian colony in Constantinople, which had been destroyed when that city was taken by the Turks, regained its strength fairly quickly, and the naval victory of Lepanto (1571), in which Venice, with the help of Spain and the Papacy, crushed the Turkish power, gave the republic a respite. Besides, at the end of the sixteenth century Turkey was constrained to turn her back on the Mediterranean in order to confront Iran.

The conquest of Syria and Egypt by the Turks in 1516 was a still more serious threat to Venice than the fall of Constantinople. There again she managed to come to terms with the enemy and kept her right of access at Beirut and Alexandria; but in the hands of the Turks, who were little concerned with trade, the decline of those long celebrated markets was not slow in coming. Egypt in particular, reduced to the rank of a Turkish province and torn by domestic strife, was to experience a long period of decline.

The very fact that the Portuguese went to seek spices directly at the source in the Indian Ocean abolished the intermediaries and completely upset the market system. But as Braudel has shown, Venetian pepper managed none the less to hold its own against Portuguese pepper until the end of the sixteenth century.

Even after the discovery of the Cape route, Venice still had one means, and that the best of all, of penetrating into the Indian Ocean: the reopening of the former Suez canal, sanded up since 767; she considered this in 1504, and made proposals to that effect to the Sultan of Cairo But the project was not managed energetically enough. 'Venice', writes Diehl, 'gave up rather casually the only project that would have been able to retrieve her fortunes; and finally, powerless, she had to resign herself to going along with the general trend and seeking her spices like the rest of the Occident, on the market at Lisbon.'[1]

Moreover, the Venetians did not attempt to follow the Portuguese in the Indian Ocean, although Ludovico di Varthema, who travelled in Arabia, Persia, India, and the Malay Archipelago from 1502 to 1508, showed them the way. There is a good account of his voyage, which closely followed da Gama's, in Jacqueline Pirenne's recent work, *A la découverte de l'Arabie* (Paris, 1958). Actually, Varthema was imitated by only one of his compatriots, Pietro della Valle, who travelled through Persia and India in the seventeenth century, learned oriental languages, and brought back to Venice information that could have been put to account by the merchants. It was not until the end of the nineteenth century, however, that the Italians once again turned their gaze to the Indian Ocean.

5. THE PORTUGUESE ADVENTURE

There were two ways in which the Westerners might cut down the Moslem colossus The first was to attack it in the Erythraean Sea itself; the second, to take it from the rear by going round Africa.

The first way was tried in 1182 by Renaud de Châtillon, lord of the land of Transjordan. After having separate segments of vessels built on the shores of the Mediterranean and then carried on camels to the Gulf of Aqaba, he managed to disorganise Moslem commerce in the Red Sea and even got as far as Aden, but ended by being overpowered by enemy forces.

The project was taken up again, about 1300, by the Dominican Guillaume d'Adam, who proposed the building of a fleet by the Holy See, either at Ormuz, in the Persian Gulf, or at Bombay, or on the Malabar Coast, with the object of severing relations between Egypt and the Far East by cruising in the Indian Ocean. Blocked in the direction of the Red Sea and abandoned by the merchants of the Mediterranean, Egypt would not have been long in succumbing. This daring project came to nothing.

The first attempts by western nations to take the Moslem

[1] C. Diehl, *Une Republique patricienne: Venise*, Paris, 1915, pp. 197–8.

barrier from the rear and clear a way to the Indies around Africa began in the thirteenth century, and its instigators were Genoese.

About the year 1270, shortly before the Polo brothers took off for their second journey to the Orient, a Genoese fleet commanded by Lancelot Malocello entered the Atlantic, and after a long voyage reached the Canaries, which had been known to the ancients as the Fortunate Isles, but whose existence Europe had long since forgotten. In 1291 another Genoese, Tedisio Doria, pushed still farther along the west coast of Africa to the vicinity of Cape Noun.

Why did the Genoese not persist in their explorations, which, had they been carried out vigorously, would have allowed them to round the Cape of Good Hope well before the Portuguese? The question is rather difficult to answer. The fact is that, instead of continuing to sail on their own, they preferred to enter the service of Portugal, a small country which had just won its independence and had as yet no navy.

With crews supplied by the Genoese, the Portuguese navy was gradually built up and was soon to work wonders. When we say soon, we must not forget 170 years that had elapsed between the time when the Portuguese king Diniz enlisted the Genoese in his service (1317), and the time when Bartholomeu Dias rounded the Cape of Storms (1487). For Portugal, at war with the Moors and Castilians, and rent internally by civil dissension, did not really begin to breathe until the reign of João I (1385–1433).

In the meantime, navigators from Dieppe in Normandy, descendants of the ancient Vikings, had rounded Cape Noun and established trade relations with the coast of Guinea which lasted for almost forty years. When the unfortunate condition of France forced them to give up that trade, the men of Dieppe, so as not to let it fall into the hands of others, spread most fantastic rumours about the dangers of sailing beyond Cape Noun. These rumours were believed to such an extent that when King João I wanted to send a fleet into those regions in 1417 he had great trouble finding sailors to man it.

Another event was to delay the Portuguese advance towards the Indian Ocean: the exploitation of trade along the coast of Guinea. Like the navigators from Dieppe who had preceded them, the Portuguese devoted considerable time to this. In addition to gold, and slaves, they also found there a pepper-like plant called 'malaguetta', which they managed to sell fairly well in Europe; in fact, it subsequently withstood the competition of real pepper.

Given new impetus by Prince Henry the Navigator and King João II, who added to his title King of Portugal the designation King of Guinea, the Portuguese explorations along the African coast went steadfastly on until the day Bartholomeu Dias rounded the Cape of Storms, christened by João II (1487) the Cape of Good Hope.

At the same time that he dispatched Dias on the ocean route, João II, determined to reach the Indies by land as well as by sea, entrusted two emissaries, Pero da Covilham and Affonso de Payva, with the search for the kingdom of the mysterious Prester John. After having collected some information on the trade of India from Arab merchants, the two emissaries separated at the port of Aden. Payva went to visit Abyssinia, and Covilham made his way to India's Malabar coast. He was the first Portuguese to travel in the Indian Ocean, and his story is rather curious. On his return, having learned in Cairo of Payva's death, he decided to go out himself in search of Prester John; he therefore sent a Jew to the king of Portugal with his report and set out for Abyssinia. Welcomed by the king of that country, he married, and settled there for the rest of his life. However, he did send the king of Portugal detailed information on navigation in the Indian Ocean and on the possibility of entering it by way of the Cape of Good Hope. In the interval King João II died, and the honour of organising the final expedition fell to his successor, Manoel I. Under the command of da Gama, the expedition was to enter, for the first time, the seas of India and reach Calicut.

According to Estancelin, one Captain Cousin, from Dieppe, beat da Gama by seven years, but up to now this has never been proved conclusively. Braudel also points out that very shortly after da Gama, ships from Ragusa came to the Indian Ocean.

Even if we admit that the voyages from Dieppe and Ragusa took place, still they came to nothing, whereas da Gama's voyage opened a new chapter in the history of the world. The

Portuguese perhaps took their time to get to the Indian Ocean, but once they were there, they certainly did not rest on their laurels.

6. THE ATTRACTION OF THE ORIENT

This flashback on the relations between the Orient and the Occident during the Middle Ages was necessary in order to show that the maritime invasion of the Orient by the Occident, initiated by da Gama's exploit, was the result of persistent endeavours, and that it represents the last phase of a long quest for the Orient, dating from the Roman era.

Since the time Rome made Eastern products fashionable and her Egyptian subjects went out to seek them in the Indies, since the time she launched out on a large scale into that 'splendid and trifling' trade mentioned by Gibbon, the European world had been possessed by the mirage of the East. And when the Arabs shut off all access to the Indian Ocean, Europe continued to supply herself from the markets of Asia through the caravan routes of the Levant.

According to Burckhardt, this trade was a natural development; the Mediterranean and the world that extends it to the Indian Ocean making up one 'single living entity'. Braudel thinks, on the contrary, that this trade was not a natural development; all the desert land from Egypt or Syria to the waters connected with the Indian Ocean constituting a real obstacle, whereas the Mediterranean and the ocean are areas capable of flourishing economically in independence of each other.

Natural or not, this trade had become as necessary to the Mediterranean world of the Middle Ages as to that of the Roman Empire, even more so perhaps, for the contact with the Moslem world could not but develop a taste for magnificence and luxury in the peoples of Europe.

This applies mostly to the peoples of the Iberian peninsula, to which the Moors had brought their Oriental customs and splendour. According to W. D. Cooley,[2] there can be little

[2] See W. D. Cooley, *History of Maritime and Inland Discovery*, 3 vols., London, 1830-31, I, p. 351.

doubt that the pearls, perfumes, and other commodities of Eastern luxury were brought into Spain chiefly by the Moors; and that as the hostilities between this people and the Spaniards became daily embittered and implacable, the supply of the luxuries now come into vogue grew continually less adequate to the demand. The markets of Venice and Genoa could hardly have been so copiously stocked or so advantageous to the Spanish merchants as those offered by the Moors. It appears, therefore, that the expulsion of the Moors from the peninsula of Spain may be reckoned among the motives for seeking a new course to India by the ocean.

However, the lure of spices and other products is perhaps not sufficient to explain the breakthrough of the West into the Indian Ocean at the end of the fifteenth century. In fact, this breakthrough was not the work of those Mediterranean peoples most interested in trade with the East. We have seen that the Venetians themselves, for whom that trade was practically a matter of life or death, made only feeble attempts to open a seaway through the Isthmus of Suez; in that case self-interest alone proved an inadequate motive.

The success of the Portuguese can be explained by the fact that the interest in trade went along with a real crusading spirit still alive in the Iberian peoples, whereas it had in the other peoples of Christendom all but disappeared. The persistence of that spirit can itself be explained by the fact that, from the tenth to the thirteenth centuries, the Portuguese and Spaniards had fought against the Moors in at least three thousand battles, and that it was in terms of struggling against the Moslems that they had created a national consciousness.

7. THE CARAVEL

Let us now turn to the instrument that made it possible for the Portuguese to launch out on the conquest of the Indian Ocean; the caravel, which La Verande calls '*le petit navire-roi* of the fifteenth century'.

Experts are not in agreement on the origins of the caravel. Even the etymology of the word is uncertain. Some think it comes from *cara-bella*, meaning a beautiful shape; others, from *carabos*, a kind of lobster. Technically, the word designates a ship with three masts, lateen rigged, that is, rigged with triangular sails, a length of about 100 feet, rather low on the water, with a hull wider at the stern than at the bow, and of not over 200 tons burthen. There are two kinds of caravel: the *caravel latina*, using only lateen sails, and the *caravel redonda*, using square sails. The caravel in which Dias rounded the Cape of Storms in 1488 was of the second type.

We must also distinguish between the caravel and the *nau*, which likewise has three masts, but is of 400 tons burthen and sometimes more, and uses a *mistic* or combined rigging, with square sails on the mizzen mast and mainmast, and a lateen sail on the foremast. For his first voyage around the Cape, Vasco da Gama used a *nau*.[3]

In Spain the *nau* gave rise, in turn, to the galleon, which was still larger and had a more complicated rigging and a very special sterncastle. In the sixteenth century the galleon soon became the ocean-going ship *par excellence*, used mostly in the Atlantic and the Pacific (the well-known Acapulco galleon), but also in the Indian Ocean.

Before the caravel, the Europeans were familiar with only two kinds of vessel: the Mediterranean galley, which had its origin in the Roman *navis longa*, and the Nordic *kogge*, which traces back to a Norman vessel, itself a modified form of the Vikings' *drakkar*.

In a very remarkable work on the evolution of ships and their influence on social evolution, an American, S. A. Reeve, showed how the advent of the caravel, completely different from both the galley and the *kogge*, led to a real revolution in maritime history; but whereas he considers it of European provenance, a French writer, Amsler, is more inclined to believe that its origin was in the East.

The hull of the caravel, wider at the stern than at the bow, tends to be modelled on the body of aquatic birds, and consequently is of the same nature as the Chinese junk (and, to a lesser degree, the Arab dhow). Now, as Amsler makes clear, the European navies up to then had, on the contrary, been faithful to symmetrical profiles, which had their origin in the ancient *drakkar* or the galley. As for the lateen rigging of the

---

[3] The Iberian *nau* was called a *caraque* or *carrack* by the Dutch, English, and French, but neither the Portuguese nor the Spaniards used the term.

caravel, we have already seen that the lateen sail was actually an Arab sail that spread westward with the influence of the Crusades.

Jean Amsler concludes that the caravel was of Eastern origin, and puts forward the following theory:

> The arrival on the scene of the expert Jafuda Cresquez and the end of Don Pedro's stay in Venice coincide with the advent of the caravel. Those two active and cultivated minds sensed the need for a renewal of naval construction. They found in the Infante Henriquez a willingness to set to work, at Lagos, establishing official shipyards, securing capital, and recruiting men ready for adventure. Thus the caravel, with its Asiatic hull, its African derivation, and its sails three-quarters European, was to carry to the ends of the earth the man born of the contact between the three sectors that went to make up the Old World: the Mediterranean man. Iberia, the bridge between Europe and Africa, was predestined to serve as his starting base. Portugal pocketed the first results.[4]

This is an attractive hypothesis which very nicely weds the East to the West. But it was not exactly a typical Mediterranean man, that is, a privileged being, who was carried to the ends of the earth in a caravel, but rather a new species, whom Toynbee calls *Homo occidentalis*. The Orientals, he adds, first saw him as no more than a kind of rather inoffensive animalcule that came from the sea; but he was soon to change into a marine monster and later into an amphibian as formidable on land as on water. That, in brief, is the genesis of the conquistador.

[4] L.-H. Parias, *Histoire universelle des explorations*, II, Paris, 1955, 28–29.

VIII. The Conquistadores

I. FIRST HOSTILITIES

UNTIL the arrival of the Portuguese, the Indian Ocean had never been the theatre of very serious conflicts. Doubtless piracy had always been fairly active there, especially in the Gulf of Kutch and the region of the Sunda Straits; from the tenth to the thirteenth centuries, the Chola and Shrivijaya navies had often come to grips; but all that was sham fighting compared to the raging battles that closely followed the first Portuguese expeditions.

In the account of da Gama's first voyage, we read that the Arab pilot who showed him the route from Malindi to Calicut warned the Portuguese navigator that war with his coreligionists was inevitable. 'You will see', he said, 'that you will have to conquer, whether you want to or not.' Da Gama had already come up against undisguised hostility in Mozambique and Mombasa, and it was not till he reached Malindi that he had met with a fairly friendly reception.

When da Gama reached Calicut in May 1498, it had become the most important port of all India. The enlightened policies of the kings of the country, called Zamorins, had attracted thither merchants from all the countries of the Indian Ocean. The most numerous were the Moslem merchants who had a veritable colony there of about 15,000 people. Naturally, they did not look kindly upon the newcomers. Had it rested with them, neither da Gama nor any of his companions would ever have seen Portugal again. But since the Zamorin was opposed

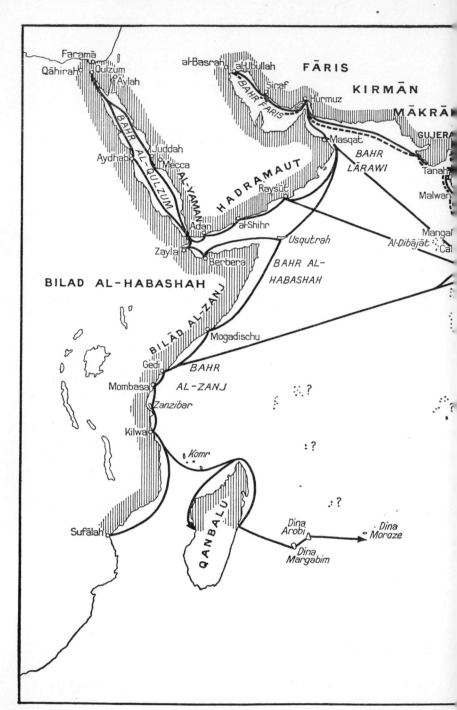

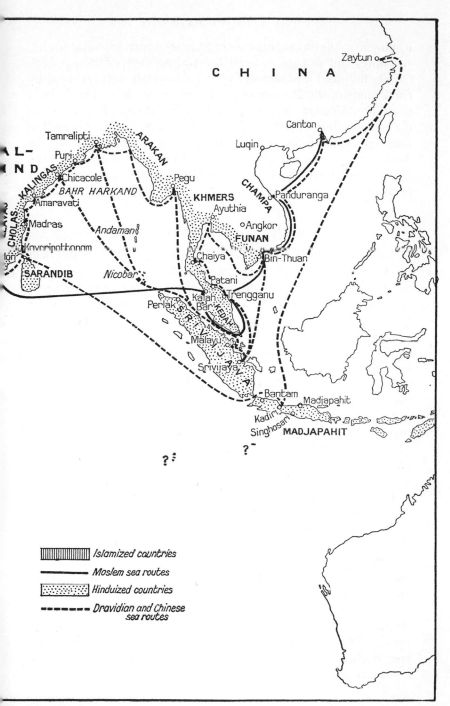

to violence, the Portuguese were able to return safe and sound.

Things did not go so well for Cabral's expedition, which closely followed da Gama's (1500). Although well received by the Zamorin, the Portuguese were no sooner settled in Calicut than the Moslem merchants fell upon them. The counter-thrust was immediate. Cabral, who had at his disposal a fairly powerful force, 13 vessels and 1,200 men, sank all the Arab ships that happened to be in the port and bombarded the city for two days. Hostilities had begun; they were to last for more than a century.

2. ALBUQUERQUE'S GRAND DESIGN

It had taken the Portuguese about two centuries to discover the Cape route. It took them less than fifteen years to secure all the key positions of the Indian Ocean, and they did it despite very active resistance. As a matter of fact, it had to be done quickly, before the Turks took possession of Egypt, which happened as we have seen, in 1517.

While waiting to gain a foothold in India, the Portuguese used at the beginning the ports of Cochin and Cannanore on the Malabar coast, whose rulers, then at war with the ruler of Calicut, made them welcome.

In 1505 the Portuguese forces in the Indian Ocean were placed under the command of a viceroy. At that time Sofala, on the coast of Mozambique, captured in 1503, was already in Portuguese hands. Then came the turn of Kilwa and Socotra, and Socotra controlled the entrance to the Red Sea.

Panic-stricken, the Arabs and the Zamorin of Calicut appealed to Egypt, where the Venetians, terribly apprehensive about their own trade, urged the sultan to intervene against the Portuguese. In 1507 an Egyptian fleet, comprising twelve caravels built in Suez by Venetian engineers and placed under the command of an experienced sailor named Mir Hussein, entered the Arabian Sea and headed for Diu, on the Indian coast. The small fleet at the Zamorin's disposal soon joined it. At the first encounter the Portuguese were beaten, but they returned to the charge immediately and this time scattered the enemy forces. Until 1538 they would have no more to fear from forces sent out from Egypt.

While this was going on at Diu, the celebrated Albuquerque destroyed an Arab fleet at Ormuz, wreaking such havoc there that it upset the entire historic balance of the Arab world, which was as surprised as it was terror-stricken. Becoming viceroy of the Indies in 1510, Albuquerque first tried to take Calicut; failing in this, he attacked Goa, which he managed to capture after a hard battle and made it the seat of the Portuguese power in Asia. He was then able to turn towards the eastern region of the Indian Ocean.

In Ceylon and Pegu he signed treaties with the native kings; but his main objective was the emporium of Malacca, which was taken in 1511. Then returning west, after having sent out a fleet to explore the Moluccas, Albuquerque launched out against Aden, from which point he hoped to conquer Egypt. He had grandiose plans in that connection, aiming at nothing less than the permanent occupation of the country. Repulsed after having suffered heavy losses, he made a second expedition against Ormuz, where he managed to set up a Portuguese station. Death overtook him on his way back to Goa in 1515.

Albuquerque's work must not be underestimated. He was a very great sailor, endowed with a really oceanic vision.[1] His strategy can be summed up in three points: (1) the organisation of a real colony in Goa, where, in order to ensure Portuguese settlement, he did not hesitate to encourage marriage with native women; (2) the building of forts or strongholds at all the strategic points of the ocean; (3) the signing of treaties with the rulers of territories of importance for trade. This strategy, which aimed not at territorial conquest but only at the control of trade routes, was to be adopted almost unchanged, at the beginning at least, by all the Western peoples who followed the Portuguese in the Indian Ocean. The fortified trading post, as conceived by Albuquerque, remained the classical type of European establishment in the Asian seas until the nineteenth century.

For the Orientals this type of establishment was an innovation. In every large Eastern port, colonies of foreign merchants did exist, but those colonies did not really form separate worlds, states within the State. The fortified trading post was a real

[1] On Albuquerque, see especially Elaine Sanceau, *Indies Adventure: the Amazing Career of Afonso de Albuquerque, Captain-General and Governor of India, 1509–1515*, London, 1936.

stronghold, with its life completely apart from that of the territory that surrounded it and constituting a perpetual threat to that territory.

The religious intolerance of the Portuguese was also something new for the world of the Indian Ocean. Until then, the most diverse religions had got along together quite well; the Moslems alone occasionally proved to be somewhat fanatical. It is clear that in this matter the Portuguese were on the wrong track, and far from encouraging the diffusion of Christianity, their attitude, on the contrary, merely strengthened Islam's position in such regions as the Malay Archipelago.

3. REACTIONS OF THE TURKS AND HINDUS

At Albuquerque's death the Portuguese unquestionably held the Indian Ocean, but they did not succeed in ousting the Moslems or in completely annihilating the Hindu naval forces on the Malabar coast.

Albuquerque's failure to take Aden allowed the Turks to resume the offensive in 1538 and to establish themselves in Aden; a fleet commanded by Suleiman, the Pasha of Egypt, was then about to attack Diu, but the Portuguese managed to save it just in time.

In 1549 the fortress of Diu was again threatened. In 1551 and 1553 two Turkish fleets broke into the Indian Ocean; the first, commanded by Piri Reis, had come from the Red Sea; the second, commanded by Sidi Ali, from the Persian Gulf. Both were beaten.

Braudel attributes the Turks' defeats to the fact that they fought against the Portuguese with Mediterranean equipment. It was a struggle between the galley and the caravel. While Mir Hussein's fleet in 1507 was composed of a few caravels built in Suez by Venetians, those of Suleiman, Piri Reis, and Sidi Ali consisted of nothing but galleys.

The galleys were transported in separate parts by camel across the Isthmus of Suez; launched on the Red Sea, they were capable of manoeuvring in the narrow Red Sea and Persian Gulf, but not always of entering the vast Indian Ocean and there coming up against sailing boats of great height, abundantly provided with artillery, the ships that made up

Portugal's strength. Each encounter was to be a real disaster for the Turks.

Moreover, at that time Turkey was compelled to fight both against the Christians in the Mediterranean and against the Shiites in Persia.[2] Braudel points out that the Turkish thrusts into the Indian Ocean occurred fairly regularly between the periods of war with the latter power.

In about 1585 there was a lull in the Persian war, and as the Turks were no longer fighting in the Mediterranean, the Turco-Portuguese war was resumed in the Indian Ocean. This time its theatre was mainly the east coast of Africa. We shall return to it later.

The Marakkars or Hindu 'admirals' of the Malabar coast also gave the Portuguese trouble. In 1524 the latter laid waste their base, Ponnani, to the south of Calicut; in 1528 they captured their leader, Kuttiali; but the Marakkars established a new base at Kattakal and replaced Kuttiali by a new and equally capable leader, Kunjali, and the struggle went on.

In 1538 the Portuguese prevented the consolidation of Kunjali's forces with those of Suleiman of Egypt. In 1558 Kunjali was defeated a second time off Cannanore, and this was followed by a blockade of Calicut, put into effect by a powerful Portuguese squadron of thirty vessels and six thousand men under the command of Luis de Mello. The recall of de Mello to Portugal gave Kunjali a respite. He took advantage of this by making several fruitful raids on the Portuguese along the Indian coast. In 1569 he again successfully pushed back a fleet dispatched from Goa. The struggle did not end until Kunjali's death in 1595.

Yet these constant struggles against the Turks and the Hindus did not prevent the Portuguese from establishing themselves securely on the west coast of India, at Goa, Diu, Daman, Salsette, Bassein, Chaul, and Bombay, as well as on the island of Ceylon, which was under the jurisdiction of Goa. Along with Goa and Malacca, Colombo, in Ceylon, was one of the essential elements in the Portuguese holdings.

[2] The Moslems were divided into Sunnites and Shiites. From the very beginning of Islam, the Shiite doctrines found favour in Persia. The coming to power of the Safawid dynasty at the beginning of the 16th century awakened the old quarrel between the two sects, and placed Persia and Turkey in permanent opposition to each other.

They did not undertake anything in the Persian Gulf or the Arabian Sea, but contented themselves with Ormuz, which they held until 1662 and from where they could watch the Turks, limiting their commercial activities in that region to Masqat and Aden, whose ruler at one point even stood by them against the Turks.

Thus, during almost the whole of the sixteenth century, the Near East remained open to the spice trade; it was crossed by many caravans, some going from the Persian Gulf to Aleppo, others from the Red Sea to Cairo; in about 1550 the Egyptian pepper trade alone totalled between seven and nine million pounds a year, an enormous amount, higher even than that brought to Lisbon via the Cape route; trade in the Levant prospered, and for a time Venetian pepper even competed with Portuguese pepper.

4. THE CONTRA COSTA

On the African coast, the *Contra Costa*, as they called it, the Portuguese remained in a rather precarious situation during the entire sixteenth century; for the Arabs who held the coast refused to submit to their dominion. The main centre of resistance was the stronghold of Mombasa, which the Portuguese were to subjugate several times during the century, but without ever managing to neutralise it completely.

The first expedition against Mombasa took place in 1528; it was masterfully led by Nuno da Cunha, who put the town to fire and sword. A longish truce ensued, of which the Portuguese took advantage to explore the hinterland of Mozambique, and to exploit the gold and silver mines of the ancient land of Punt; but by so doing, they drew upon themselves the animosity of the African tribes of Monomotapa.

In 1585 Turkey intervened on the African coast, this time with sailing ships. A Turkish captain named Ali Bey left Jidda with two vessels, and succeeded in rousing Mogadiscio and other coastal cities against the Portuguese. Having managed to take several Portuguese vessels, he soon found himself in command of a real fleet, which he used to devastate the entire *Contra Costa*. The king of Malindi, still faithful, sent a warning to Goa and asked for reinforcements, but when they arrived,

Ali Bey had already returned to the Red Sea, taking with him a rich booty and fifty Portuguese prisoners.

In 1589 Ali Bey returned and again stormed all the points on the coast except Malindi, Patta, and Kelipe, but this time Portuguese forces sent from Goa succeeded in engaging his at Mombasa and in exterminating them.

In order once and for all to subdue Mombasa, whose sultan declared himself a vassal of the Porte, the Portuguese again sacked it in 1592, deposed the sultan, and put in his place their ally, the king of Malindi, and so as to avoid any new rebellion, built the famous Fort Jesus, whose imposing mass still rises today at the entrance to the old port of Mombasa.

At the end of the sixteenth century, another danger threatened the Portuguese on the coast of Africa: the arrival of the English and the Dutch. Hostilities began in 1607 with an attack on Mozambique by a Dutch fleet under the command of Van Caerden; but the Dutch were pushed back, and the Portuguese succeeded in holding the *Contra Costa* for yet another century, until 1698.

In the African waters around Madagascar, or in the Mascarenes, the Portuguese never tried to establish themselves securely. In the year 1500 Diogo Diaz, a captain in Cabral's expedition, arrived on the eastern coast of Madagascar and gave it the name *São Lourenço*, because he reached it on 10 August, St. Lawrence's day. In 1510, according to Kammerer, the island was correctly located on Portuguese maps and fairly accurately drawn. Again according to Kammerer, in about 1529, and until 1545, small Portuguese settlements would appear to have existed both at Ranofotsy Bay, or the Bay of Galleons, and on the coast of Fanzahira, or the False Bay of Galleons, almost at the southern tip of Madagascar; but it was not until 1615 that the Portuguese really tried to gain a foothold on the island, and then unsuccessfully.

As for the Mascarenes (Réunion, Mauritius, and Rodriguez), they were discovered by the Portuguese between 1510 and 1539. According to Visdelou-Guimbeau, Pero Mascarenhas, who gave his name to the archipelago, discovered only Réunion, about 1512. Mauritius was discovered by another navigator, Domingos Fernandez, about 1511, and Rodriguez by Diego Rodriguez in 1538. Although the islands were beautifully situated on the route to the Indies, the Portuguese founded no settlement there. The same was true for the Seychelles and the Chagos Archipelago, which they also explored during the first half of the sixteenth century. Several islands in the Mascarene, Seychelles, and Chagos groups still bear Portuguese names.

The Amirante Islands of modern maps were the *Ilhas do Almirante*, Islands of the Admiral, situated between the so-called Seychelles and the Comoros. Indeed, it was on his second voyage to India that da Gama, then an admiral, came upon these islands.

The islands of Agalega (the Galician), situated about midway between the Seychelles and the Mascarenes, took its name from the nationality of its discoverer, the Galician Juan de Nova, whose name was also given to two other islands in that region.

Peros Banhos and Diego Garcia, in the Chagos Archipelago, still bear the names of Portuguese navigators. The same is true of Cosmoledo (which no doubt should be written Cosmo Ledo), near the Seychelles group. The name Chagos itself is but a corrupt form of the Portuguese *Chagas*. Also, the reef of Cargados Garajos (to the north-east of the Mascarenes) must originally have been called *Coroa dos Garajãos*, or Reef of the *Garajãos*, sea birds that swarm in the vicinity; and finally, there is the reef of Saia de Malha (Coat of Mail, because it vaguely resembles one), situated to the north of Cargados Garajos.

5. THE PORTUGUESE IN THE FAR EAST

In the eastern region of the Indian Ocean Portuguese activity was far more noteworthy. Besides the trading posts of Negapatam and São Tomé, near Madras, there were two other settlements on the Bay of Bengal; one at Hooghly, near present-day Calcutta, and the other at Dianga, near Chittagong, in the kingdom of Arakan. These two settlements, particularly Dianga, founded by adventurers outside the jurisdiction of Goa, lived mainly on what was later called 'country' trade, that is, between one Asian port and another, a trade intended at that time to supply the court of the Moguls with luxury items from the Far East.

As the revenue from that trade was insufficient, the Dianga adventurers finally entered the service of the king of Arakan, who used them to protect his state against Mogul invasions. The activities of the Portuguese of Dianga in the Bay of Bengal lasted for more than a century, and it was not until 1665 that Aurangzeb managed to get rid of them and to extend his own dominion to the kingdom of Arakan.[3]

In the Malay region the Portuguese held Malacca until 1641, but they were constantly on the alert, having to hold their own against the Malays and the Achinese, who among themselves, however, never managed to get along well enough to form a common front against their adversaries.

In the general scheme of Portuguese dominion in Asia, Malacca was even more important than Goa, for she made it possible to control the whole group of the Moluccas, then the centre of the spice trade.

The Moluccas originally included the islands of Ternate, Tidore, Motir, Makian, and Bachan, along with their dependencies; later, the name was extended to cover Amboina and the Banda Islands. The Spaniards also coveted these islands. In 1521, during his famous circumnavigation of the globe, Magellan, a Portuguese 'traitor' in the service of Spain, had annexed Tidore.

The quarrel over the Moluccas finally ended in a compromise. In 1529 Spain ceded its rights over them for the sum of 350,000 ducats. After a vain attempt to regain a foothold in the Moluccas in 1544, the Spaniards established themselves on Manila, in the Philippines (1564) where they managed to attract a great part of the Far Eastern trade and enter into stiff competition with the Portuguese settlement of Macao in China.

Actually, then, the Portuguese found themselves isolated at Malacca. The fact of neglecting the other islands of the Malay Archipelago, in particular Java, where they never gained a foothold, and the fact of having inadequate naval forces at their disposal were to make their control of the entire region precarious in spite of everything. When the Dutch succeeded in establishing themselves in the Malay Archipelago, the Portuguese were soon done for.

[3] On the history of the Portuguese of Dianga, see the memoirs of Friar Manrique, translated by Maurice Collis in *The Land of the Great Image*, London, 1943.

In China they had better fortune. From the beginning of the sixteenth century, their vessels frequently visited the ports of Canton, Ningpo, Chuanchow (Tsinkiang), and Foochow (Minhow), and succeeded in evicting the Moslems, who then had almost a monopoly of trade with China. In 1557 the Chinese authorities put Macao at their disposal, and it was subsequently to become the favourite place of residence for foreign merchants in China. At first rented by the Portuguese, the port of Macao became their entire property from 1887. They still hold their own there today, though they have lost all their other possessions in Asia.

6. THE PORTUGUESE FAILURE

The causes of the Portuguese failure to retain the Indian Ocean are various. It has been attributed to their intolerance in religious matters, to their lack of commercial organisation, to Spain's annexation of Portugal in 1580, to the transportation crisis on the Cape route due to the deterioration of ships towards the end of the sixteenth century, and to the discovery of Brazil, which diverted their energies toward the New World. In reality, it was due above all to the fact that they never managed to exercise real control over the vast spaces of the ocean.

The Portuguese exploits themselves have been judged very differently; like Helen of Troy, they have in turn been much admired and much disparaged. Camoens' flights of poetry and the pompous accounts of the Portuguese historians intent on praising to the skies their national epic in Asia are answered today by such harsh criticism as that of the Hindu professor Nambiar, who sees the Portuguese exploits in India as a series of piratical acts.

Both sides, clearly, have exaggerated. One would not, of course, go to Camoens' *Lusiads* for an accurate picture of Portuguese activities in the East in the sixteenth century; on the other hand, no serious historian would lower those activities to the level of vulgar acts of piracy.

The truth, as Braudel points out, is that general history has not yet been as enlightening as it should be on the vast oceanic exploits of the Portuguese. Even the great syntheses of Jaime

Cortesão, Prestage, and Danvers are neither complete enough nor very vigorously drawn. The archives of Torre do Tombo have been, even today, most inadequately exploited, and we must wait for contemporary historians such as Botelho de Sousa, Boxer, and Axelson to make the most of them, so that we can be well informed on this chapter of the history of the Indian Ocean.[4]

7. EASTERN TRADE

As for the economic scope of the Portuguese conquest, we shall try to evaluate it in the light of the works of van Leur and Braudel.

According to van Leur, the Portuguese régime hardly changed the structure of Eastern trade, which continued to exist in its traditional form, although obviously hampered by the constant battles between Moslems and Christians.

The volume of trade did not increase to any appreciable degree during the whole of the sixteenth century. In fact, it remained what it had been for centuries: a rather small luxury trade, strictly controlled by the State, as much on the Portuguese side, as on the Asian; and its fundamental characteristics, whose origins go back to Byzantium and the first caliphs, were introduced into Portugal itself by Jewish and Italian merchants. Far, then, from introducing new economic elements into the trade of the Indian Ocean, the Portuguese did no more than strengthen it in its previous character. This they did to such an extent that for van Leur the Portuguese period, although the first phase of European expansion in the East, should be linked up not with the subsequent phases of that expansion but rather with the Eastern history of the Indian Ocean.

The mercantile bourgeoisie, which was just beginning to develop in other European countries, did not as yet exist in Portugal, where the class of *fidalgos* were in control. In India there was a merchant class, but it was not powerful enough to defeat the feudal system of the Moguls;[5] besides, this class did

[4] For the description of the archives of Torre do Tombo, see Eric Axelson, *South-East Africa, 1488–1530*, London, 1957.

[5] For a good descripton of this class, see the recent work of T. V. Mahalingam, *South Indian Policy*, Madras, 1955.

not have enough ships to launch out into large commercial operations. For this reason, they at first welcomed the Portuguese, seeing them as possible associates. Portuguese liberalism in social matters was to encourage that kind of association; and as a matter of fact, although the Portuguese reserved to themselves the monopoly of the distribution of Eastern products in Europe, they willingly worked on a fifty-fifty basis with the Asian merchants in everything relating to the 'country' trade.

In the sixteenth century that trade consisted essentially in the exchange of products from the Moluccas and the Malay Archipelago, pepper and spices, for the muslins and cotton goods of India. The exchanges between India and China also played an important though secondary part.[6]

Malacca was the great centre of that trade, a kind of Alexandria of the Indian Ocean, and consequently the Portuguese valued it highly. Goa was the centre of the trade with Persia and Ormuz, from which it received horses, dates, almonds, raisins, silk, pearls, and cotton fabrics. Goa was also the place where expeditions for Lisbon were organised. Yet Goa came only second, after Malacca.

All was not profit for the Portuguese in their trade in the Indian Ocean. Braudel points out that, after having extended his dominion to include Portugal in 1580, Philip II of Spain proposed reselling Portuguese pepper in Europe, at Venice, Milan, Genoa, and Florence, but in vain. If those cities refused his offer, it was because they did not find the prospect sufficiently attractive. In fact, as we have already said, the Near East remained open to the spice trade until the effective control of the ocean by the Dutch, that is, until about 1625, the year which marked the beginning of what was really not the second but the first European age in the Indian Ocean.

On this point Braudel's thesis only reinforces van Leur's, by showing that the exact date of the definitive decline of Eastern trade with the Mediterranean by land route must be sought after 1600, that the triumph of the oceanic route was not immediate, and that the struggle of the two rival routes lasted for more than a century.

---

[6] On the trade of the Portuguese with China, see T'ien-tse Chang, *Sino-Portuguese Trade, 1514–1644: a Synthesis of Portuguese and Chinese Sources*, London, 1934.

8. CARTOGRAPHERS AND EXPLORERS

If, from the viewpoint of economic history, the period of the conquistadores did not really mark a new era and differed little from the preceding age, from that of the history of geography and exploration it really marked the beginning of an era, and a very important beginning at that.

Doubtless, Arab geographers had described large areas of the oceanic world fairly well, and the Chinese had begun writing the *Wu-Pei-Chi* before the arrival of the Portuguese; but at the beginning of the sixteenth century, Eastern cartography for the Europeans was practically limited to the great tradition of Ptolemy, and as the remarkable studies of Cortesão, Kammerer, Destombes, and Bagrow have shown, the mapping of the Indian Ocean unquestionably came into being with the Portuguese.

According to Kammerer, the oldest Portuguese map of the Indian Ocean, and the first scientific map of it as well, is an anonymous portolano in the ducal library of Wolfenbüttel, which remained unknown until its publication by Uhden in 1939. Uhden attributes it to the year 1509, but as it bears a reference to the naval battle of Diu, which took place on 3 February 1509, and could not have been known of in Lisbon until the beginning of 1510, Kammerer prefers to date it 1510.

During the next twenty years Portuguese cartographers gave proof of remarkable activity, evidenced by the magnificent portolanos of Franciso Rodriguez (1513–15), Lopo Homem (*c.* 1516), the Reinel brothers (1519–22), and Diogo Ribeiro (1523–29), all of which were discovered in recent times and are today well known, thanks mainly to Bagrow's superb reproductions. The only land of the Indian Ocean not represented on those portolanis is Australia; Cortesão has shown, however, that there is reason to believe that the Portuguese had discovered it as early as 1522, but that the secret of that discovery had been jealously kept. Indeed, we know that the Portuguese kept their discoveries secret so that other European countries could not benefit from them.

It was also during the first decades of the sixteenth century that the famous roteiros or sailing directories were written, as well as the remarkable descriptions of the eastern coast of Africa by Duarte Barbosa, of the Red Sea by Francisco Rodriguez, and of Indonesia and the Far East by Tomé Pires and Fernão Mendez Pinto.

Tomé Pires' *Suma Oriental* dates from 1512–15, and the manuscript found its way, by heaven knows what chance, to the Library of the Chambre des Députés in Paris, where it was recently discovered by Cortesão. In itself it constitutes a first-rate document on the whole region of the Indian Ocean to the east of India. For that region, then almost unknown in Europe, it represents what the *Periplus* represented in the first century A.D. for the so-called region of the Erythraean Sea, with the advantage of being far more exact.

The official organisation of Portuguese cartography deserves particular mention. After each cruise, the commanders submitted their ships' logs and the pilots their reports, as well as their instruments, to the *Casa da India e da Mina*, the 'Office of India and Mines', a sort of combined Ministry of the Navy, the Colonies, and Overseas Trade. It was also a school for pilots, a kind of Central Astronomical Office. The ships' documents were given to the chief pilot and to the head cartographer, whose charge it was to keep up to date what was called the *padrão*, a standard map of the world, on the largest possible scale, devoid of any doubtful indications, ornamentations, or embellishments.

The Portuguese school for pilots, men who were really very learned for their times and had tested methods at their disposal, was quite remarkable. There was also a brilliant school for official cartographers attached to the Casa da India. Most of their works are now to be found outside Portugal, partly for mercenary reasons and partly because, as those maps were the best in the world at that time, all the kings of Christendom tried to procure them, and as soon as Portugal found herself impoverished, she derived some income from them; moreover, the dreadful Lisbon earthquake of 1755 destroyed the Casa da India and all its archives.

Those interested in seeking out the scattered elements of the former Portuguese science of cartography must really undertake extensive research in both time and space, a difficult but fascinating exploration, to which a scholar like Kammerer, for example, has devoted his entire life and in which he has found the materials for a monumental work that does him the greatest credit; but as already pointed out, not all the pieces of what we might call the Portuguese puzzle have yet been reassembled, and that puzzle still continues to intrigue historians.[7]

[7] For a collection of reproductions of old Portuguese maps, see Armando Cortesão and Avelino Teixeira da Mota, *Monumenta Portugalis Cartographica*, 4 vols., Lisbon, 1960.

IX. The Gentlemen Merchants

I. ANTWERP AND AMSTERDAM

THE Portuguese could not hope to exclude the other European countries indefinitely from the Indian Ocean, especially as they themselves had not enough ships at their disposal to ensure the resale in Europe of the products they obtained from Asia, and so had to place them in the hands of an international consortium in which the Netherlands were well represented.

It was also in a city of the Netherlands, Antwerp, that they raised the money necessary for buying pepper and spices in the East. According to Braudel, Antwerp thus became the most 'colonial' city of the sixteenth century, after Lisbon, to which it was bound by close trade relations. But after 1565 the troubled situation in the southern Netherlands brought about the decline of Antwerp to the benefit of the Dutch ports, Amsterdam in particular, and when Philip II's troops occupied Antwerp in 1585, the finance and business of the Netherlands was reconstituted definitively in Amsterdam.

Even if Philip II had not involved Spain and Portugal in a war against the Netherlands and had not forbidden the access of Iberian ports to the Dutch 'heretics', officially, at any rate, for they came all the same, the merchants of that region would have been sure sooner or later to come into conflict with the Portuguese in the Indian Ocean, for the development of their trade was to lead them inevitably to take, in their turn, the route to the Indies.

118

They sought that route at first through the Mediterranean by way of the Levant and in the north of Europe through the ice of Spitsbergen and Novaya Zemlya, but as soon as they were able to obtain information on Portuguese voyages in the Indian Ocean, they did not hesitate to take the Cape route.

One figure loomed large during the beginnings of the Dutch adventure in the East, that of Linschoten. As a very young man, he was sent to Lisbon and managed to get a berth on a Portuguese ship on its way to the Indies. He made the most of it by gathering important information about the Cape route and about navigation in the Indian Ocean. On his return to Holland, after a five years' stay in the East, he published, in 1595 and 1596, two guides to navigation (*Reysegeschrift* and *Itinerario*), which disclosed the oceanic world to his compatriots and circulated geographical knowledge which the Portuguese had always endeavoured to keep secret. The *Itinerario* in particular soon became the Bible of Dutch navigators in the East.

2. THE DUTCH ESTABLISHMENT

The first Dutch expedition to the Indies, led by Keyser and Houtman and financed by Amsterdam merchants who had formed the so-called 'Distant Lands Company', dates back to 1595, the very year Linschoten's first work came out. Its objective was not India itself but Indonesia, the centre of the spice trade, and it was at Bantam, on the island of Java, that contact was made with the natives. The island of Java had been chosen because the Portuguese rarely went there.

Claiming to be 'gentlemen merchants' ready to help the Javanese in their struggle against the Portuguese of Malacca, the Dutch were well received. Houtman brought back a cargo whose profits, although not considerable, stimulated other shipping ventures. From 1594 to 1601 no less than fifteen expeditions to Indonesia, comprising a total of sixty-five ships, were organised by the trading companies of Holland.

In 1597 the attack against the Portuguese began. In 1602 the Dutch were securely established in Bantam. In 1602 they sent envoys to Ceylon and later chased the Portuguese from

Colombo. In 1602 also a trading company was formed in Holland, called the 'Vereenigde Oostindische Compagnie', or United East Indies Company for the exploitation of eastern trade.

In 1619 Jan Pieterszoon Coen, one of the first governors named by the company to direct its operations in the Indian Ocean, moved his headquarters from Bantam to Jakarta, which he rechristened Batavia, and there laid the foundations for a European city. Charliat calls Coen 'an Albuquerque with a strain of Protestant rigidity'. The description would seem more suited to another Dutch governor, Anthony van Diemen, for it was in his 'reign' (1636–45) and not in Coen's that Batavia really became an important stronghold and that the Dutch supplanted the Portuguese once and for all in Southeast Asia by seizing Malacca (1641).

Under Van Diemen's government, the Dutch secured yet another important 'stepping stone' in the Indian Ocean by establishing themselves in 1638, on the second island of the Mascarene group, discovered about 1511 by the Portuguese Domingos Fernandez. They rechristened it Mauritius, in honour of Prince Maurice of Nassau.

The Dutch were not interested in the large neighbouring island of Madagascar, which produced neither pepper nor spices, except as a place from which to procure slaves; but in spite of the slaves imported from Madagascar and the convicts sent over from Batavia, Mauritius hardly developed. Some years later (1652), the Dutch found that the Cape of Good Hope, whose value the Portuguese had never suspected, was a better port of call than Mauritius, which they gave up in 1658. A second attempt at settlement on that island was made from the Cape in 1668, but it was no more successful than the first, and the island was relinquished definitively in 1710.

The settlement on the Cape, launched by two men, van Riebeck and van der Stel, was the first actual colony to be planted by Europeans on the route to the Indies. Neither Goa, nor Malacca, nor Batavia, where the Asian element was predominant, were really European cities. At the Cape, on the other hand, the absence of any native substratum (the Hottentots did not count) and the excellent subtropical climate were to make it possible for the Dutch to establish a real colony.

Yet during the seventeenth century and even later, Batavia was considered much more important than the Cape, which, despite everything, was looked upon as a second-class settlement.

3. AN UNSTABLE HEGEMONY

When they became established at the Cape of Good Hope, could the Dutch really consider themselves masters of the Indian Ocean? With the founding of Batavia, the seizure of Malacca, and the annexation of the principal Spice Islands, they undeniably held the entire region of South-east Asia. Yet in Ceylon they had not completely eliminated the Portuguese. The struggle for the conquest of Ceylon continued with ups and downs until 1658, and it was only then that the whole island was to fall under Dutch control.

In India itself, the evicting of the Portuguese from their factories on the Malabar and Coromandel coasts did not become an accomplished fact until about 1663, and even then these were only secondary factories, for the Portuguese held their own in Goa, Daman, and Diu, their main strongholds, and their navy was far from destroyed. Dutch activity on the Indian coasts was concentrated on the Coromandel coast, especially at Pulicat, and had to do mostly with the purchase of textiles for Indonesia, where they were exchanged for spices. The exploitation of the pepper trade on the Malabar coast is of less interest.[1]

In the western region of the Indian Ocean, the fact that in 1622 the Persians had recaptured Ormuz from the Portuguese opened a new trade route for the Dutch and weakened their rivals' position in that region. Persia, having emerged victorious from her battle against the Turks in the previous century, played a very important part in the history of trade between the East and the West during the entire seventeenth century. Now the Dutch, who tried to reach the East by way of the Mediterranean before launching out on the Cape route,

[1] The Dutch pepper came mainly from Java, Sumatra, Malaya, and Borneo. The great centre of the pepper trade in Indonesia was Bantam (Java). The pepper from the Malabar coast was of interest to the Dutch principally for trade with Persia.

did not neglect that region, and the progress they made in the Indian Ocean did not distract their attention from trade in the Levant.

But the Portuguese were not the only rivals the Dutch had to reckon with in the Indian Ocean. Indeed, they were very closely followed by the English, the Danes, and the French, and although those three peoples did not, like the Dutch, aspire to capture the spice trade, and at the beginning were satisfied with far more modest operations, they nonetheless made their presence felt, especially the English.

4. ENGLISH COMPETITION

England's quest for the Orient actually began with the English voyages in the Mediterranean, which have been studied by Braudel. Starting in 1573, English ships made their way as far as the Near East; at the same time that Anglo-Turkish negotiations were getting under way, the Levant Company was formed (1581), preceding the East India Company by twenty years. 'The Englishman looked, above all, to Syria and its land routes; it was with Syria that he dreamed of doing business and there that he organised a trade of merchandise for merchandise, which the second discovery of the Cape of Good Hope, by the Dutch, was not immediately to destroy.'[2]

The English entered the Indian Ocean itself for the first time, with Drake, by a route not commonly used, that of the Pacific, which had been opened up by Magellan in 1521; but Drake's voyage (1577–80) was a privateering operation against the Spaniards rather than a commercial enterprise. The first commercial expeditions were not sent out until 1591, and took the normal Cape route. Although they had defeated Philip II's Armada in 1588, the English did not yet feel strong enough, and they approached the spice islands as junior partners of the Dutch.

The beginnings of the East India Company in India were rather modest: a small trading post at Surat, on the west coast (1613), and another small trading post at Masulipatam, on the east coast (1611). The watchwords were prudence and circumspection. In 1616 Sir Thomas Roe, an envoy of the

[2] Braudel, *La Méditerranée et le monde méditerranéen*, Paris, 1949, p. 486.

East India Company at the court of the Great Mogul, declared that war and trade were incompatible.

In 1619 the English and Dutch signed a treaty of alliance against the Portuguese, but the alliance was short-lived. Portugal's separation from Spain in 1640 facilitated a reconciliation with England, and peace was definitively concluded on that side when the Portuguese recognised the right of the English to free trade in Asia (1654). The Dutch then became the enemy number one.

Moreover, in 1623, relations between the English and the Dutch became very strained, following the 'Amboina massacre',[3] which is judged very differently by historians of the two countries. In 1628 the English, horrified by the 'massacre', shut up shop in Batavia. From then on, though they had factories in Macassar till 1667 and in Bantam till 1685, it was clear that they could not gain a foothold in Indonesia, where the Dutch were determined to defend their monopoly fiercely. They thus clung even more tenaciously to India, where the Dutch hold was not so strong.

At the beginning, the English made very slow progress on the sub-continent. On the west coast it was only with the acquisition of Bombay (1661), received as part of the dowry of Catherine of Braganza to her husband Charles II and ceded to the Company (1668) that the English secured a good base of operations; in 1687 Bombay definitively supplanted their first trading post of Surat, on the same coast.

On the east coast they gave up Masulipatam in 1626 for Armagaon, but as that place was situated very near the Dutch trading post of Pulicat, they soon had to abandon it also. In 1639 they finally obtained from the ruler of the state of Vijayanagar a concession at Madras; there they built Fort St. George, which became their main base of operations on the Coromandel coast.

To the north on the Bay of Bengal, they tried to establish themselves successively at Hariharpur, Balasore, Hooghly, Patna, and Cassimbazar, but it was not until the eighteenth

[3] (This is the name traditionally given to an incident which greatly embittered Anglo-Dutch relations. In spite of an agreement between the two countries permitting the English to trade on the island of Amboina in the southern Moluccas, the Dutch governor, alleging an English conspiracy to capture the fort by surprise, arrested and tortured 18 English traders, twelve of whom were executed.— Tr.)

century that they succeeded in gaining a foothold in the region of Bengal.

During the entire first half of the seventeenth century the situation of the English company in India remained somewhat precarious. Far from finding, as it had hoped, an outlet in the Indian markets for fabrics, linen goods, and other English products, it was forced, on the contrary, to buy textiles from the Indians so as to exchange them for spices.

5. THE DANISH ADVENTURE

Whereas in Holland and in England the first expeditions to the Indies had preceded the creation of trading companies, in Denmark the opposite occurred. A Danish East India Company was first formed in 1618, and it was this company that organised the first voyages in the following year.

As the Portuguese were then holding the Malabar coast and the Dutch held Indonesia, it was to the Coromandel coast that the Danes turned their attention. In 1621 they obtained a concession at Tranquebar from the Rajah of Tanjore, and there they immediately built Fort Daneborg.

Besides the expedition sent out by the Danish company, there were also some expeditions made by adventurers to Mauritius, which at that time (1622) the Dutch had not yet occupied. The object of these expeditions was the exploitation of ebony, in which the island abounded; a study of them has recently been made by Dalgard.

In 1619 another adventurer of Dutch extraction, named Boshouwer, who during a trip to Ceylon had received letters of nobility from the king of that country, convinced the Danish company that it would be easy to found a settlement on the island, at Trincomalee. An expedition sent out for that purpose ended in failure, for Boshouwer died *en route* and his Sinhalese friends refused to deal with the Danes.

For some time the Tranquebar settlement prospered, and the Danes even extended their operations to the Malabar coast and to the north on the Bay of Bengal, where they opened trading factories; they also managed to establish themselves in Bantam, on the island of Java, but in 1634 the Danish company went bankrupt. A second company was immediately formed to replace it, followed by a third in 1686, and a fourth in 1732.

By the end of the seventeenth century the situation of the Danes in India had become that of 'poor whites', living by their wits and sometimes even by piracy. Without the help of the English, they would probably have lost their trading post in Tanjore. Not until the eighteenth century did they prosper anew, and even then, not for long.

6. FRANCE IN THE EAST

The first French voyages to the Indies were all made by adventurers, and were organised at Dieppe, Honfleur, and Rouen, in Normandy; but it was in Brittany, at Saint-Malo, that in 1604 the first French company was formed, following on the extraordinary excursion of two Breton adventurers, Martin and Pyrard, the former of whom published an enthralling account of it in 1601.[4] However, the first shipping enterprise of that company, called the 'Compagnie des Moluques', was not undertaken until 1616. Its destination was Java, but the Dutch kept a careful watch on the island and the French had to return empty-handed. They then fell back on the Mascarenes and Madagascar, which had been explored by Martin and Pyrard and by other adventurers who had gone there in search of cargoes of ebony at the beginning of the century.

In 1638 an expedition sent out to occupy the Mascarenes found the Dutch established on Mauritius and had to content themselves with the island of Bourbon (Réunion), which was larger and more fertile but devoid of good anchorages.

In 1642, at the instance of Richelieu, a 'Société de l'Orient ou de Madagascar' was formed, with the objective of founding a 'France in the East' in Madagascar, which offered little in the way of resources, but could serve as a stepping-stone to the Indies. Entrusted to an incompetent leader by the name of Pronis, the settlement formed at Fort-Dauphin, at the south of the island, in 1643 was soon in a bad way. From 1648 to 1660 Flacourt attempted to rehabilitate it. In 1674 a frightful

---

[4] The very first French voyage to the Indies, that of the Parmentier brothers (1521), had been made almost a hundred years before.

massacre put an end to the settlement of Fort-Dauphin. Those who escaped took refuge on Bourbon, but even that colony was to vegetate until the beginning of the eighteenth century.

Meanwhile, Colbert launched the first fairly well organised East India Company, the 'Compagnie des Indes orientales' (1664). This time the objective was neither Indonesia nor Madagascar, but India itself. Colbert's company also differed from its predecessors on the choice of a route. First the overland route through the Levant was tried, and agents were sent to Persia. With a more or less similar idea in mind, the philosopher Leibniz suggested to Louis XIV, in 1672, a plan for conquering Egypt, which would have opened the Red Sea route to France. Fantastic at first view, the plan was not at all impracticable, according to Castonnet des Fosses, but Louis XIV was then interested in the Rhine, from which Leibniz meant to distract him, and not in the Red Sea. And so the French finally reverted to the Cape route.

In 1668 the first French trading factory in India was opened at Surat, then the great market of the west coast of the peninsula. From Surat, expeditions were sent to the Persian Gulf to try to open up a caravan route there from Baghdad to Aleppo in Syria. But Caron, who was directing the operations, wanted to do too much, and instead of sticking to the Persian Gulf region, he suggested to the company that it establish trading factories on the Bay of Bengal, in Ceylon, in Indonesia, and even in China and Japan.

In 1672 Caron tried to seize the port of Trincomalee, in Ceylon, by force, with the help of the first French squadron sent to the Indies under the command of de la Haye. Repulsed by the Dutch, the French managed to lay the foundations for a settlement at Pondichéry, where the survivors of Caron's expedition took refuge and succeeded in holding their own under the command of François Martin. In 1688 Pondichéry was definitively conceded to the French company by Aurangzeb. In the eighteenth century Dupleix was to try to make it a bridgehead for the conquest of southern India.

In the region of the Bay of Bengal, soundings made by Caron led to the opening of a small trading factory at Chandernagore (1673) and, what is more important, brought the French into contact with the king of Siam. Anxious to secure allies against the Dutch, he offered to cede Bangkok and Mergui to France. It was a magnificent opportunity for the French to gain a foothold in South-east Asia, even though Siam offered little in the way of resources from an economic viewpoint, but the enterprise was so badly managed that in 1688 Bangkok and Mergui had to be evacuated. Almost a century passed before the French again made themselves felt in the region, with the celebrated Pigneau de Behaine.[5]

By the end of the seventeenth century the French had not made much progress in the Indian Ocean. Like the English, they did not succeed in disposing of any of their products there. Still worse, the cotton piece goods imported from India proved such serious competitors with the products of the home industry that, at the request of the French textile manufacturers, their importation was forbidden in 1685.

7. TRADING COMPANIES

In his study of European activities in the Indian Ocean in the seventeenth century, van Leur concludes that from a strictly commercial point of view those activities had not yet succeeded in seriously breaking ground in the East. Yet there is no doubt that the Dutch and, after them, the English, the Danes, and the French brought in a new element of great consequence: trading companies called 'India Companies', an idea that had never occurred to the Portuguese.

To understand properly the workings of those companies, we should have to review the history of the mercantile bourgeoisie in Europe at that time, which would be irrelevant here. Suffice it to say that the trading companies were not purely peaceable enterprises and that they all aimed at conquest.

At first sight nothing was less like the sixteenth-century conquistadore than the seventeenth-century 'gentleman merchant', who brandished neither sword nor Cross, and merely asked his Asian brothers to grant him a small concession on their territory so that he could indulge solely in his small trading operations. We have only to glance at the 'professions

[5] We will not enlarge in this book on the history of French activities in the Indo-Chinese region, which is outside the Indian Ocean. On that subject see especially G. Taboulet, *La Geste française en Indochine*, 2 vols., Paris, 1955–56.

of faith' of any of the merchants of that time. Sir Thomas Roe's statement has already been mentioned. In France, Colbert also proclaimed on the subject of India 'We should have no other aims in that country but trade'. The Dutch and the Danes said the same, and denied that they had any plans for conquest. In point of fact, the seventeenth-century 'gentleman merchant' represented an even more formidable species than the conquistador.

There are several fairly detailed works on the India Companies; the most recent is Glamann's, dealing with the activities of the Dutch company from 1620 to 1740. A few important studies on the origins of mercantile capitalism should be mentioned, especially the recent thesis of the Indian historian R. Mukerji. Nevertheless, the history of mercantilism in the seventeenth century has not yet been adequately examined, and it still poses a host of problems.[6]

The world of the Indian Ocean was vast enough for all the Europeans who had entered it to make a place for themselves and to devote themselves to the peaceful pursuit of profits; but on this point, seemingly very simple, economists are not in agreement. Mukerji tries to show that the trade of the Europeans in the Indian Ocean in the seventeenth century could pay only if it were a 'colonial' trade, based on monopoly. Among the examples he gives in support of his thesis is the following seemingly paradoxical fact. When Cromwell threatened to dissolve the English company and to make trade in India free, those who became most agitated about it were the members of the Dutch company, well knowing that they themselves would suffer as much as their rivals, for the measure would have weakened their own position in Holland and would have left the coast clear for English interlopers. It would even have been better for competition to be limited to that between companies with monopolies.

But although monopoly assured the companies the exclusive privilege of buying and selling, it did not secure for them the possibility of buying *cheaply* the products they wanted to procure on the Eastern markets. For that they had no alternative but to secure political control of those markets; in other

[6] On mercantilism, see especially E. F. Hecksher, *Mercantilism*, 2nd edn., London, 1956.

words, the India Companies were drawn inevitably into the path of imperialism.

A thesis opposed to this has been put forward by the American Holden Furber, who thinks, on the contrary, that imperialism was not an economic necessity and that its origins should be sought rather in the weakness of Eastern society, which had become an easy prey to the cupidity of the Westerners. 'Economic contact between India and the West,' he writes with regard to India, 'was inevitable, but imperialism was not inevitable. It grew out of the weaknesses and diversities of Indian society, and in particular out of Indian powerlessness at sea.'[7] Van Leur says in the same context on the subject of Dutch activities in Indonesia: 'the progress of Dutch power must be attributed not to more diplomatic insight, to greater courage and greater impetuosity, to greater economic reserves, but to the sturdier rigging and the greater speed of the ships, the more powerful cannon-royal, the greater mobility of armed troops.'[8]

Particular emphasis, for not enough importance has been attached to this point, should be placed on the preponderant role played by the agents to whom the trading companies entrusted the management of their operations in the Indian Ocean. It was they who most often induced the companies to become involved in extraordinarily ambitious projects. The first in date was the Dutch Jan Pieterzoon Coen, who in 1614 wrote to his directors: 'Trade in India must be conducted and maintained under the protection and favour of your weapons, and weapons must be supplied from the profits enjoyed by the trade, so that trade cannot be maintained without war or war without trade.'[9]

As for the English, as early as 1669, that is, exactly fifty years after Sir Thomas Roe expressed his cautious views, Gerald Aungier, chief of the factory at Bombay, wrote to the directors of the company in London: 'The time now requires you to manage your general commerce with the sword in your hands.' The directors took some time to make up their minds,

[7] H. Furber, *John Company at Work*, Cambridge, Mass., 1952, p. 321.
[8] Van Leur, *op. cit.*, p. 189.
[9] Quoted by F. B. Eldridge, *The Background of Eastern Sea Power*, London, 1948, p. 237.

but in 1687 they came to a definite decision, and ordered their agents in India 'to establish such a politie of civil and military power . . . as may be the foundation of a large, well grounded, secure English dominion in India for all time to come.'[10] Clearly, a very complete programme, and one that was to be carried out to the letter. And the intention was obviously not to colonise, like the Dutch, but to rule, like the Portuguese.

In the case of the French, we have already seen the ambitious Caron at work. In the eighteenth century we shall see the megalomaniac Dupleix invent 'nabobism' and, taking advantage of the weakening of Mogul power, try to conquer the whole of southern India between 1746 and 1753.

Actually, the race of conquistadores glorified by Camoens did not disappear in the seventeenth century. It merely changed its aspect and countenance. There always have been, and there always will be, men who dream of conquering the eastern El Dorado, even though that El Dorado is, at the time, no more than a deceptive mirage.

8. THE EASTERN MIRAGE

Here we touch on another extremely interesting question, and one which has not yet been completely elucidated. What exactly, at that time, was the value of Eastern trade? Were the riches of Asia real or only apparent? On this point Charliat's opinion is worth quoting:

> Asia at that time showed no more than signs of wealth. In the cities and temples one perhaps came upon riches that had been immobilised for centuries, even since antiquity. This money was not often invested and hardly circulated. The competition of European sailing ships was not the only reason for the decline of the Islamic navies in the Indian Ocean and for the forsaking of land routes.[11]

In order to come to any conclusion on the matter, it would be necessary to know the exact figure of the profits and losses of the trading companies. Unfortunately, the statistics we so far possess are most inadequate. Glamann's study, mentioned

[10] R. C. Majumdar (ed.), *An Advanced History of India*, London, 1956, p. 639.
[11] In Parias, *Histoire universelle des explorations*, III, 12.

above, which was not published until 1958, shows, for example, that the book-keeping of the Dutch company was extremely complicated and that it never had any central accounting system. Each of the six 'chambers' of Holland drew up a yearly financial statement. Batavia did the same for the company factories in the Indian Ocean. By comparing the accounts kept in Holland and in Batavia, a total balance was arrived at, but no account was kept of capital or of profits and losses.

Glamann also shows that the alleged stability of Dutch trade in the Indies was only a myth. For the period he examines, from 1620 to 1740, he found great variations in the prices of the main articles of Eastern trade, which at that time were, in order of importance, pepper, spices, silk, cotton goods, sugar, copper, coffee, and tea.

The Dutch company held a monopoly of the spice trade, but in the case of pepper, which grew almost everywhere in the East, it had to reckon with competition from rival trading companies. The spices themselves (nutmeg, cloves, and cinnamon) did not yield much profit. In fact, smaller quantities of cloves were sold in India in the seventeenth century than in the sixteenth, during the period of Portuguese dominion. There was also strong competition in the trade in silk, which came from Persia, Bengal, and China. In that line the English finally got the better of the Dutch at the beginning of the eighteenth century.

The same can be said for cotton goods, whose main centre of production was the Coromandel coast. At first sight, we might believe that the restrictions imposed in England and France on the importation of cotton piece-goods at the end of the seventeenth century were to the profit of the Dutch. But nothing of the kind was true. Glamann stresses the fact that during the years 1702–05 Holland imported yearly from England about £95,000 worth of textiles made in India.

As for sugar, that which the Dutch produced in Java sold fairly well on the Eastern and European markets in the seventeenth century. The same is true for coffee, but the cultivation of the plant did not spread in Java until the end of the seventeenth century and the beginning of the eighteenth. Indeed, it was not until then that Europe began to acquire a taste for coffee, though it was soon to be all the rage. Coffee from Java, however, never supplanted that from Arabia, which European merchants procured from Mocha and Hodeida, on the Red Sea.

Tea, at that time produced only in China, likewise did not appear among the commodities of trading companies in the East until rather late. But in the seventeenth century Chinese junks brought it regularly to Batavia, along with silk, gold, copper and porcelain. The Dutch were unable to make a profit in this trade, and eventually it was the English and Americans who, at the end of the eighteenth century, were almost to monopolise the Chinese tea trade.

All things considered, we might well ask whether, during the seventeenth century and a good part of the eighteenth, the trade carried on by Europeans in the Indian Ocean really brought much profit to Europe itself. Much as the companies may have gained from it, it is clear that the East continued to drain Europe of precious metals in the form of Spanish dollars and Venetian ducats, which were then monies of high standard, whereas at the same time countries such as India devalued their own money. Of beating the Oriental on his own ground and eliminating him as a competitor there was still no question.

X. The Interregnum

I. THE STRUGGLE FOR THE ATLANTIC

THE second European age of the Indian Ocean, which was actually the first, as we have seen, does not correspond exactly with the seventeenth century. According to Admiral Ballard, indeed, it began toward the middle of that century and lasted until the middle of the next. He calls that period the 'interregnum', for he sees it as a period of unstable equilibrium, during which no one maritime power really controlled the Indian Ocean.

When Portuguese supremacy came to an end with the seizure of Malacca in 1641, three European peoples found themselves face to face in the seas of Asia: the Dutch, the English, and the French (the Danes hardly counted), and each wanted exclusively to take the place of the Portuguese. Yet before they came face to face here, they had met elsewhere, in the Atlantic, and it was really there that the game was to be played out, a game of prime importance, for this was no simple commercial rivalry but a far more serious conflict, in which the stake was nothing less than the command of the seas.

From the very beginning, as Godechot shows in his *Histoire de l'Atlantique*, the conflict moved on the political level. In 1609 the Dutch jurist Grotius, in a famous work, maintained that the freedom of the seas was an 'unassailable axiom of the law of nations'. In 1615 and 1635 the English jurists Welwood and Selden answered him that the sea was not common to all men either by natural right or by the law of nations, but was, on the contrary, open to appropriation.

Yet in the sixteenth century it was in the name of the freedom of the seas that the English attacked Portuguese and Spanish vessels. But at that time they still had no national navy. The ships that had defeated the Invincible Armada were the private property of Queen Elizabeth. In the seventeenth century, the situation changed. Thanks to ship money, a special tax, Charles I built up England's first navy. Cromwell strengthened the English position on the seas with the Navigation Act of 1651, which forbade all foreign ships to transport anything to England other than the merchandise of their own country. Its object was to free English commerce from its dependence on the Dutch carriers.

There followed a long struggle with the United provinces, which ended by the latter's being obliged to recognise England's absolute sovereignty over a large part of the Atlantic in the region called the 'British seas'. By sheer weight of naval power, the hypothesis of Welwood and Selden prevailed over that of Grotius.

Taking advantage of the quarrels between English and Dutch, the France of Richelieu and Colbert tried, in turn, to gain the mastery of the Atlantic. At the end of the seventeenth century she was on the point of succeeding, but the defeats at La Hogue and Vigo put an end to that attempt, and the treaties of Utrecht (1713) left the field to the English.

In the eighteenth century, says Godechot, the Atlantic was virtually an English lake. 'Of course,' he adds, 'English dominion had its fluctuations, its ups and downs; it was at its height between 1763 and 1775, but at the beginning as at the end of the century, the British hold on the Ocean remained powerful, extensive, and even overwhelming.'[1]

Control of the Atlantic did not necessarily mean control of the Indian Ocean, but it is clear that any power dominating the Atlantic could, at any moment, intercept ships going to or returning from the Indies. This is what happened at the end of the eighteenth century; but during the entire seventeenth and at the beginning of the eighteenth, the English navy was too busy in the Atlantic theatre to be able to show itself in the

[1] J. Godechot, *Histoire de l'Atlantique*, Paris, 1947, p. 162.

Indian Ocean. In the conflicts that broke out there during the interregnum, the only ships that took part were the Indiamen, merchant vessels of the East India Company, equipped it is true for war. On the other hand, the Dutch and the French sent out veritable squadrons to the East Indies.

Although in 1713, by the time of the treaties of Utrecht, England had won the battle of the Atlantic, she had not yet won that of the Indian Ocean. Indeed, she had not yet even begun it. In this connection there is perhaps good reason to extent the end of the interregnum to the treaties of Vienna of 1815, which sanctioned definitively the British hegemony in the Indian Ocean; for although the victory at Plassey in 1757 marks Britain's supremacy in India itself, it cannot be said that she had at that time complete command of the ocean.

According to van Leur, the victory at Plassey in itself brought about no immediate change in the situation of the English in India, for it was merely a victory over a provincial authority, the Nawab of Bengal; its significance became apparent only in the light of later events. British supremacy in India, van Leur believes, was not really assured until after the defeat of Bonaparte's expedition against Egypt (1799).

This chapter, however, will deal only with events that occurred between the seizure of Malacca in 1641 and the beginning of the Anglo-French duel in 1740. These events belong, above all, to the realm of military history. They were primarily conflicts among the Europeans themselves on the one hand, and between them and the Orientals on the other. Afterwards, there was an extensive activity by pirates, who were so constantly in the picture during the interregnum that this chaotic period might equally be called the age of pirates.

Yet it would be a mistake to depict it as having been solely a period of conflict. If war plays a large part in it, so likewise do exploration and discovery play important parts. For this reason, although the history of exploration, which has already been written, is not our concern, the last part of this chapter will be devoted to noting the main stages in the acquisition of knowledge about the oceanic world in the seventeenth century and at the beginning of the eighteenth.

2. THE ANGLO-DUTCH CONFLICT

Like the 'Amboina massacre', the Anglo-Dutch conflict in the Indian Ocean in the seventeenth century has been judged very differently by historians of the two nations. On the one hand, Colenbrander, Stapel, and Vlekke say that the English contrived to follow the Dutch everywhere so as to try to rob them of the fruits of their endeavours; on the other hand, Foster, Moreland, and Hall say that the Dutch tried unfairly to do the English out of a natural right.

The claim of the Dutch to reserve the monopoly of the spice trade for themselves was no doubt excessive; the claim of the English to exercise in the seas of Asia a 'natural right' which they refused to the Dutch in the seas of Europe was no less so.

One thing is certain: in the beginning the Dutch proved superior to the English from every point of view; first of all, because they were better organised and knew exactly what they wanted, whereas their rivals had no well-defined policy for a long time, and secondly, because the Dutch navy was clearly in advance of the British.

That advantage was not to be maintained. As early as the first Anglo-Dutch war (1652–54), caused by the proclamation of the Navigation Act, the Dutch Admiral Tromp was beaten in the English Channel by Blake, a soldier turned admiral or, more precisely, a 'general at sea', but who proved to be a figure of very great ability and when the British fleet blocked its ports, Holland had to capitulate.

Yet everywhere in the Indian Ocean the Dutch Company's ships got the better of the English East Indiamen. At the same time, so as to secure the route to the Indies, the Dutch occupied the Cape of Good Hope (1652).

The second Anglo-Dutch war (1665–67) again ended in defeat for the Dutch in spite of Admiral de Ruyter's successes. It took place once again in the seas of Europe, for the English did not have enough forces at their disposal to trouble their rivals seriously in the Indian Ocean.

The Dutch company suffered heavy losses of ships in metropolitan waters, but the respective situations of the belligerents in the East were not noticeably affected.

From 1672 to 1678 England, now in alliance with France, endeavoured once again to break Dutch economic power, which had remained intact despite the reverses suffered during the previous wars. For the Dutch Republic the result of this third conflict was the loss of its settlements in North America, and the dissolution of the Dutch West India Company, created in 1621 as a counterpart to the Dutch East India Company.

The Vereenigde Oostindische Compagnie itself was scarcely affected. Its vessels, as we shall see, even gained a clear victory over a French squadron sent to the Indies to seize Ceylon. In fact, it was during the Anglo-Dutch wars that the company had its period of greatest prosperity, its 'golden age', which, according to Dutch historians, lasted from 1639 to 1693. During that period it established itself securely in India, Ceylon, Java, the Moluccas, and at the Cape, transforming its purely commercial policy of the beginning into a policy of territorial conquest. In Indonesia, at the end of the century, the Dutch power made itself felt more and more.

Yet there is no doubt that the wars with England considerably weakened Dutch economic power. For although the Vereenigde Oostindische Compagnie sent some sixty richly-laden vessels yearly to Holland and paid annual dividends of from 20 to 40 per cent, the fact is that because of the vast expenses involved in its territorial conquests, its profits remained lower than the profits of the British East India Company during the same period.

Another more serious fact was that in naval construction Holland allowed herself to be out-distanced. Whereas at the beginning of the seventeenth century the builders of the British navy copied Dutch models, at the beginning of the eighteenth it was the Dutch who were to call in English technicians. In another respect, as Godechot points out, the general development of naval construction in the seventeenth century was to be fatal to the Netherlands, because only vessels of small tonnage could enter Dutch ports, and the average tonnage of ships rose in the seventeenth century from about four or five hundred tons to eight hundred or a thousand.

3. THE FRANCO-DUTCH CONFLICT

The Franco-Dutch conflict extended over a period of forty years and was divided into three phases: the Dutch War, in which France allied with England to attack Holland (1672–78); the War of the League of Augsburg, in which France had to face a coalition of England, the Netherlands, and Spain (1689–97); and the War of the Spanish Succession, in which France and Spain fought against a coalition made up principally of England, Holland, and Austria (1702–13).

In the beginning the conflict was motivated by the same reasons that set off the Anglo-Dutch dispute: the desire to free French trade from its dependence on the Dutch navy; subsequently, the main adversary was actually not Holland but England, which was securing more and more of a hold on the Atlantic. The combats that took place on the seas of Europe are of no interest to us here, and we shall keep to the skirmishes on the Indian Ocean, undoubtedly a very secondary theatre of operations.

Yet although the seas of Asia were not the main concern of the great powers, France took it upon herself to send a squadron there in 1670, even before the Dutch War broke out, with the obvious intention of impressing the peoples of the Indian Ocean. Auber says that it was made up of forty-five vessels and three storeships, but Lieutenant-Commander Delort, in his very detailed monograph on this first French squadron in Indian seas, mentioned only six vessels and four hookers, the hooker being a ship with a shallow draught and easy to manoeuvre, first used in Holland and then adopted by the other navies. This fleet carried four companies of infantry, as well as merchants, colonists, etc., 1688 men in all. It was called the 'Persia fleet', and had as its commanding officer a military man, Lieutenant-General Jacob Blanquet de la Haye. Two directors of the India Company accompanied it, De Faye and Caron.

After calling at Madagascar, where the troops and colonists disembarked, and the island of Bourbon, where a few soldiers were put ashore, the squadron sailed to Surat where de la Haye assumed the title 'Viceroy of the Indies', a most presumptuous title, corresponding to nothing concrete, for the affairs of the French trading factory at Surat were in a very bad way. The presence of the squadron could have restored French prestige, but only by a show of force. On Caron's advice, a *coup de main* against Ceylon was decided upon. On its way, the French squadron passed a Dutch squadron, under the command of Admiral Rijklof van Goens making its way up the Malabar Coast, but as war had not yet broken out between the two nations, de la Haye did not want to attack.

The Ceylon operation failed; and so did an endeavour at São Tomé, on the Coromandel coast. In fact, after having taken that stronghold, the French had to give it back to the Dutch, for Van Goens succeeded in neutralising, in the waters of Madras, a British force sent in 1673 to join the French, and the French fleet itself was in the greatest need of refitting, after four years of campaigning, during which it had received no assistance from France.

In 1675 de la Haye returned to France, having lost his squadron, most of his captains, many other officers, and more than two-thirds of his troops and crew. He also brought with him the remaining members of the Madagascar settlement, whom he picked up on his way back. As one small compensation for what might be termed a resounding disaster, after de la Haye's departure Baron, who succeeded Caron, obtained for the French the right to establish themselves in Pondichéry.

They were not to remain there long without being disturbed. As soon as the War of the League of Augsburg was declared, the Dutch began 'swaggering around Pondichéry and threatening to burn up the French "chief" in his fortress'. The arrival of a squadron under the command of Duquesne put an end to this, but as soon as it left, Pondichéry had to capitulate (1693).

This settlement, the only one in the Indies that France possessed in her own right, was restored to her by the treaty of Ryswick (1697), but through a subtle distinction made by the Dutch between the fort and the town itself, the treaty was not applied until 1699.

Fortunately, the War of the Spanish Succession did not greatly affect the Indian Ocean. This time the French were troubled neither by the Dutch nor by the English. François Martin took advantage of the respite to develop Pondichéry actively. However, on his death, in 1706, the 'city' numbered only 700 Europeans, 300 *topas* (half-breeds), and 30,000 Hindus, and from then on it made little progress until Lenoir's arrival in 1721.[2]

4. THE ARAB RECONQUEST

While the Dutch, English and French were fighting each other on every sea, the Portuguese found themselves once more in conflict with the local powers in the western region of the Indian Ocean.

Persia held unquestionable sway over the west of the Asiatic continent, playing a part similar to that of France in Europe during the same period. Persia was the first Moslem state to react against the weakened Portuguese, chasing them out of their stronghold of Ormuz in 1622. She did not, however, manage to do this alone, and had to appeal for help to the English company. All-powerful on land, with a permanent army of 150,000 men, Persia was in fact completely without a navy.

In the neighbouring state of Oman the Moslems, on the contrary, learned a lesson from the naval defeats that had been inflicted upon them by the Portuguese during the previous century They built up a navy that even included vessels copied from the Portuguese caravels and rigged with square sails.

In 1648, with their own resources, the Arabs of Oman drove the Portuguese out of Masqat. Somewhat later they were bold enough to raid Diu and Daman, but their attacks were directed mostly against the Portuguese possessions in Africa. The first attack against Mombasa took place in 1660. At the end of a long siege, the Portuguese had to evacuate Fort Jesus, but shortly afterwards they managed to reconquer it and then inflicted terrible reprisals.

In 1698 a real armada, patiently got together by Seif-ibn-Sultan, the ruler of Oman, again set sail for the *Contra Costa* from Masqat. Mombasa finally fell, despite Portuguese resistance. Then, moving down the coast, the Arab fleet forced the recognition of Seif-ibn-Sultan's sovereignty over Pemba, Zanzibar, and Quiloa. No longer was the whole coast

[2] On the beginnings of Pondichéry, see Mme M. V. Labernadie's thesis, *Le Vieux Pondichéry*, Pondichéry, 1936.

north of Cape Delgado part of the Portuguese possessions in east Africa. The Portuguese were pushed back to Mozambique and managed to drive away the Arabs only by means of a stratagem. It was the first time in the history of the Indian Ocean that the Orientals gained a decisive victory over the Europeans.

Admiral Ballard judges the Arabs' reconquest as follows: 'it must be admitted that the project was a singularly bold conception for an Oriental ruler, which none of the many Princes of India, or even the Sultans of the Malay Archipelago, would ever have thought of attempting.'[3]

The activities of the Omani sailors were not limited to the east coast of Africa. They next turned against Persia, from which they managed to take most of the islands of the Persian Gulf except Ormuz, where they were repulsed. At the same time, they engaged in privateering operations against the Portuguese vessels of Goa.

'In Anno 1715,' says Hamilton, 'the Arabian Fleet consisted of one Ship of 74 guns, two of 60, one of 50 and 18 small Ships from 32 to 12 Guns each, and some Trankies or rowing Vessels from 4 to 8 Guns each, with which Sea Forces they keep all the Sea-coasts in Aw, from Cape Comerin to the Red Sea.'[4]

The Persians finally made common cause with the Portuguese. In 1719 a Portuguese squadron transporting Persian troops inflicted a serious defeat on the Masqat fleet. Masqat itself was not attacked, for the Persian force was not large enough. For the same reason, the Portuguese did not attempt to re-establish their authority on the coast of Africa north of Mozambique, for they would have needed imposing forces to wipe out the large Arab population that had settled in the region. In 1728, however, a Portuguese commando succeeded in recapturing Mombasa and held its own there for some time.

After a pause, the attacks of the Omani privateers (or should we say pirates?) against Persia began once more. Nadir Shah, who ruled in that country, then bought a few ships from Europeans who were trading in the gulf and, adding them to those he had had built in Surat, sent out an expedition in 1742 against Masqat, which had to recognise his sovereignty.

[3] G. A. Ballard, *Rulers of the Indian Ocean*, New York, 1928, pp. 220–1.
[4] A Hamilton, *A New Account of the East Indies*, Edinburgh, 1727 I, 74.

In the region now called Trucial Oman on the Coast of Pirates, piracy continued all the same to prosper through the entire eighteenth century to the beginning of the nineteenth. In his book on the Indian Ocean, Villiers describes the activities of these pirates at length, and says that it took no less than three expeditions organised in Bombay, in 1809, 1816, and 1819, to wipe them out once and for all and to make navigation safe in the Persian Gulf.

5. THE PIRATES OF ASIA

Besides the activities of the Omani sailors, we must also mention those of the Marathas on the Malabar Coast, whose history has been written by Biddulph, Hill, Mookerji, and Panikkar. The battles they fought between 1655 and 1758, first with the troops of the Great Mogul and then with European forces, are among the most memorable engagements that took place in Indian waters.

We recall that in the sixteenth century emperor Akbar had organised a real war fleet, and that the main body of that fleet, known as the *nowwara*, was concentrated at Dacca on the Bay of Bengal. Aurangzeb pursued a similar policy: he had no fleet based on the western coast of India. That mistake allowed the Maratha leader Shivaji, when in 1657 he rebelled against Aurangzeb, to organise on the Malabar coast a fleet powerful enough to defy the authority of the Great Mogul on the sea as well as on land. The Maratha had never previously distinguished themselves, but they were 'seafaring people' perfectly capable of building vessels and of turning them to good account. Their main base was Kolaba, and later Gheria, which for a long time was thought to be impregnable. As for the Mogul forces, they were based on Janjira, where Aurangzeb had made the Siddis of Janjira his 'admirals', entrusted with the protection of the trade of Surat.

Until 1683 the Siddis held their own against the Marathas, but when the famous Kanoji Angré took command of the Marathas, the situation changed. What had originally been a national movement then became a vast piratical enterprise, Angré's 'navy' at that time including not only Marathas but also a large number of European, Arab, and African sailors.

Angré soon dominated the entire coast south of Bombay and directed his attacks not only against the Mogul's vessels but also against those of the East India Company. To guard against the danger, the company had to organise a special force in Bombay, known as the Bombay Marine. In 1717 and 1722 that force itself began to attack, but did not manage to oust Angré from his hideout. In 1724 and 1728 the Dutch company, whose vessels had also been plundered by Angré's men, tried in turn to subjugate Gheria, but without success. It was not until 1756 that a powerful English squadron under the command of Admiral Watson and Colonel Clive managed to disperse the pirates and occupy Gheria.

In the Bay of Bengal Aurangzeb's *nowwara* proved at first to be powerless against the two groups of pirates that infested the region in the seventeenth century: the *Muggs* and the *Feringhis*. *Mugg* is a corrupt form of the word *Magh*, a name given by the Bengalis to the people of Arakan. The word *feringhi* means 'foreigner', and designated the Portuguese adventurers of Dianga, of whom we have already spoken. Chased out of Dianga in 1607, following a quarrel with the king of Arakan, they then established themselves on Sandwip Island, in the waters of Chittagong, where their numbers were soon increased by a motley assemblage of individuals from various European settlements in the Indies. The *Feringhis* were much better organised than the *Muggs*, and consequently far more dangerous.

In that region the Mogul naval forces had also to confront the fleets of the kingdom of Assam, which began to attack Bengal in 1638. In 1662 a *nowwara* of 323 units managed to crush them, but the *nowwara* itself emerged from the battle in such poor condition that it took a long time to build it up again. Shortly afterwards (1664), it was attacked at Dacca by the *Feringhis*, who destroyed half its complement.

Aurangzeb's navy finally managed to neutralise the Arakan pirates, but not until its commander, Shaista Khan, had succeeded, through clever bargaining, in separating the Portuguese *Feringhis* from their 'brothers', and in addition had secured the support of the Dutch in Batavia for an expedition against Sandwip Island. The Portuguese defection also allowed the imperial fleet to get the better of the pirates, even before the arrival of the reinforcements it had asked for from the Dutch.

With regard to piracy in the Bay of Bengal during the interregnum, the astonishing career of the English pirate Samuel White must also be mentioned. Entrusted by the king of Siam with organising a fleet for him at Mergui, on the coast of Pegu, in 1683, White used that fleet for fruitful privateering operations of his own.

Finally, we should consider the activities of the Malay pirates and the Bugis of Macassar in the Indonesian archipelago at the end of the seventeenth century, which are described at some length in Hall's work on South-east Asia, but this would obviously lead us too far afield. Suffice it to say that even Indonesia, where the Dutch had gained a foothold, had constantly to reckon with the great plague of the Indian Ocean in the seventeenth century: piracy, a veritable hydra with hundreds of heads forever springing up anew.

6. THE PIRATES OF MADAGASCAR

The *Feringhis* were not the only European brotherhood of pirates in the Indian Ocean during the interregnum, nor the most important. Indeed, the prize, so to speak, should go to the extraordinary pirate 'Republic' formed at Diégo-Suarez in northern Madagascar about 1685, which held its own until around 1730. It has been the object of many studies, which Deschamps used in 1949 to produce a fascinating book.

Large-scale piracy in the Indian Ocean sprang from the buccaneering in the West Indies, which was at its height between about 1550 and 1685. At that time the buccaneers, because of the settlement of the West Indies, were forced to seek refuge elsewhere. They removed, bag and baggage, to Sierra Leone, on the west coast of Africa, but as the Indian Ocean offered better prospects, they at length settled once and for all in Madagascar. Since the Fort-Dauphin massacre (1674), the French had forsaken the island; consequently the place was unoccupied.

There they founded a real communist republic before its time, whose mere name was a whole programme: *Libertalia*. Like any self-respecting state, it had a code of summary laws (which were not to be trifled with), various administrative departments, and even an international language which must have been a kind of Esperanto or highly colourful Volapük. This republic was mainly the joint work of Misson, a French adventurer, and Caraccioli, a defrocked Italian monk. Deschamps calls them the 'pirate philosophers'. Besides those two, the most celebrated of the freebooters of Libertalia were the Englishmen Read, Teat, Williams, Avery, and Kidd; the Americans Tew, Burgess, and Halsey; the Irishman Cornelius; the Jamaican Plantain; and the Frenchman Le Vasseur, alias La Buse, or the Buzzard. The brotherhood included, in addition, a whole group of minor pirates of all nations, in which the English element predominated, or so it would seem from the *Pirates' Who's Who* compiled by Gosse in 1924. Their operations were not limited to the regions of Madagascar and the Mascarenes, but covered practically the entire Indian Ocean. They attacked Arab, Indian, and European vessels indiscriminately, and the preponderance of Omani Arabs in the western region of the Indian Ocean does not seem to have bothered them very much. Besides, they had accomplices in all the ports. Deschamps recounts that certain merchants of the Malabar coast informed them of shipping movements and then bought the booty from them. In 1696, if we are to believe the French merchants of Surat, the English governor of Bombay himself joined up with the pirates and protected them at the expense of his company's own vessels. The booty was so considerable that a veritable 'market of the Jolly Roger' was formed in Madagascar, where, around 1700, traders from North America regularly came to lay in supplies, thus making their first appearance in the Indian Ocean. More remarkable still, real shipping enterprises in piracy, bound for the Indian Ocean, were organised in New York, Boston, and Philadelphia. The operation was known as the 'grand round'.

Deschamps finds that there were three main periods in the development of piracy in Madagascar: the period of Avery, Misson, and Kidd, which lasted from 1685 to 1701; that of the small or minor pirates, which reached its height about 1705; and finally, that of the last freebooters, beginning in 1718 and ending about 1726.

Two events provoked the breaking up of Libertalia in the

second decade of the eighteenth century. The first was the heavier armament of the trading-company ships, which rendered their capture more difficult; the second was the intensification of French colonisation in the Mascarenes which had begun, as we have seen, in 1674, but did not become really effective until the stimulus given to the island of Bourbon by Desforges-Boucher from 1721 to 1725 and the occupation of Mauritius, rechristened Île de France, in 1721.

In a recent thesis Lougnon has shown how Desforges-Boucher succeeded in attracting a great number of pirates from Madagascar to Bourbon and in making them contribute to the settlement of the island. Those who did not want to accept his offers were mercilessly attacked. One of the last to resist, the Frenchman La Buse, was captured and hanged at Bourbon in 1730.

The children that the pirates had had by Malagasy women, principally of the Betsimisaraka tribe, and their children's children continued to indulge in piracy during the whole of the eighteenth century and even at the beginning of the nineteenth. But despite everything, theirs were minor operations, although they sometimes gathered together up to 500 dugouts and 18,000 warriors, directed solely against the Comoro Islands. Occasionally, but rarely, they pushed out as far as the African coast. Their activities were really no more than sidelights on history. But the exploits of the great pirates of Libertalia, Masqat, Malabar, and Bengal are far more important, and if we have described them at some length, it is because they show that during the entire interregnum the trading companies did not have a firm hold on the Indian Ocean and could not even lay down the law there, except perhaps in extremely limited areas.

7. DUTCH CARTOGRAPHY

Although none of the European nations then trading in the Indian Ocean really dominated it during the interregnum, one of them at least managed to explore it fairly extensively, and delineated it on magnificent maps that show real progress over the Portuguese portolani. The important work accomplished by the Dutch in this realm must not be passed over in silence.

In a book on the discovery of Australia, Professor G. Arnold Wood was very hard on the story of the Dutch discovery:

> It is not a very interesting story. It is, in fact, a story of unsurpassable dryness. We have been told that 'it was the spirit which had cut the dykes that gained the Spice Archipelago for Holland'. But there was very little of 'the spirit of the dykes' in the use which the Dutch made of their gain. The trail of business is over the whole story; indeed the whole story is nothing but a trail of business. Complete and singular is the contrast between the Spaniard and his successor. It is the contrast of the Cathedral full of men with all human virtues and vices, and the Factory wherein is neither virtue nor vice, nor even man, but one thing only, desire to make money.[5]

The comparison between the Iberian conquistador and the Dutch merchant is fair enough; but it can apply to the English, the French, and the Danes, just as well as to the Dutch, for like them they were all, at the beginning, exclusively concerned with money-making.

The Australians of today may perhaps still nurse a grudge against the Dutch for having formerly set such little store by their country; but that is no reason for refusing to give them credit for having contributed very considerably to the knowledge of the oceanic world.

Opposed to Professor Wood's opinion is that of Destombes, who made a thorough study of the Dutch nautical maps of the seventeenth century, 'As a whole, he concludes, 'this collection of maps gives a sufficiently good idea of the perfection of the Dutch technique and of the enormous work accomplished by the pilots who laid the foundations for the maritime cartography of all Asia in the seventeenth century.'[6]

At its beginnings, Dutch cartography owed everything to the Portuguese. Linschoten's *Itinerario* is merely a collection of seafarers' manuals copied in Lisbon, but towards the middle of the sixteenth century Holland already had two cartographers of world renown, Mercator and Ortelius. In the seventeenth these were succeeded by Hondius, Blaeu, van Loon, Goos,

[5] G. A. Wood, *The Discovery of Australia*, London, 1922, p. 223.
[6] M. Destombes, *Cartes hollandaises: la cartographie de la Compagnie des Indes orientales* (*1593-1743*), Saigon, 1941, p. 18.

Doncker, van Keulen, De Hooge, De Wit, etc. In 1645 Blaeu still indicated no more than a few Dutch names on his maps of the Indian ocean, but from 1645 to 1743 the particulars were entirely Dutch.

It would seem that a cartographic centre was at work very early in Batavia, in addition to the one in Amsterdam. The Vereenigde Oostindische Compagnie at first kept their maps secret; certain of them were not found until this century (Wieder published some very curious ones in his *Monumenta Cartographica*), but around 1700 the policy of secrecy changed, and several atlases were published in Holland for the use of all the navies of the world. They were far more sumptuous than anything of the kind that subsequently appeared.

The Dutch explored mostly in the south-eastern part of the Indian Ocean. At the very beginning of the seventeenth century they reached the coasts of Australia. In 1642 Van Diemen sent Tasman to see whether that new land had any relation to the *Terra Australis Incognita* of the ancient geographers. During his circumnavigation of Australia, Tasman discovered Tasmania and New Zealand as well, and their names still recall the fact that it was the Dutch who were the first to get there.

Australia itself, which was then named New Holland, was imperfectly explored by the Dutch. As soon as they were certain that it produced no spices, they lost interest.

The Dutch are also responsible for the discovery of a more direct route from the Cape of Good Hope to the East Indies than that taken by the Portuguese. Whereas the latter, like the Arabs, merely navigated with the monsoon, and thus had sailed up north of the Equator and then come down through the Sunda Strait, the Dutch preferred to use the roaring forties, which carried them directly from the Cape to the Malay Archipelago. This route, followed for the first time by Brouwer in 1611, which for ships on their way to the Indies meant saving a year's time, was immediately adopted by the Company. It was the route that the clippers were to take in the nineteenth century to get to Australia.

The Dutch contribution to oceanic literature was also quite remarkable. Valentijn's work (*Oud en Nieuw Oost-Indien*) was itself a monumental one, not to mention the accounts of Tasman, Schouten, van Twist, etc. Moreover, Barthold points out that in the first half of the seventeenth century Holland possessed a whole school of outstanding orientalists.

Although not completely negligible, the contribution of the other European nations to the knowledge of the oceanic world during this period was far smaller. The cartographic work of the English and the French did not really attract attention until the eighteenth century. As for the oceanic literature of these peoples, there were a few great works in the seventeenth century such as those of Tavernier and Thévenot in France, and of Fitch in England, but nothing that can be compared with, for example, the *Summa* of Valentijn.

XI. The Anglo-French Conflict

I. THE DECLINE OF ASIA

THERE is no doubt that the most important happening in the world of the Indian Ocean during the eighteenth century was the decline of the great Asian states. This decline was not only political and military but economic and maritime as well. Two factors contributed in equal measure to the conquest of Asia by the West: the inner disintegration of the Oriental States, and a fundamental maritime revolution.

In the sixteenth century the very fact of possessing a strong navy when no Asian state had one made it possible for a small European nation from the other end of the world to seize all the strategic points of the Indian Ocean in a relatively short time; but as we have seen, that was not enough to disorganise the maritime economy of the Asian world. Despite all their efforts, the 'gentlemen merchants' of the seventeenth century did not succeed in seriously shaking the Asian economy any more than had the Portuguese conquistadores. The Dutch Company itself, in its golden age, had to reckon with strong competition from Eastern ships. But as a result of the maritime revolution of the eighteenth century, that competition was eliminated and the 'country' trade completely changed hands, passing from the Asians to the Europeans. We shall return to this phenomenon in the following chapter. For the moment, we shall deal only with the first factor, namely, the political and military decline of Asia:

In the middle of the seventeenth century, Asia still had a far more important place in the world than Europe. As against 125 million Europeans, there were 300 million Asians; India had over 100 million inhabitants and China even more. The riches of Asia were incomparably greater than those of the European states. Her industrial techniques showed a subtlety and a tradition that the European handicrafts did not possess. And there was nothing in the more modern methods used by the traders of the Western countries that Asian trade had to envy. In matters of credit, transfer of funds, insurance, and cartels, neither India, Persia, nor China had anything to learn from Europe.[1]

The first signs of decline appeared in Turkey, the most powerful of the Moslem states, when she was defeated in the eastern Mediterranean by a second Holy League made up of Venice, Malta, Austria, Poland, and Russia (1684). Turkey had then to make large concessions in the Levant to Austria, Russia, England, and France. Her defeat in Europe naturally had great repercussions in the entire Moslem world. She lost her role as a dominant power to the benefit of her former rival, Persia.

In 1722 Persia herself started on the road to decline when she found herself attacked simultaneously, in the east by Afghan nomads, in the north by the Russians, and in the west by the Turks. Between 1735 and 1779, two dictators, Nadir Shah, the same whom we have already seen acting against the ruler of Masqat, and Kerim Khan, endeavoured to re-establish their position and even launched out into foreign conquests, but Persia emerged completely ruined from this terrible upheaval.

In India, Aurangzeb's reign, which ended in 1707, marked the last phase of Mogul grandeur. After him the empire of Delhi, torn by conflicts of succession, declined rapidly. The seizure of Delhi by Nadir Shah in 1739 was the final blow. In reaction to India's decline, that of Persia was hastened.

In Burma, Malaya, and Indonesia, the decline began still earlier, with the decay of the great empires of Shrivijaya and Madjapahit. The history of the various small states that succeeded them presents, in the seventeenth and eighteenth

---

[1] J. Pirenne, *Les Grands Courants de l'histoire universelle*, Paris, 1950, III, 297.

centuries, a confused picture of dynastic quarrels which gave a good opening to the Dutch in that region.[2] The only state of continental Asia that remained stable and powerful in the eighteenth century was China, but she does not really belong to the world of the Indian Ocean. The European merchants, still just tolerated in Macao and Canton, cut a sorry figure there.

Yet the decline of the great Asian states in the eighteenth century had nothing at all in common with that of the 'old regime' in Europe at the same time. It is significant that the revolutionary ideology of Europe produced no repercussions in the oceanic world at the end of the century, owing to the fact that Eastern civilisation bore no resemblance whatever to Western. Westerners, in using the decline of Asia to their own ends, employed not European but typically Asian methods. Moreover, as a consequence of that decline, the Orientals did not develop any inferiority complex, nor did the Westerners develop a complex of superiority. The East-West antithesis is a phenomenon of the nineteenth and not of the eighteenth century.

2. THE NABOBISM OF DUPLEIX

Curiously, it was those who were the last to come to the Indian Ocean, the French, who were to be the first to launch out into a great policy of expansion in India, at the time of the weakening of Mogul power, and to invent the system that was subsequently to inspire the European push throughout the East.

In his excellent study on Dupleix, Jouveau-Dubreuil called that system 'Duplexian nabobism', and showed that it bore the stamp of one personality only. Imperialism was doubtless in existence at the time of Dupleix; it was not he who invented it. Albuquerque, Coen, Van Diemen, and Aungier were imperialists in their way. What Dupleix did invent was 'nabobism', and it was his method that finally prevailed.

In what did nabobism consist? Quite simply in integrating a European into the society of India as a Nabob, that is, a Mogul prince, and then using that imperial dignity, as the other nabobs did, to take advantage of the state of anarchy

[2] See D. G. E. Hall's detailed *History of South-East Asia*, London, 1955.

prevailing in the country, so as to attain supreme authority, at least over a great part of India.

Indeed, the title of Nabob, which Dupleix managed to have granted him by a firman of the Great Mogul in 1740, was by no means a purely honorary distinction, as is generally believed. His investiture therewith gave him access to the imperial caste, and entitled him to levy taxes, command five thousand horsemen, hold a durbar, and, in short, act exactly like a Mogul general.

Dupleix's genius consisted in his having been the first to understand that the system of 'factorisation'[3] would never allow the Europeans to become solidly established in India, and that something else had to be found. He was also one of the first to understand the politics of the Eastern princes, a politics dominated by intrigue and double-dealing. In that domain he himself was to be past master, becoming the most crafty and scheming of all the nabobs. Another of Dupleix's brilliant ideas was to use Indian soldiers, Sepoys, to conquer their own country.

We shall not discuss here the stages of nabobism, for they constitute a whole chapter in the political history of India. They are dealt with in the many works that have been devoted to Dupleix, more especially those of Martineau and Jouveau-Dubreuil, which also show how, from the time he arrived at Pondichéry (1742) until his recall to France (1753), he tried to conquer southern India.

Two reservations must be made on the subject of nabobism. The first is that although it was a very ingenious and relatively inexpensive system, it was perhaps not the best means for France to gain a foothold in the Indies. Rather than to attempt the conquest of India in the wake of the Moguls and to replace, in short, Eastern despotism by European, would it not have been better to have formed, on the contrary, an alliance with the Hindus of the south against the Moslems of the north and thus become a liberator?

The second is that there was one serious flaw in Dupleix's conception: it did not take into account what Mahan has since called 'sea power'. 'A Dupleixian troop', writes Jouveau-Dubreuil, 'had four weapons: infantry, artillery, cavalry, and

---

[3] I.e., in the sense of founding trading factories.

intrigue. And the latter was the most important.'[4] He is wrong. To succeed, Dupleix would have needed an even more important weapon: a navy, and that Dupleix would seem never to have understood.

As for the English, *they* understood it very well, for when war again broke out between England and France, after the twenty-five-year truce between the treaties of Utrecht and the outbreak of the War of the Austrian Succession, they were quick this time to send units of the Royal Navy into the Indian Ocean, and to attack, despite the private treaty of non-aggression concluded in 1742 between the two companies.

La Bourdonnais, Governor-General of the Mascarenes and commander of the only French fleet in the Indian Ocean, himself understood it very well. That is why, after having made, in 1746, a successful and unhoped-for *coup de main* against the British settlement of Madras with his 'squadron', which was no more than a makeshift force, he refused to support Dupleix's nabob politics and preferred to withdraw to the Mascarenes. In his remarkable thesis on what has been called 'the Madras affair', Crépin has recently shown that it was La Bourdonnais who was right.

Although peace was concluded in Europe in 1748, Dupleix nevertheless continued to wage his own private war in India until his recall in 1753. After his departure, Clive, the English Dupleix, was to adopt his adversary's ideas with better success but with the support of the British navy.[5]

3. THE GOLDEN HOUR OF THE MASCARENES

French historians would seem to be far more concerned with Dupleix's grandiose plans in India than with the less spectacular but much more useful work carried out between 1735 and 1746 by La Bourdonnais in the Mascarenes, making them the best French bases in the Indian Ocean.

To call this work a transformation is not enough. It was a real creation *ex nihilo*, to which there is nothing comparable in the history of the Indian Ocean except that accomplished by

[4] G. Jouveau-Dubreuil, *Dupleix*, Pondichéry, 1941, p. 182.
[5] On the role of the British navy in the eighteenth century, s ee the classic work of Admiral A. T. Mahan.

the first Dutch governors of the Cape of Good Hope; there also, everything had to be created from nothing. In both cases, unfortunately, the European settlement was insufficient, and so, in addition to the colonists, they had to use slaves. We say unfortunately, because it would have been far better to spare those still virgin lands the vicissitudes of the slave system from the very beginning.

In this matter, however, La Bourdonnais had an idea which the Portuguese had already put into practice in Goa, and the Dutch in Batavia: this was to use the slaves to make up a native island-navy. The utility of this conception was shown at the time of the seizure of Madras, when the crews of the French fleet included a great number of slaves.

An island-navy: that was the main idea of La Bourdonnais who tried, above all, to give the Mascarenes a 'look of buccaneering', as he put it, and to make Port Louis, the capital of Île de France, into a great seaport. Indeed, it was essential for France to have a shipbuilding centre in the Indian Ocean. As the Coromandel coast was very exposed, it was of no use for that purpose. On the Bay of Bengal the only favourable spot at that time was the Burmese port of Syriam. Between 1689 and 1740 the English and the French tried to set up shipyards there, but a revolt of the natives finally chased them out.

On the other side of the Indian sub-continent, however, the English had the possibility of establishing shipyards in Bombay. In 1735, just as La Bourdonnais was beginning to get organised at Port Louis, they themselves set to work at Bombay in collaboration with a great family of Parsi builders, the Wadias, of whom a history has just been written by one of their descendants (Ruttonjee Ardeshir Wadia, *The Bombay Dockyard and the Wadia Master Builders*, Bombay, 1955). Most of the vessels of the Bombay marine were built by the Wadias.

In 1780, when the English were securely established in the region of Bengal, they opened other shipyards at Hooghly and Chittagong. They never had a Bengal marine comparable to the Bombay marine, but the warships built in Bengal revived, in a sense, the former *nowwara* of the Moguls.

In 1760 the French managed to establish themselves once more at Syriam, where La Noë and Pruel built several ships for Pondichéry, but the political situation in Burma was so disturbed that in 1780 they finally had to give up; in the meantime, some attempts were made at shipbuilding in Rangoon in 1768, but without much success, so that during the entire eighteenth century Île de France was the only important French base in the Indian Ocean. We shall see later what a help it was during the Anglo-French conflict, which began with the War of the Austrian Succession and lasted until 1815, and how the effectiveness of the squadrons sent into the seas of India during those wars was constantly dependent on the state of preparedness of the Mascarenes.

In the eighteenth century, naval construction made giant strides in the seas of Europe, and France unquestionably held the lead in that domain, as even English writers are willing to admit. Unfortunately, the scarcity of wood considerably limited the activity of the naval architects. In a study entitled *Forests and French Sea-Power*, the American historian P. W. Bamford has recently shown how the difficulty the French had in procuring wood for their ship-building forced the navy to remain constantly on the defensive during the eighteenth century. In that respect the resources of the Indian Ocean were almost inexhaustible. The teak of Burma and Siam was highly superior to the oak of Europe as a building material. What the French ought to have done was to direct all their energies to the pursuit of La Bourdonnais's suggestions and to create the equivalent of a Bombay Marine in the Mascarenes. Unfortunately, his ideas never took hold in France. Instead of building enough ships in the Indian Ocean to compensate for the weakness of their complements, the French preferred to follow Dupleix's policy, however impracticable, without the support of a powerful navy.

Another of La Bourdonnais's dominant ideas was to use the Mascarenes as points of departure for permanent settlements in the Seychelles, in Madagascar, and on the Mozambique coast. 'The Mozambique coast', he wrote to the Company as early as 1740, 'is one of the most beautiful and luxuriant that there is. If the French could have it, it would be *their* coast of Brazil!'[6]

These plans also were to come to nothing. Explored in 1742

[6] La Bourdonnais, *Memoire des isles de France et de Bourbon*, (ed.) A. Lougnon and A. Toussaint, Paris, 1937, p. 78.

during the governorship of La Bourdonnais by an expedition that he had organised especially for that purpose, the Seychelles islands were not colonised until 1770, and then in such a half-hearted way that they never performed a very important function. The attempts at settlement in Madagascar during the eighteenth century were also clearly inadequate, and resulted in no more than a few slave-trading posts on the east coast of the island. As for the plans to settle on the African coast, one attempt at founding a settlement on Kilwa was made in 1772 by a private individual, a captain from Île de France named Morice, but it failed for lack of support. Thus, while France was chasing after a chimera in India, she was neglecting a region where, with a little perseverance, she could have created a real France in the South Seas.

In the Mascarenes themselves, the French East India Company at first left La Bourdonnais's work in peril, and it needed the disasters of the Seven Years' War, which led to the Company's own ruin, for the French government to intervene and take control of the islands.[7]

4. DUEL OF THE FLEETS

The Anglo-French duel in the eighteenth century can be broken down into five very distinct phases: (1) the War of the Austrian Succession (1740–48); (2) the Seven Years' War (1756–63); (3) the American Revolutionary War (1778–83); (4) the Wars of the French Revolution (1793–1802); and (5) the Napoleonic Wars (1803–15).

There is no comprehensive work in French on the repercussions of all these wars in the Indian Ocean, except perhaps Saint-Elme le Duc's unfinished study, which still exists in manuscript in the Bibliothèque Nationale. In English there is only one worth mentioning, that of Colonel Malleson, already very out-of-date but not yet superseded, despite the more recent works of Admiral Ballard and Professor Northcote Parkinson.

As naval history is of minor relevance to this study, we shall deal only with the most important operations; however, we

---

[7] The French East India Company's transfer of the Mascarenes to the royal government took place in 1767.

would point out at the very beginning that large-scale naval operations did not play a very great part in the Anglo-French conflict, except during the War of American Independence.

During the War of the Austrian Succession, the only incidents worth mentioning are the seizure of Madras in 1746 by the makeshift squadron got together by La Bourdonnais in the Mascarenes, and the demonstrations of Boscawen's squadron against those islands and Pondichéry in 1748. However, despite the fall of Madras, the British were in control of the sea and were able to attack French trade with impunity. The Mascarenes themselves were saved only by a stratagem. As for the Dutch, they were not involved in this war and thus need not be discussed. When peace was concluded, the belligerents found themselves in much the same situation as before, but while the Mascarenes were vegetating under the moribund régime of the French East India Company, the English were consolidating their position in India.

During the Seven Years' War, France sent out a great expeditionary force under the command of Lally against Clive's troops and Pocock's squadron. It was a bad choice. Lally, who had had no experience with India, piled up mistake on mistake and was beaten at Wandiwash (1760). Pondichéry and Mahé surrendered in 1761. On the sea, d'Aché, who was in command of the fleet, was unable to undertake anything against Pocock. Besides, he had to think above all about keeping his force in good shape, for far from being able to count on the Mascarenes, which were then in extreme destitution, he found himself, on the contrary, obliged to supply them with provisions. It was a total failure. When peace was concluded, France recovered Pondichéry, but in what a state! The company was going into liquidation, and Lally paid for his errors on the scaffold.[8]

Under the control of the Ministry of Marine, which then took over their administration, the Mascarenes experienced a genuine renaissance between the years 1767 and 1778. During the same period the English continued to make headway in Bengal, which they had controlled since the victory of Plassey (1757). Clive having departed, Warren Hastings completed what he had begun. The East India Company's policy of

[8] He was later to be rehabilitated, after long proceedings taken by his son.

territorial expansion was subjected to severe criticism in Parliament, but it emerged victorious. The Dutch did not become involved in the conflict, but in 1759, feeling that the interests of their factory at Chinsura were threatened by Clive's advance in Bengal, they sent a fleet there from Batavia to make a demonstration. They were soon obliged to retreat and apologise.

When hostilities were resumed in 1778, the Mascarenes were ready at length to give all the support necessary to the powerful squadron sent to the Indies under the command of Suffren, who was the first great sailor since Albuquerque that Europe had sent to the Indian Ocean. Faced with only a mediocre adversary in Admiral Hughes, he should have succeeded. Unfortunately, his genius was reduced to impotence by the insubordination of his officers.[9]

At this time Holland was on France's side, but her navy was in a pitiful state and could be of no help. It was Suffren who at La Praya (1781) neutralised Johnstone's British squadron, which had been sent to seize the Cape of Good Hope. It was he again who, by his brilliant campaign in Indian waters, recaptured Trincomalee from the English and saved the Dutch East Indies.

The names Sadras, Providien, Negapatam, Trincomalee, and Cuddalore all recall Suffren's memorable engagements with the British forces. Constantly harassed, the British had to remain on the defensive, and for the first time the French really controlled the sea, but the lack of discipline of his officers, who let him down in the very midst of every battle, kept Suffren from reaching his main objective: the complete destruction of the enemy forces. The opportunity was not to return.

At the beginning of the Wars of the Revolution, France had, in the Indian Ocean, only a small naval division under the command of Saint-Félix. His arrest by the Jacobins of Île de France completely disorganised the French forces. A large expedition to the Indian seas, decided upon in 1793 by the Convention, had to be called off. It was not until 1796 that a small squadron under the command of Sercey could be sent

---

[9] It must be said also that Suffren's difficult disposition contributed more than a little to creating a very strained situation between him and most of his officers.

to the Mascarenes, but Sercey soon had to give up any plans he may have had for large-scale operations against the much greater forces that the English had at their disposal.

The English also got the better of the Dutch, when Holland came into the war on the side of France. The Cape of Good Hope, Ceylon, Malacca, and Amboina fell rapidly into the hands of the English. In 1796 a squadron sent from Holland to recapture the Cape surrendered without fighting in Saldanha Bay. The Mascarenes never managed to join forces with Java.

In 1798 the Egyptian expedition came in time to create a diversion and saved what remained of the French and Dutch colonies by compelling the English to send their forces into the Red Sea.

During the Napoleonic wars, the English maintained their superiority. Given back to the Dutch at the Peace of Amiens, the Cape was recaptured in 1806. The French squadron sent into the Indian Ocean in 1803, under the command of Linois, was paralysed by its leader's indecision. When he finally left the Indian Ocean in 1805, after having quarrelled with Decaen, the Governor of the Mascarenes, the French naval forces in that theatre had been reduced to a few frigates. Once again they did not manage to make a junction with forces from Java. In 1810 and 1811 both the Mascarenes and the Dutch East Indies surrendered. Later we will give some details of the operations that marked the last phase of the conflict.

5. THE WAR OF THE PRIVATEERS

The French were apparently the first to practise privateering in the Indian Ocean. As early as 1508 one of the ships of Tristan da Cunha, who was in command of one of the first Portuguese expeditions, was captured by the French in the Mozambique Channel. In 1526 three privateers took off from Dieppe, one of which reached India, another Sumatra, and the third Madagascar. In 1642, shortly after the first French settlement in Madagascar was founded, two privateers left Fort-Dauphin for the Red Sea. These first expeditions, however, were greatly similar to piracy. Those which used the

Mascarenes as their starting point during the Anglo-French duel in the eighteenth century were, on the contrary, unquestionably part of the history of privateering.

Buccaneering was clearly what inspired the first expeditions organised in the Mascarenes, and there is no doubt that more than one of those who took part in them had pirate blood in his veins, for, as we have seen, the repentant pirates of Madagascar had contributed greatly to the settlement of the island of Bourbon. Still, the seventeenth-century pirates, who were outlaws and professional bandits, should not be confused, although they often have been, with the eighteenth-century privateers, who were fighting for their country.

The first privateering expedition organised in Île de France dates from the War of the Austrian Succession: it was none other than the operation devised by La Bourdonnais against Madras. He himself was first of all a privateer, a 'commando' man, and not an orthodox strategist like Suffren.

During the Seven Years' War at least two privateering expeditions again took off from Île de France. The first was under the command of the renowned D'Estaing and was made up of two ships armed at his expense, with a crew of five hundred men, a hundred of whom were French and four hundred, slaves. With those two ships, operating for twenty-two months against the English settlements on the Indian Ocean, from Bander-Abbas to the Sunda Strait, D'Estaing led an extraordinary campaign, described in detail by Calmon-Maison. The second was under the command of M. de La Pallière, of d'Aché's squadron. In 1762 he captured seven Indiamen, which had a total value of 2,500,000 *livres tournois*.

During the American Revolutionary War, privateering increased considerably. The Île de France archives show that from 1779 to 1782 there were no less than twenty-nine privateering expeditions, not counting several others fitted out 'for war and trade'. The most important year was 1781, with fifteen such expeditions. The most celebrated of the privateers then operating from Île de France was Deschiens Kérulvay. His first cruise, in the vicinity of Ceylon, by itself brought in 1,670,000 *livres tournois*.

The history of privateering in the islands during the Revolu-

161

tionary War has still to be written; Saint-Elme le Duc and Malleson give only a very sketchy account of it. We are better informed on privateering during the wars of the Revolution and the Napoleonic wars, thanks to the works of Cunat, of Garneray, Surcouf's grandson, Bourde de la Rogerie, and a few memoirs of privateers, some of which are still unpublished. All things considered, however, 'privateering' literature is neither very voluminous nor very reliable, and we must still go to the archives, until a definitive work on the question is written.

For the years 1793–1810, the statistics compiled from the Mauritius archives show 193 cruises, 122 of which were made by merchant ships and 71 by naval vessels. A breakdown of this figure of 193 for the two periods of war is as follows: 111 for the wars of the Revolution (1793–1802), and 82 for the Napoleonic wars (1803–10). If we compare the figure of the first period with Canon Robidou's figure of 149 for privateering at Saint-Malo during the Revolution, we see that such activity at Port Louis, in Île de France, was almost as great as that of the well-known Breton port.

Moreover, for a long time the two ports had had close ties, and in fact most of the privateers who then distinguished themselves in the Mascarenes had some relation to Saint-Malo. Among the foremost was Robert Surcouf, who earned the title 'king of the privateers'; but although they were not so well known, Lemême, Dutertre, Ripaud, Malroux, Hodoul, Le Vaillant, and Tréhouart were in no way inferior in audacity and courage. The boldest of all, bolder even that Surcouf, was probably Ripaud de Montaudevert.[10]

The total value of the prizes taken from the English has not yet been established. Milburn estimates them at £2,500,000 for the period 1793–1802 alone, the period that was the most fruitful. According to the same writer,

> So numerous and valuable were the prizes taken, and carried into the Isle of France, that the markets were over-stocked with the manufactures and staple commodities of the

---

[10] In the work of Saint-Elme le Duc there are biographical notes on several of the Mascarene privateers, but there are many whose exploits have so far remained in the dark.

British possessions in India; and American vessels frequently resorted thither to procure them on terms more favourable than they could have obtained in Calcutta.[11]

Further details on this subject will be found in the next chapter.

Braudel calls privateering, in any age, 'une petite guerre'. And that is perfectly true. Privateering by itself could not have beaten down British power in the Indian Ocean; still, it often kept it in check. The capture of Indiamen, which were all well-armed vessels, by privateers that were often no more than wretched little *barques* shows that, had privateering been better organised in the Mascarenes in other respects, it could have really exhausted the English. Besides, had the Mascarenes been able to build up the equivalent of the Bombay Marine, that is, a real auxiliary navy, they would probably have been able to hold out victoriously against the British until the end of the war in 1815.

6. THE EGYPTIAN EXPEDITION

Although the Indian Ocean was not the theatre of Bonaparte's expedition to Egypt in 1798, that expedition deserves special mention, for it had a very marked influence on the course of operations in the ocean. It is also quite clear that his success seriously threatened England's position in India. Finally, this operation was not, as is generally believed, a mere caprice of General Bonaparte's. It was very much in keeping with French policy in the Levant, where France was predominant in the eighteenth century.

Bonaparte's mistake, as well as the Convention's, was to believe that British power was based primarily on the Indies. Now at that time England's supremacy was far from being definitively established in India, and a defeat there would not necessarily have led to a setback to British power in the seas of Europe.

As for keeping England in check in India, this was perfectly possible, even after the destruction of the French fleet by Nelson at Aboukir. According to Northcote Parkinson, if Bonaparte

[11] W. Milburn, *Oriental Commerce*, II, London, 1813, 569.

had had a few ships built at Suez and had added them to the vessels that he might have procured from the Mascarenes and from Tippoo Sahib in India, he could well have got together a flotilla large enough to put ashore at Mangalore, on the Malabar coast, at least a complete brigade, or 3,000 men, more than enough to inflict serious losses on the English in India.

That the English were prepared for this contingency can be seen from the fact that the Admiralty expressly sent a special force from England, under the command of Captain Blankett, to block the entrance to the Red Sea. The British authorities in India, for their part, sent an expedition to occupy the island of Perim, with the same purpose in mind. Blankett himself was all for occupying Aden, but his suggestion was dismissed so as not to upset the Arabs.

To guard against the threat of a French army in Egypt, the English also gave up any plans for attacking the Mascarenes and Java. In 1801 a new expedition under the command of Popham was sent from England to make a landing at Suez. By the time it arrived on the spot, the French were no longer masters of Egypt, but their intervention in that country had not been useless.

There is nothing to indicate that Bonaparte himself had considered an invasion of India by sea, using the Red Sea route, as the English feared, but the result was the same. Northcote Parkinson's opinion on the Egyptian expedition is that it was

> a striking demonstration of what can be done by an army against a fleet. For the remaining enemy settlements were saved by Bonaparte and by his indirect threat to India. With Tippoo's help, he saved Manila by the military successes which led up to the Treaty of Campo-Formio. He saved Mauritius by landing in Egypt. He saved Java by threatening to retain Egypt. In assessing the relative failure of his Egyptian campaign, these indirect results should be borne in mind. To put British India on the defensive from 1797 to 1801 was, in itself, no mean achievement.[12]

In the realm of history, archaeology, and ethnography, the results of the French push in Egypt were also very remarkable.

[12] C. Northcote Parkinson, *War in the Eastern Seas, 1793–1815*. London, 1954, p. 182.

The scholars attached to the expeditions got together a vast amount of documentation which was to make it possible to shed light on that country and on its millenary past.

Finally, the Egyptian expedition not only did a great deal for the past but also prepared the future. Among the projects entrusted to the scholars with the expedition was to study the possibilities of a canal linking the Mediterranean waters with those of the Red Sea. In this connection, Bonaparte was bent on personally retracing the ancient canal of the Pharaohs, and it almost cost him his life.

The ultimate failure of the Egyptian expedition did not interrupt the work of the engineer Lepère, whom Bonaparte put in charge of setting up a plan for the canal. The work went on for a period of thirty-nine months and the plan itself was not published until 1809. Although it brought no final solution to the problem and contained many errors, it at least laid out a direct line for the digging of the canal. It also gave useful information on navigation in the Red Sea, the difficulties of which tended at that time to be exaggerated.

7. THE END OF THE CONFLICT

The presence of one of Napoleon's generals as governor of the Mascarenes in 1803 lends very special interest to the last phase of the Anglo-French duel in the Indian Ocean. It was also a period about which we are well informed, thanks to Prentout's remarkable thesis on Decaen, which is usefully complemented, from the English point of view, by Northcote Parkinson's work.

When hostilities were resumed in 1803, the situation was as follows: the French had lost their settlements in India and held only the Mascarenes; their allies, the Dutch, had lost Ceylon and several of their trading posts in India, but had retained the Cape of Good Hope, Java, and their other possessions in the Indonesian archipelago; the English were in complete control of the two sides of India, of the Red Sea and the Persian Gulf, and also held Ceylon.

The naval forces involved were a French division at Île de France under the command of Linois; a Dutch division under the command of Hartsinck at Batavia; and the British East Indies squadron commanded by Rainier, whose main bases were Bombay and Madras. The English were superior in number, but their vessels, which had had to remain constantly at sea from 1793 to 1802, were in poor condition. The Linois division, just arrived from France, was fresh and included, in addition, a first-rate vessel, the *Marengo*, which in itself was a great asset.

Instead of taking advantage of the situation and striking a decisive blow at the English, Linois preferred to use the *Marengo* for privateering operations. As Northcote Parkinson very rightly noted, it was like using a sledge-hammer to crack a nut. When Napoleon learned of this, he was absolutely furious.

At Île de France Decaen was also fulminating, and soon the disagreement between the two leaders reached such a point that Linois, after two cruises that, though fruitful, were without any great significance from a naval point of view, decided to return to France with his best units, leaving Decaen to shift for himself with a few frigates (1805).

How, under such conditions, was it possible to conduct the great war of which the general dreamed, especially since the English recaptured the Cape of Good Hope in 1806, thus isolating the Mascarenes? To reinforce his effectiveness, Decaen had to requisition privateering vessels, including those of Surcouf, who got angry and also returned to France. Decaen could expect nothing from the Dutch, who prudently remained on the defensive and were finally beaten in an engagement between Pellew and Hartsinck in the waters of Batavia in 1806. Nor could he expect anything from France. From 1806 to 1810, he received in all only six frigates.

Decaen vainly tried to interest Napoleon in a major attack on India, and sent dispatch after dispatch on the subject. Napoleon, who saw things on a large scale, thought that Decaen's plans were inadequate, hesitated and beat about the bush, and when he finally made up his mind to arrange for an expedition to the Indian Ocean, it was too late.

After having eliminated the privateers and set up a tight blockade around the Mascarenes, the British forces, from both the Cape and India, in 1809 occupied the island of Rodriguez. The following year, the island of Bourbon and Île de France surrendered in turn in the space of a few months despite the brilliant victory won in the bay of Grand Port (Île de France) by the small division of the Mascarenes over the advanced guard of the British squadron in August 1810. In 1811 the English were able to concentrate all their forces against Batavia and get the better of them by force of arms. The Dutch settlements on the coast of Sumatra were also captured.

Until the end of the war, in 1815, the English, who had taken command in the Indian Ocean, experienced only one moment of alarm, when the United States declared war on them in 1812. It is true that the Americans had only nineteen warships at the time, which meant very weak striking-power. On the other hand, the United States was in a position to bring more than five hundred privateers into the campaign. During the three years the war lasted, the British merchant marine suffered more losses because of them than the Americans themselves suffered. Several of those privateers reached the Indian Ocean, but since they had no bases, they were unable to do much harm to their adversaries.

XII. Searching for Gold
and New Horizons

I. 'COUNTRY' TRADE

THE port-to-port trade in the East, which the English called 'country' trade and the Dutch *Handel von haven tot haven,* long remained the prerogative of the Orientals. It was a lucrative trade, and responsible for the accumulation of vast fortunes, as the following example, mentioned by Pirenne, shows: at the beginning of the eighteenth century the 'prince' of the Surat merchants, that is, the head of their corporation, Virji Vora, died and left a fortune estimated at 22 million gold francs.

This trade comprised three distinct branches: (1) the coastal trade along the Indian seaboard; (2) the trade between the ports on the west coast of India and the region of the Persian Gulf and the Red Sea, as well as the ports on the African coast; (3) that between the ports on the east coast and Burma, Malaya, Indonesia, and China.

Of the three branches, the most important at the beginning of the eighteenth century was the second. The two great Indian ports of the west coast were then Surat and Bombay, and their trade was mainly directed towards Persia and Arabia. Goa, Cochin, and Calicut came next.

According to certain travellers, Surat was then the most beautiful city in India. One small detail will give an idea of the unparalleled luxury that prevailed there: certain streets were paved with porcelain. François Martin in his *Mémoires* calls it 'a real Babylon'. Bombay at that time had also become a very active port. The Parsis, descendants of the Mazdeans who had emigrated from Persia in the seventh century, formed a very enterprising and active mercantile community there and had large interests in the country trade.

Most of the boats used for this kind of trade ('country' ships or 'country' *wallahs*) were native boats at first built in Bombay (the activity of the Wadias in Bombay has already been mentioned) and later in Calcutta as well. The boats from Bombay were the best and largest, of from 600 to 1000 tons burden, whereas those from Calcutta rarely exceeded 400 tons. Their design was much the same as that of European vessels, which the Indians had not taken long to copy.

As the teak of which these boats were built was almost indestructible, eighteenth-century 'country' ships could still be seen sailing in the Indian Ocean during the nineteenth century and even at the beginning of the twentieth. Northcote Parkinson states that one of the boats built in Bombay at the end of the eighteenth century was still in existence in 1928. He says also that a comparison between them and the Indiamen built in England for the East India Company's trade with the metropolis was to the advantage of the 'country' ships, except that the Indiamen were larger and better-looking.[1]

Engaged at first by the native shipowners to command their vessels, the European captains gradually began to work for themselves. It was actually the 'country' captain, says Furber, who was responsible for the considerable development of trade in the Indian Ocean at the end of the eighteenth century:

> This obscure and unsung soldier of fortune charted new trade routes in the Eastern Seas and redeveloped old ones. With a crew of obedient lascars at his back, he dared undertake voyages which few Mohammedan commanders would attempt. Whenever several such voyages were successful, he was able to buy a ship of his own and become independent of the Indian or European merchant-princes who employed him. His widespread operations had their share in bringing about a commercial revolution in the Indian Ocean in the mid-eighteenth century.[2]

[1] On the Indiamen, see Sir Evan Cotton, *East Indiamen: the East India Company's Maritime Service*, London, 1949.
[2] Furber, *op. cit.*, p. 161.

As we have already pointed out, this revolution consisted in the country trade's passing from the hands of the Asians into those of the Europeans. It was naturally the English who benefited from it the most. But all the same, the Dutch, the French, and the Danes took a large share of the trade, often in association with the English.

The wars between their respective countries at that time made no difference whatsoever. A phenomenon on which Furber dwells at length and which was quite peculiar to the eighteenth century was the fact that although the French, Dutch, and English were often at war among themselves during that period, nationalism did not enter into their relations. The Europeans were far less busy killing one another in the Indian Ocean during the eighteenth century than they had been in the seventeenth, and they should be seen rather as a large international association, in which business came before everything else.

There were even quite extraordinary cases, such as that of the collusion that existed between certain agents of the English company at Madras and the privateers of Île de France, the proofs of which can be found in the Madras archives. We shall also see later that the English company often joined up with the interlopers. Actually, all the companies' employees took part in 'country' trade. It might even be said that they lived on it, for their salaries were negligible.

Also, the social distinctions then prevailing in Europe no longer existed in the region of the Indian Ocean. Across the equator, as the old saying goes, all men are equal. The French *gentilshommes* of the *ancien régime* did not feel it beneath their dignity to 'do business' in the Indies, and the same was true for English gentlemen. (It should be noted, however, that from the very beginning the East India Company had decided not to employ gentlemen.)

All the same, in the various countries of the Indian Ocean in which the Europeans had established themselves, especially in India and in the Mascarenes, a real merchant caste was formed, which launched out into large-scale 'country' trade after the French company's charter was cancelled in 1769.

In India the appearance of that caste and the substitution of the East India Company's sovereignty for that of the

Mogul authority in Bengal was, according to Mukerji, accompanied by a decline of the Indian mercantile bourgeoisie. At the end of the eighteenth century, he says, the great merchants of India had almost disappeared in Bengal and elsewhere. Those who remained played a secondary part as *banians* and *gomastahs*, serving as intermediaries between the company agents and the mass of natives.

Still, the eighteenth-century European 'nabobs', whether merchants or company agents, which came in the end to the same thing, were largely 'Asianised', as it were, did not disdain the Eastern customs, and even lived in the Eastern way. On this subject we may consult William Hickey's Memoirs and Spear's interesting study of the English nabobs in India.

It should also be noted that they were a class of men whose horizons were singularly broadened by their frequent voyages and business habits, and who, while not being exactly philanthropists, were undeniably open-minded on many questions.

2. THE ROUTE TO CHINA

About 1770 there was an extraordinary development in the third branch of 'country' trade, that between the region of Bengal and the Far East: to the Indies route was soon added a real route to China. The burden of the vessels engaged in this traffic increased from 4000 tons to 25,000 in the period 1780 to 1790 alone.

It was a one-way trade, for the Chinese themselves did not go to India, and at first would accept no European articles in exchange for their tea, silk, and china, but only Spanish dollars, which since the sixteenth century had become the real monetary standard of the Indian Ocean, and were not to be replaced by Indian rupees until the nineteenth.[3]

Moreover, the only Chinese ports open to the 'Western barbarians' were Macao and Canton, particularly the latter. The corporations of Chinese merchants specially established to deal with them were known as *Hongs*, whence the term *Cohong* given to the system as a whole. It was also called the 'Cantonese system' by the Europeans, and had a vague and rather remote

[3] On the various rupees in circulation in the region of the Indian Ocean, see Furber's work mentioned above.

similarity to the organisation of their own India companies. The system remained in force until 1842.

The spice trade was not large enough to ensure the East India Company profitable returns. When in 1721 it had also to give up exporting textiles from India to England, something else had to be found. Tea from China was about the only item whose use could be expanded without affecting the metropolitan industry. The history of tea in Europe and America was to have very extensive developments. Suffice it to say that its consumption in England, insignificant at the end of the seventeenth century and the beginning of the eighteenth, went up to six million pounds in 1783, fifteen million in 1785, and almost thirty million about 1800. In less than half a century, tea had become the national drink of the English people. It alone made the East India Company prosperous.

There was one shadow in the picture: the necessity of paying for Chinese tea in Spanish dollars. But it did not take the English Company long to realise that although the Chinese had no taste for English products, with the exception of 'singsongs', which had very small exchange value, they were ready to accept two products from India: raw cotton and opium. Of those two products, opium was the most prized, for China itself produced cotton, but no opium, and opium, although strictly prohibited, was in great demand among the Chinese.

Officially, of course, the Honourable Company had nothing to do with such traffic. It did grow and harvest opium in India, but it was the 'country' ships and not the East Indiamen that transported the opium to China. Moreover, the traffic was carried on outside Canton and by intermediaries other than the *Cohong* merchants. Yet, as Greenberg has shown in his study of the question, the opium trade was by no means, as might be thought, a small contraband trade but, on the contrary, a very vast operation which probably had no equal in the world during the eighteenth and nineteenth centuries.

Two factors contributed to making this illicit trade an extremely profitable operation: the venality of the Mandarins and, more especially, the absence of a Chinese navy, which would obviously have protected the splendidly isolated coasts of that country better than the imperial edicts. For a long time all went relatively well, but finally in the nineteenth century the reactions of the Chinese were to provoke a bloody conflict.

Thus European trade in the Indian Ocean in the eighteenth century had two very different sides to it, just as it was maintained by two very separate routes: a quite honourable side, carried out by means of the so-called Indies route, which linked Europe with Asia by way of the Cape of Good Hope; and a far less honourable one, indeed, one not at all honourable, even considering the eighteenth-century mentality, carried on via the route to China, which linked India with the Far East.

On the one hand, there was the royal sea-way, in principle travelled solely by the majestic vessels of the great companies, with the 'blue ribbon' going unquestionably to the English Indiamen. These were the most beautiful ships of the time, maintained far better than those of the Royal Navy, commanded by East India captains, the elite of their profession, and laden with the rarest and most marvellous commodities of the East. On the other hand, there was the smugglers' route used by the 'country' ships. Though far less spectacular, these were often better sailing ships than the Indiamen, indeed they had to be. They were commanded by hardbitten masters, and carried in their flanks the most subtle of poisons.

All that can be said in defence of this immoral traffic is that it contributed to the progress of navigation by giving rise to a special type of ship known as the opium clipper and by turning out absolutely first-class sailors.

3. THE DANISH INTERLOPERS

If piracy was the major factor in the history of the Indian Ocean during the seventeenth century, it can be said that clandestine trade played a similar role in the eighteenth. Indeed, the development of country trade was not long in attracting to the seas of Asia adventurers of all nations, who came to defy the monopoly of the large trading companies and were most of the time in league with the company agents: these were the interlopers. Their activities have been studied by Furber in a major work on the economic history of the Indian Ocean in the eighteenth century, in which the shady side and the intrigues of the mercantile bourgeoisie of the time are clearly exposed.

Foremost among these interlopers were the Danes, whose moribund company at the beginning of the eighteenth century was to prosper anew only through this kind of operation. But it must be emphasised that they were not the only ones, and that the interlopers were recruited from other countries as well.

The beginning of the eighteenth century saw the appearance in the Indian Ocean of adventurers from several European nations which as yet had played no role there. In 1718 a company for Eastern trade was formed at Ostend. In 1720 a vessel from Ostend reached Mauritius, which the French had not yet occupied, and took possession of it in the name of the Emperor of Austria. From there it went on to India, where the members of the expedition founded a settlement at Koblon, about fifty miles from Pondichéry.

The Swedes, who had tried to form an India Company at the end of the seventeenth century, made another attempt to do so in 1731. In Prussia the Elector of Brandenburg had also tried to make his country into a colonial power by founding a trading company and a settlement on the coast of Guinea. Prussian ships appeared in the Indian Ocean, mainly in Bengal. In 1730 Polish vessels came several times to look over the coasts of India and tried to establish relations with the natives. It would seem that Russia as well sent a few vessels into the Indian Ocean, which she tried to reach also in another way, by making Persia, whom she had attacked in 1722, grant her certain commercial facilities. Finally, towards the end of the eighteenth century, vessels from Hamburg, Genoa, Trieste, and Spain made their way to the Indian Ocean.

Of all the new 'India Companies' created at that time, the most curious was certainly the Ostend company. Dissolved in 1732, at the intervention of France, Holland and England who looked on it unfavourably, it was reconstituted clandestinely, first in Denmark and later in Trieste.[4]

The fourth rebirth of the Danish company in 1732, which has already been mentioned, was brought about with the help of capital from Ostend. There was one special feature about

---

[4] On the Trieste company, see F. von Pollack-Parnau, *Eine österreichische ostindische Handelskompagnie, 1775–1785*, Stuttgart, 1927.

the company in its new form: it carried on its operations with two kinds of capital, an 'assured capital' and a 'non-assured capital'. The former consisted of 400 shares at 250 rix-dollars each, and the latter, of investments made by the shareholders in proportion to the shares they held in the 'assured capital'.

During the entire eighteenth century the Danish factory at Tranquebar was a very active centre of contraband. As the Danes were not involved in the Anglo-French conflict at that time, their position as neutrals allowed them to do good business in trading with the belligerents. Especially during the wars of the Revolution and the Napoleonic wars, trade between Tranquebar and the Mascarenes was established, and it was equally profitable to the Danes and to the colonists of the islands, who thus had the possibility of provisioning themselves despite the English blockade and, at the same time, of profitably selling off the booty brought in by the privateers. This trade has recently been the object of an interesting study by Aage Rasch.

As the East India Company was then the largest of the European companies in the Indian Ocean, its French and Dutch rivals having practically disappeared in 1769 and 1798 respectively, it might be thought that it would be the one to suffer most from the competition of the interlopers. Furber's work shows that this was not the case.

Actually, the East India Company was a very cosmopolitan association. At least one-fifth of its nominal capital of £3,200,00 was in Dutch hands, and a large proportion of that capital came also from other European countries, so that not only in London and Amsterdam but in Paris, Copenhagen, and Lisbon the financiers were directly concerned in the company's affairs. It was the cosmopolitan nature of the East India Company that gave it its strength. Its own rivals were unable to do without it, and Furber concludes that the commercial activity of the French, the Dutch, and the Danes in the Indian Ocean during the eighteenth century clearly shows that 'the time had arrived when Europeans at home or overseas who had a stake in the maintenance of European power anywhere on the Indian continent were one and all forced to take part in the work of building a *British* empire in India.'[5] As we shall

[5] Furber, *op. cit.*, p. 31.

see further on, the Abbé de Pradt said much the same thing at the beginning of the nineteenth century, declaring that it was in Europe's interest to maintain British sovereignty in the Indies.

4. THE AMERICANS IN THE INDIAN OCEAN

Little is known of American activities in the Indian Ocean during the eighteenth century, although they have been the object of several studies, among which should be mentioned the works of James Duncan Phillips and a few other members of the Essex Institute and the Peabody Museum of Salem, Massachusetts, where today the main sources relevant to the subject can be found.

The first Americans to sail in the Indian Ocean were, as we have already said, traders from New York, Boston, and Philadelphia, who went to the pirates' market in Madagascar to procure supplies at the end of the seventeenth century. The English colonies of North America had at that time still not separated from their mother-country to form the United States. That, of course, did not happen until the Revolutionary War, and it was also at that time that the American adventure in the Indian Ocean really began, for the expeditions to Madagascar during the previous century ended with the disappearance of the pirates.

The first legitimate American expedition to the Indian Ocean dates back to 1784. Its destination was China. The same year, tradesmen from Baltimore gave financial support to the Hungarian adventurer Benyowsky in his second endeavour to create a settlement at Madagascar, an attempt that ended in failure.[6] In 1786, American vessels reached Île de France and India for the first time.

The objective of those expeditions was to procure spices, tea, and other European products without using the English as intermediaries. In ships and sailors the United States was not lacking. The Revolutionary War had given rise to a type of very rapid sailing vessel known as the Baltimore clipper, because the first ships of the kind came from the Baltimore

---

[6] On Benyowsky's endeavour, see his own memoirs, the first edition of which was issued in London in 1790, and the various works subsequently devoted to him.

shipyards. As for sailors, they were easily recruited from all the maritime regions of the United States. What the Americans lacked was a good port of call in the Indian Ocean, for the route from North America to distant China was a long one, the Pacific route having not yet been opened.

They quickly learned that they could procure all they needed from the Mascarenes. Indeed, those islands had a very active trade with China, India, and the ports of the Red Sea. The declaration of freedom of trade at the time of the French East India Company's liquidation in 1769 had been greeted enthusiastically there, and when Louis XVI decided to re-establish the former company's charter on behalf of Calonne's India Company in 1785, he was forced by the protests of the colonists to give up any idea of including the Mascarenes in the charter. On the other hand, the islands, which had always been very badly supplied by France, offered the Americans an excellent outlet for their own products, which consisted mainly of food and of nautical rigging and gear.

As the Americans were neutral, the wars of the Revolution and the Napoleonic wars did not interrupt the traffic between the United States and the Mascarenes. On the contrary, they intensified it and gave it new sustenance: the booty captured from the English by the privateers. That booty was also sought by the Danish interlopers, but the Americans, who could offer more, since they were able to furnish the Mascarenes with Baltimore clippers for privateering, soon eclipsed their Danish rivals.

Trade with the Mascarenes became so important for the United States that at the time of the 'quasi-war' with France in 1799 they sent a special mission to the islands to negotiate a private treaty of non-aggression with the government of the Mascarenes, which was then not on the best of terms with France in regard to the abolition of slavery.[7]

Under the Empire, relations with the Mascarenes were further developed, actually reaching their peak in the years 1804–05. Napoleon's policy towards the neutrals caused President Jefferson to declare an embargo on American ships in 1807 and consequently put an end to American voyages to

[7] The documents on this mission are reproduced in A. Toussaint, *Early American Trade with Mauritius*, Port Louis, Mauritius, 1954.

the islands. This was a great misfortune for the Mascarenes, for the cessation of trade contributed more than a little to the loss of those colonies.

The American expeditions in the Indian Ocean did not all stop at the Mascarenes. The voyages to China, begun in 1784, continued without interruption until the Chinese ports were definitively opened to the Americans in 1844. Latourette has given a very detailed account of them during the whole of that period.[8]

The Americans had no opium to offer the Chinese in exchange for their products. On the other hand they had ginseng, a plant to which the Chinese attributed extraordinary qualities and which grew abundantly in the Hudson Valley.[9] The time came when the Chinese market was over-saturated with ginseng, but that did not happen before the first decades of the nineteenth century. Until then the Americans were able to do excellent business by exchanging a valueless root for the most precious products of the Celestial Empire. An American historian has devoted to this trade a book entitled *Gold of Ophir*.

5. THE SPICE CONQUEST

No one ever protected a monopoly more jealously or more fiercely than the Vereenigde Oostindische Compagnie did its monopoly of spice. It lost its monopoly of pepper very early, for the English, the French, and the Danes were able to procure as much from India as could the company itself from the Indonesian archipelago; but for a long time it retained its monopoly of cloves and nutmeg.

In order to prevent any clandestine trade in its precious commodities and to eliminate all competition, the company had organised in the Moluccas, as of 1625, expeditions called

---

[8] See K. Latourette, 'History of Early Relations between the United States and China, 1784–1844,' *Trans. of the Connecticut Academy of Arts and Sciences*, XXII (1917), 1–209, and 'Voyages of American Ships to China', *ibid.*, XXVIII (1927), 238–71.

[9] The ginseng root is small, fusiform, and aromatic, and comes from *Aralia Ginseng*. It was in great demand in China as a tonic and particularly as an aphrodisiac.

hongitochten, with the object of systematically destroying the spice trees in the archipelago, except at Amboina, where the cultivation of cloves was concentrated, and on three small islands of the Banda group, where they kept only the nutmeg trees.

The result of this system was to impoverish the population of the Moluccas. In place of spices, the natives had to plant sago and rice, but as they never managed to produce enough of those commodities, they were finally forced to buy rice from the Dutch. These made the situation even worse by importing slaves to cultivate the 'spice farms'; these were made over, at a nominal price, to former soldiers, on condition that the entire harvest was sold to the company at whatever price the company fixed. When the harvest was too plentiful, part of it was destroyed to maintain prices. Glamann reports that in 1710 the directors of the company in Holland 'were distressed' by the news of an exceptionally fine harvest of cloves at Amboina, and that, so as to reduce the harvest the following year, 150,000 clove trees had to be cut down.

Such a system, of course, necessarily encouraged theft and contraband, which the company never managed to do away with, any more than it managed to do away with piracy, in spite of the severe penalties inflicted upon those who indulged in it, whether Dutch or natives. Hall reports, for example, that in 1722 governor Zwaardekroon had at least twenty-six of the company's employees, convicted of fraud, beheaded in a single day.

An enterprising man, the Frenchman Pierre Poivre (or Pepper, a predestined name) did manage to steal clove and nutmeg plants from the Dutch in the course of the eighteenth century and spread their cultivation to the Mascarenes and other countries of the Indian Ocean. The story of that 'spice conquest', merely outlined in Sonia Howe's work, has just been told in detail for the first time by Mlle Ly-tio-Fane, of Mauritius, in an interesting study which we shall summarise here.

From the very beginning of the colonisation of the Mascarenes, the French East India Company had contemplated cultivating on the islands not only coffee but spices as well. They had no trouble with coffee, which they imported from Arabia to Bourbon for the first time in 1715. The whole story of the beginnings of coffee cultivation on that island can be found in Lougnon's thesis. As for spices, the attempts made to procure them from the Moluccas between 1719 and 1729 never got beyond the planning stage.

The project was taken up again in 1747 by Poivre and was finally carried through in 1755. In the course of that year, during an adventurous voyage around the spice archipelago, Poivre succeeded in procuring clove and nutmeg seeds at Zamboanga in the Philippines, and on the Portuguese part of the island of Timor, and in bringing them back to Île de France, to which in 1753 he had dispatched a first shipment of nutmeg. The hostility and ill will of the botanist in charge of acclimatising the plants to the islands reduced Poivre's efforts to nothing. He made another attempt when he was named administrator of the Mascarenes in 1767. In 1770 and 1771 he sent two expeditions to the Moluccas that were highly successful. In 1776 and 1778 respectively, the first cloves and nutmeg were solemnly picked on Île de France. From there the clove and nutmeg spread to Bourbon, the Seychelles, Madagascar, Tranquebar, and the French colonies in America. In the Mascarenes the yield was disappointing, except at Bourbon, where the cultivation of both spices became important, but was not carried on to any great extent until the nineteenth century. From Bourbon the clove was taken to Zanzibar and Pemba in 1818, and it was finally there that the plant really throve. When the British occupied the two islands in 1890, they thus became the main beneficiaries of Poivre's efforts. Today, Indonesia still furnishes three-quarters of the world's nutmeg, but Zanzibar and Madagascar supply most of the cloves consumed in the East or imported to Europe and America.

As Sonia Howe so rightly says,[10] Poivre's activities can obviously not be compared to the exploits of the first Portuguese navigators in search of the maritime route to India, but he 'certainly is a worthy member of that great company of courageous men, who devoted their lives to the search for such apparently insignificant products of nature as pepper, cloves, and nutmegs'.

[10] S. E. Howe, *In Quest of Spices*, London, 1946, p. 259.

6. THE NEPTUNE ORIENTAL

Historians who specialise in exploration often call the eighteenth century 'the century of Cook', because of that navigator's important discoveries in the Pacific, but with regard to the region around the Indian Ocean it could be more suitably called 'the century of d'Après de Mannevillette'.

From the beginning of the century, Eastern cartography was completely transformed by Delisle (1675–1726) and D'Anville (1697–1782). But both of these eminent geographers applied themselves primarily to the Asian continent, and it was d'Après de Mannevillette, the hydrographer of the French East India Company, who drew up a set of nautical charts, called the *Neptune oriental*, which was to replace all previous collections.

The first edition, published in 1745, was limited to the northern region of the Indian Ocean. The part concerning the southern region was not drawn up until 1753, after d'Après had determined, for the first time and with the help of the Abbé de La Caille, the exact longitude of the Cape of Good Hope and that of Madagascar and the Mascarenes.

In 1766 d'Après again revised his work with the help of data furnished by Dalrymple, the hydrographer of the English company. Finally, in 1775, the definitive edition was published, and it included the observations the Chevalier Grenier had meanwhile made in 1772. It was accompanied by a guide to navigation entitled *Instructions sur la navigation des Indes orientales et de la Chine pour servir au Neptune oriental*.

In the eighteenth century, sailors generally said 'the d'Après' to designate the *Neptune oriental*, just as during the previous century they had said 'the Linschot' to designate Linschoten's collection. Until the publication of the British Admiralty's *Indian Ocean Pilots* in the nineteenth century, d'Après's monumental work remained the last word in matters of ocean cartography.

D'Après's name ought to be closely associated with that of the Abbé de La Caille, the man who drew up the first celestial map of the southern hemisphere. More than two centuries after da Gama had opened the vast expanses of the southern seas to European navigators, the sky of the southern hemisphere was still almost unexplored. The only astronomical observations sailors had at their disposal for that part of the world were those of Houtman the younger (*c.* 1600) and those which Halley made at St. Helena in 1676, showing only 341 stars and lacking in precision. That is why, at the time when French influence was becoming stronger in the Indian Ocean, the Académie des Sciences entrusted one of its most capable members with the mission of going to an observation post better located than St. Helena, the Cape of Good Hope, to draw up the celestial map of the southern hemisphere.

The young Abbé, who was not yet forty, and we know that youth for academicians begins at fifty, was destined, quite simply, to do wonders. In a year's work he determined the position of no less than 9766 stars, and his catalogue of them still excites the admiration of scholars throughout the world.

This modest scientist, who applied himself to locating the constellations of the southern sky with the help of a rudimentary telescope, or the 'nabob' Dupleix, who during the same period tried to carve out an empire in the Indies for France by force and by guile—which was the greatest? Which served his country best? On this point the judgement of history two centuries later leaves no doubt.

Today, Dupleix's work is wiped out; France's imperialist dream has vanished, as have those of her rivals; but La Caille's *Coelum Australe Stelliferum* and d'Aprés de Mannevillette's *Neptune oriental* remain as lasting monuments of European genius, a genius that the African and Eastern peoples will continue to admire in men like La Caille and d'Après, whereas no doubt they will have forgotten Dupleix along with so many other ephemeral proconsuls.

D'Après's name should also be associated with that of his English colleague Dalrymple, the hydrographer of the East India Company, to whom d'Après himself paid full tribute in the preface of his *Neptune oriental.* It may be said that Dalrymple's whole life was devoted to the Indian Ocean, for he went into the service of the English Company at the age of fifteen. But luck unfortunately refused to smile upon this extraordinary self-taught man and creator. After having carried out cartographic work of great value in the Eastern seas, it was not he but Cook who was chosen to command the expedition that resulted in the exploration of the east coast of Australia in 1770. Later, after disputes with his superiors, he was shamefully dismissed from his post as head of the hydrographic department of the Admiralty, a department he had created. He died three weeks later of a broken heart, and it was only after his death that his enormous services were acknowledged. A great part of Cook's glory unquestionably belongs to him.

7. THE ANTARCTIC REGIONS

D'Après, La Caille, and Dalrymple were not the only prospectors for horizons in the Indian Ocean during the eighteenth century. We have granted them a special place because their work was of prime importance, but besides them, there was a whole collection of scientists and explorers who contributed in varying degrees to the knowledge of the world of the Indian Ocean. As it would be impossible to do all of them justice here, we shall merely refer mathematicians to Marguet's work, travellers and orientalists to Barthold's, and explorers to Heawood's.

Here we shall give only a few brief particulars on the discoveries in Australasia of the southlands which, in the realm of exploration, was the great event of oceanic history in the eighteenth century, for it rectified an error of long standing on the configuration of the Indian Ocean, and to the already known ocean lands added several new ones, at least one of which was subsequently to play a leading part.

On the strength of Ptolemy and the ancient geographers, there was still in the eighteenth century a belief in the existence of a vast southern continent stretching to the south of the three oceans and filled with extraordinary riches. The Portuguese, the Spaniards, and the Dutch had gone out to seek it in the sixteenth and seventeenth centuries, and their search had led them to the shores of what is today Australia; but although, since Tasman's voyages in 1642, the existence of a vast land in the south-eastern region of the Indian Ocean was well established, nothing was yet known about its exact configuration, its inhabitants, or its resources.

'The entire southern portion of our globe is still unknown,' wrote de Brosses in his *Histoire des navigations aux Terres australes*, the first edition of which came out in 1757. And he added: 'The greatest, most noble, and perhaps most useful venture that a ruler could undertake, and one that is the most likely to make his name illustrious forever, is the discovery of the Southlands.'[11]

Twenty years later, the main southern islands of the Indian Ocean had all been explored by French navigators. Their discoveries made no great stir, for they were merely rocks covered with sparse vegetation and inhabited only by seals, penguins, and sea birds. Thus the Île des Froides, discovered in 1772 by Marion Dufresne, was rechristened Prince Edward Island by Cook in 1776, since Marion's discovery had not yet been officially announced, and Kerguelen was put in prison for having discovered nothing but valueless lands, the islands that still bear his name, instead of the famous southern continent.

Cook's exploration of the east coast of Australia in 1768–70 and his companion Banks's observations on the subject were far more important, but they did not settle the question. Cook himself had no idea of the importance of his discovery. Completely neglecting Australia in the course of his subsequent voyages, he searched the whole of the South Pacific for the southern continent.

For several years no one bothered any further with Australia. After the American Revolutionary War, the British government contemplated sending the Loyalists, the American colonists who had remained faithful to the king of England, to establish themselves there, and giving them convicts to develop the country; but as the plan dragged on, the Loyalists, tired of waiting, settled in Canada. As no one else wanted to go to Australia, only the convicts were finally sent.

In 1788 the first contingent disembarked on the south-east coast of the country which Cook had christened New South Wales eighteen years before. At the time the event went unnoticed. Yet it was the beginning of the largest European settlement in the Indian Ocean. Indeed, today, Australia alone contains more Europeans than all the other ocean lands put together.

[11] C. de Brosses, *Histoire des navigations aux Terres australes*, Paris, 1756, pp. 4–5.

The English arrived in Australia just in time, for France also had her eye on it. La Pérouse reached Botany Bay, where the English had disembarked, exactly eight days later, just eight days too late. And when in 1801 Baudin arrived on the west coast of Australia with the expedition sent by Bonaparte to explore the southlands, he found Flinders already at work. Just as France missed the opportunity of creating a southern France in Africa, so she missed the opportunity of making a place for herself in Australia at the end of the eighteenth century.[12]

8. MISSIONARY WORK

Back in the twelfth century, as we know, those who had taken the route to the Orient in search of souls had very closely followed, and sometimes even preceded, those who had taken the same route in search of gold, and their accounts had contributed more than a little to Europe's information about the Eastern world. In the sixteenth century they had sailed out in caravels to spread the Gospel in the Portuguese possessions in Asia; and although they can be reproached with having lighted the fires of the Inquisition at Goa,[13] they did, on the other hand, present the Indian Ocean with an extraordinary and admirable missionary in the person of St. Francis Xavier, whose radiance itself was enough to excuse his confrères their momentary mistakes.

The stages in the propagation of Christianity in the Indian Ocean belong to the history of religion. It is in the pages of the numerous works devoted to that subject that a detailed account must be sought. Yet we should not revive here the memories of captains of war and of trade, of nabobs, explorers, and scholars who left their more or less durable mark on the oceanic world since da Gama, and leave in the shade those of the Christian missionaries, both Catholic and Protestant, who also played their part in the history of the ocean.

Their activities go back a long way, as we have seen, but it

[12] On the French activities in that part of the world, see J.-P. Faivre's thesis, *L'Expansion française dans le Pacifique de 1800–1842*, Paris, 1954.

[13] On the Inquisition at Goa, see Dellon's account, *Voyages de M. Dellon avec sa relation de l'Inquisition de Goa*, 3 vols., Cologne, 1711.

was in the eighteenth century that they multiplied, and broadened in scope. The conquests of Christianity in the oceanic lands are perhaps not comparable to those of Islamism, Buddhism, and Hinduism, whose inroads during the 'pre-Gamian' era, to use one of Toynbee's favourite expressions, has already been briefly mentioned. Yet on the whole they were just as real and in some cases very noteworthy.

Christianity never succeeded in becoming a serious competitor with the Eastern religions in any Asian country, not even in Ceylon, where today it occupies a favoured position. But here we are dealing with an undertaking that cannot be evaluated in purely quantitative terms; phenomena of a religious nature are subject to all sorts of imponderables. It would perhaps take no more than a few men of the stature of a St. Francis Xavier, or indeed no more than one, to transform completely Christianity's position in the East from one day to the next.

On the other hand, in the ocean lands such as Africa, the Mascarenes, and Australia, where they found no well-defined religion at all, the missionaries' work was always fruitful. If the colonisation of those countries, often involving questionable elements, did not bear the stamp of total amorality, or indeed, immorality, it is, above all, to the missionaries that the credit is due.

Accompanying those in search of gold, and often at their mercy, the missionaries were constantly forced to come to terms with them, but it would be a mistake to see the missionaries invariably as accomplices of the conquistadores, the nabobs, or the opium traffickers. Rather, we must deplore the fact that the crimes of the latter too often rubbed off on the former.

We must also deplore the fact that Christianity in the Indian Ocean, instead of presenting itself as one doctrine, a seamless robe, should have appeared in the garb of a harlequin, a condition imposed upon it by the Reformation and the wars of religion, and that, because of the additional factor of national rivalries, it was often sectarian. Taking everything into account, however, if the work of the missionaries in the theological sense was not dazzling, on the whole it was undeniably beneficent.

Considering only the secular level, attention must be drawn to the fact that generally, and in the eighteenth century in particular, the missionary was also a conscientious observer and often even a scholar, whose contribution to linguistic, archaeological, and geographical knowledge was very marked. To cite a classic example, we may mention the voluminous collection of *Lettres écrites des missions étrangères*, published by the Society of Jesus throughout the eighteenth century and up to 1820. Another fact of prime importance: it was the missionaries who spread the use of the printing press through all the countries of the Indian Ocean and translated the Bible into almost all the Eastern languages.

Although printing was invented in China and was known in the Far East long before its introduction into Europe, it was the Europeans and not the Orientals who disseminated it through all the Indian Ocean lands. The first press in that part of the world was set up at Goa, in 1556, by the Jesuits. In the eighteenth century, India had several missionary presses. The lay press did not make its appearance in that country until 1778. In the course of the seventeenth century, the missionaries introduced the printing press into various countries of the Far East: the Moluccas, Siam, Indo-China, and probably also Abyssinia.

The missionary was also the first to understand that it was to the Orientals' advantage to learn European techniques. The Jesuits' endeavours in that direction in China were particularly noteworthy. Had the Chinese listened to them, it is probable that China would have taken the road to Europeanisation far earlier than she did, and would have avoided many misfortunes.[14]

[14] It should be noted that Sun Yat-sen, the instigator of the 1911 revolution, owed his training and education to Protestant missionaries, and that his 'three principles' echoed Western thought.

XIII. British Maritime Supremacy

WE may say that in 1815 the stakes were down. Both the Dutch and the French had lost their main possessions in the Indian Ocean, and to regain their ascendancy, would have had practically to start again from scratch. The English, on the other hand, had carved out for themselves the lion's share: India, Ceylon, the Cape of Good Hope, part of Malaya, Île de France, the most important of the Mascarenes, which resumed its former name, Mauritius, and finally, Australia, which itself was as good as a new world.

Adopting Albuquerque's ideas and even giving them a new twist, for Albuquerque had not foreseen industrial capitalism, the English were to set up in the Indian Ocean the most absolute hegemony of all times, and were to impose upon Asia a yoke which was to be shaken only by Japanese cannon a century and a half later.

In the first half of the nineteenth century, English activity was limited for the most part to the eastern region of the ocean. As we have seen, in the eighteenth century there developed, in addition to the route to the Indies, a route to China. In order to control this, it was necessary to control the region of the Straits, that is, Malaya or Indonesia. When peace was concluded, England gave Java and Malacca back to the Dutch, but at the same time, she secured a sphere of influence in Malaya by establishing herself in 1819 in Singapore. The Dutch pulled a long face, but finally had to give in. In 1824 an Anglo-Dutch convention, by which Malacca went to England, fixed definitively the two peoples' respective spheres of activity in South-east Asia.

The occupation of Singapore was the result of repeated efforts on the part of the English, during the previous century, to procure a good base to the east of the Bay of Bengal: Syriam, Balambangan, and Penang had all been tried, but with no success. The occupation was, for all practical purposes, a real *coup de main*, and Raffles, the East India Company agent who organised it, was nearly disowned, but events were to prove him right. Better located than Malacca, the settlement of Singapore was not long in supplanting Malacca as the main emporium on the route to China. In 1823 the value of its imports and exports reached to over 13 million dollars.

Singapore was also a gateway to Malaya and Burma. The conquest of those two countries, all the ups and downs of which cannot be gone into here, gave the English considerable difficulty and took almost a century, with alternate periods of intervention and non-intervention, but in the end they succeeded. By 1885 Burma was completely in their hands, and the British protectorate in Malaya was definitively established in 1914.

In India itself, which in 1815 had not been completely subjugated, the English made great headway during the first half of the nineteenth century. The Marathas surrendered in 1819. The Punjab, defended by the Sikhs, was conquered between 1840 and 1850. The Indian Mutiny of 1857 led to the extermination of the last representative of the Great Moguls, the suppression of the East India Company, and the setting up of colonial rule throughout India. In 1877 Queen Victoria took the title Empress of India.

Ceylon, too, was not completely subjugated in 1815. The English at first occupied only the coastal regions of the island. The king of Kandy, in the centre of the country, had remained practically independent and had finally to be deposed following a military expedition. Ceylon then became a crown colony, withdrawn from the jurisdiction of the East India Company.

In the western region of the Indian Ocean, in Western Asia and on the African coast, England was not very active during this period. In spite of the occupation of Aden in 1839, the whole area was to remain under Arab influence for several decades more. In 1841 the Sultan of Masqat, who had controlled the entire African coast ever since his predecessors had recaptured it from the Portuguese in 1698, removed his seat of government from Masqat to Zanzibar, which thus became the centre of a new Zenj empire, drawing its main revenues from the systematic exploitation of the native resources and from the slave trade.

When England abolished slavery in her own colonies in 1835, the slave traders of the African coast often found themselves hunted down by British cruisers; yet although the English did endeavour to impede that hateful traffic, their efforts were never sustained enough to put a complete stop to it. Not until the end of the century, when the whole of East Africa passed under their protection, did they really succeed.

At the Cape of Good Hope and in the region of Madagascar and the Mascarenes, English activity was also very limited during the first decades of the nineteenth century. The Cape and Mauritius had been occupied mainly because of their strategic location. As the former was largely peopled by the Dutch, and the latter by the French, though the African and Creole population was considerable, there were many problems in forming a suitable policy.

In Madagascar, despite the emphatic protests of Farquhar, the first English governor of Mauritius, the British government at first determinedly refused to intervene and to launch out into a policy of annexation. The only order Farquhar and his successors received was to put a stop to the slave trade between Madagascar and the islands. That did not, however, keep the English civil servants from persistent scheming to frustrate French designs on Madagascar.[1]

Concerning the activity of the Portuguese, the Dutch, and the French in the Indian Ocean between 1815 and 1870, there is little to remark. All that can be said about the Portuguese is that they just about held their own at Goa, Daman, and Diu on the coast of India, and at Mozambique on the coast of Africa. They also kept part of the island of Timor in Indonesia

---

[1] On the English activities in Madagascar at the beginning of the 19th century, see S. E. Howe, *The Drama of Madagascar*, London, 1938, and R. Decary, *L'Établissement de Sainte-Marie-de-Madagascar sous la Restauration et le rôle de Sylvain Roux*, Paris, 1937.

and their settlement of Macao in China, but in all these territories there was nothing to recall their past glory.

For the Dutch the first decades of the nineteenth century proved a difficult period. Their most appreciable loss was neither the Cape of Good Hope nor Ceylon, territories that were not highly developed, but rather their trading factories in India, where they procured textiles for Indonesia. As Holland produced little in the way of textiles and the tonnage of her merchant marine was rather low, the Dutch had to resort to tariff walls to protect themselves from English competition in Indonesia. And since the spice trade no longer paid, they had also to resort to a system of forced agriculture to stimulate the cultivation of new products: mainly coffee, sugar, and indigo. Protectionism and obligatory cultivation (*cultur stelsel*) long weighed heavy on the development of Indonesia, which did not make marked progress until after 1870.

As for the French, they had resumed possession of their settlements in India: Pondichéry, Karikal, Chandernagor, Mahé and Yanaon, but there was little hope of making much of them. Nor did Réunion, which was all they had left of the Mascarenes, offer any great possibilities. They did, however, make a new attempt, after so many others, to use it as a point of departure for colonising Madagascar. But given the hostility of the Hovas, who were dominant in the great island, the counter-plots of the English, and above all, the little interest aroused by the undertaking in France itself, only trifling headway was made, despite the occupation of Sainte-Marie and several points on the northern coast and in the Comoros between 1843 and 1860. The French finally, in 1895, had to resort to military conquest to gain a foothold in Madagascar.

On the east coast of Africa, France made no move before the acquisition of Obock, in 1862, which became the base for the acquisition of French Somaliland. In the Far East as well, French activity was almost non-existent during the first half of the nineteenth century, since the effective occupation of Indo-China did not begin until 1858. In the Near East, on the other hand, France succeeded in carving out an important place for herself between 1830 and 1850, and she even gained a considerable hold over Egypt, which was later to facilitate de Lesseps' famous undertaking: the cutting of the Suez Canal.

2. WEALTH AND POWER

The British conquest of India was a unique and notable event in the history of the oceanic world. It was the first time that a European nation managed to subjugate completely a great Asian state, a state that for Europe had always symbolised Eastern grandeur and power. To be sure, India had already been conquered by the Moslems, but the Moslems were Orientals, and moreover they had never succeeded in holding more than a part of India, whereas the English held the entire sub-continent from north to south and from east to west. It was an even more remarkable achievement in that it had been accomplished with relatively small forces which had come from a great distance.

What exactly, on the national level, did that conquest represent? How much wealth and power did England gain from it? While stressing the lack of documentation on the economic consequences of English expansion in India at the end of the eighteenth century, Furber proves very reticent on this point, and is not ready to admit that England reaped great profits from her conquests in that land. And although the British imperialistic drive was intensified during the nineteenth century, it was, he thinks, for other reasons:

> Wealth is not entirely synonymous with power. No amount of evidence that British India was a wasting asset to Britain could have brought the process of European expansion in India to a halt. Whenever circumstances exist which enable a few members of one section of mankind to exercise authority over millions of other men, the power of those few will be a source of pride to their fellow countrymen long after the pure economic benefits of the relationship have begun to wane.[2]

It is interesting to compare Furber's opinions with those expressed in 1802 on the British Empire in India by a French economist, the Abbé de Pradt, in a work that once created a sensation. The Abbé de Pradt belonged to the anti-colonialist school which, before him, had had three well-known representatives in France: Montesquieu, Voltaire, and the Abbé Raynal. His argument can be summed up as follows.

[2] Furber, *op. cit.*, pp. 320–1.

Trade with India, burdensome for Europe, involved the use of metal currency and attracted the money Europe received from the New World. Now the only nation that had succeeded in dispensing with the sending of metals to India by the establishment there of sovereign rights was England; she alone possessed enough subjects and taxable commodities to be quit of the need to bring capital into India; the other European peoples had to trade there, at a loss, using metal currency. The more English sovereignty spread through India, the more she exempted Europe from the need to send capital into that country. The general interest of Europe thus became identified with that of England, and it was in fact in the interest of all Europe to maintain British power in India. 'Consequently,' concluded the Abbé de Pradt,

> the people who have enough control over India to reduce substantially the exportation of European metallic currency into Asia rule there as much for Europe's benefit as for their own; their empire is more *common* than *particular*, more *European* than *British*; as it expands, Europe benefits, and each of their conquests is also a real conquest for the latter. That fact must be clearly understood so as to avoid confusion on this subject, the vital crux of which is the nature of Europe's trade with Asia, which alone is enough to give the European states in that part of the world a level of existence quite different from what they have elsewhere. Consequently, all the sound and fury now echoing across Europe about England's hegemony in India are the shrieks of a blind delirium, as an *anti-European* uproar; it might be thought that England was taking away from every European state what it was conquering from those of Asia, whereas, on the contrary, every part of Asia that she takes for herself, she, by that very fact, takes for Europe.[3]

Up to a certain point de Pradt was right, and Furber's investigation into the relations of the East India Company with the other nations trading in Asia at the end of the eighteenth century would seem, indeed, to indicate that the interest of those nations was identical with that of England. We have dealt with this question in a previous chapter.

It would also seem that de Pradt judged accurately in advocating the total relinquishment of the small French

[3] M. de Pradt, *Les Trois Âges des colonies*, Paris, 1902, II, 452–3.

settlements in India. What interest could France, a dominant power in Europe, have in creating for herself points of vulnerability in a country that did not belong to her? What benefit could she really derive from her settlements in India after the treaties of 1815?

But what de Pradt did not see clearly was the phenomenon that Furber noted above: namely, the predominance of what might be called the sentimental aspect of imperialism. It is possible that, from one point of view, the British Empire in India served the interests of Europe, but the English certainly did not regard it in that way. They saw their Empire as essentially British and not European.

What de Pradt could not foresee either was that mercantilism was to be replaced in the nineteenth century by industrial capitalism, and that, consequently, the nature of the relations between the European and the oceanic worlds was to change completely, with imperialism taking definite precedence over any other consideration and assuming forms more absolute than 'nabobism'.

3. THE END OF MERCANTILISM

For a long time the system of monopoly had enriched the mercantile bourgeoisie, but it could not last indefinitely. In 1776 the Scottish economist Adam Smith had seriously attacked it in his treatise on the wealth of nations. In England the loss of the American colonies in 1783, for which that system was partly responsible, furnished the partisans of free trade with another argument. On the other hand, when British industry began to develop, the interests of the manufacturers demanded the opening of the Indian markets.

In 1813, when the question of renewing the East India Company's charter came up, the free traders obtained from Parliament the abrogation of the monopoly that company held on trade with India. Nor did it keep for long its monopoly of trade with China, which in turn was abrogated twenty years later. From that time on, the all-powerful Company continued to decline, until it was dealt the last blow by the Indian Mutiny of 1857. Its rivals, the French and Dutch Companies, had long since disappeared, the former in 1769 and the latter in 1798.

The disappearance of the great trading companies marked the end of a system which the French called 'le régime de l'exclusif' and the English 'the old colonial system'. The mercantile bourgeoisie had had its day; at the end of the eighteenth century, it began to be replaced in England by a new bourgeoisie, born of the industrial revolution.

In the Indian Ocean this change of system was evident in two new factors: first, the definitive conquest of the Eastern markets by products manufactured in England and later in Europe; and second, an even greater increase in the investment of European capital meant for the commercial exploitation of the countries around the Indian Ocean where the Westerners were now dominant.[4] The former nabob was replaced on the one hand by the businessman, and on the other by the colonial civil servant.

In many respects this was progress, but Toynbee has made a few cogent remarks on the subject. There was at least one thing good about the nabob: he did not live aloof from Eastern society. The 'irreproachable and unapproachable' colonial civil servant who succeeded him made the mistake of taking himself too seriously and thus set up an impassable barrier between himself and the native.

This change of system was also accompanied by solemn declarations of principle. In England, Parliament declared in 1833, with respect to India, that the interest of the natives was to come before that of the Europeans. At the same time, the English humanitarians succeeded in obtaining the abolition of slavery and of any distinction based on colour throughout the entire British Empire. In practice, unfortunately, these fine principles were often disregarded. Events soon proved that Adam Smith's gospel could serve as a pretext for new aggressions in a theatre which the treaties of 1815 seemed to have freed once and for all from the nightmare of war.

In the name of free trade, the British government, under pressure from the private enterprises that had replaced the East India Company in the opium trade, was led to undertake

---

[4] Accurate enough figures on this point are avaiable only from 1854 onward. See C. E. Carrington, *The British Overseas*, Cambridge, 1950, pp. 458 ff., who quotes figures taken mainly from the work of C. K. Colson, *The Migration of Capital*.

military intervention in China when the Chinese government, alarmed by the boom in that trade, finally decided to take drastic measures to repress it.

In 1839 began the first 'opium war', resulting, in 1842, in the treaty of Nanking, by the terms of which the Canton *Cohong* was abolished, four more Chinese ports (Amoy, Foochow, Ningpo, and Shanghai) were opened to foreign commerce, the territory of Hong Kong became a British colony, and the opium trade received official sanction. Commenting on this victory of free trade, Palmerston wrote the same year: 'There is no doubt that this event, which will form an epoch in the progress of the civilisation of the human races, must be attended with the most important advantages to the commercial interests of England.'[5]

The last stage in the abolition of 'the old colonial system' was the abrogation of the navigation acts in 1848. England then felt strong enough in the maritime and the economic fields no longer to have to fear any competition, even from the United States, although at that time American sailing ships were capable of outclassing the British, as we shall see later.

The main fact to remember in the transition from the old colonialism to the new is the following. Whereas under the former system it had been the East that in a certain sense 'exploited' the West by taking from it a vast quantity of metallic currency, henceforth it was the West that was to exploit the East, and in the full sense of the word. Not that the contribution of European capital in the East diminished; on the contrary, it increased. But for the first time the European was able to impose his conditions and to invest his money profitably as he saw fit.

It was thus that the East–West antithesis came about, and it was rapidly reinforced by the appearance of the formidable technology with which the industrial revolution provided the West, multiplying its means of conquest a hundredfold.

There has been much discussion of this antithesis; and it has perhaps been exaggerated out of proportion. It is clear that the productive effort demanded by Europe from the oceanic

[5] Quoted by M. Greenberg, *British Trade and the Opening of China, 1800–1842*, Cambridge, 1951, p. 215.

196

world in the nineteenth century was enormous, that for most of the time that production was obtained only by disorganising the life and economy of those from whom it was demanded, and that it was not work in which they collaborated willingly and joyfully but rather a burden that was imposed upon them. Yet it is undeniable that they themselves gained a great deal from it. On the other hand, even had imperialism never come into the picture, there is no doubt that the technological revolution of the nineteenth century would in itself have been enough to give rise to an antithesis between a West which had succeeded in using such forces as steam and electricity and an East bogged down in a routine thousands of years old. The mistake is to express this antithesis, as Kipling did, in a formula which tends to establish that it is in the nature of things and, consequently, irreducible. His well-known words, 'East is East and West is West', are no more than a phrase meant for effect, the kind of thing literary people are used to but of which historians must in general beware.

4. COLONIES FOR RAW MATERIALS

The advent of industrial capitalism provoked a complete revolution in the nature of Eastern trade. Until then, spices and other rare products had been the main elements of that trade. Now it was raw materials that the East was asked to furnish in order to supply European industry. The so-called colonial commodities, mainly coffee, tea, and sugar, were also in great demand. France, to take but one example, had long been deprived of colonial commodities under the Empire. The chicory root took the place of coffee, but nothing had really replaced sugar. In England tea, which from the end of the eighteenth century had become the national drink, was more and more in demand as the population increased from $6\frac{1}{2}$ million to 10 million in 1830 and to $17\frac{3}{4}$ million in 1850.

As we have seen, after 1815, sugar cane cultivation had been extensively expanded in India along with cotton and indigo. In Ceylon as well, where the main product up until then had been cinnamon, the English developed the cultivation of coffee by acclimatising saplings imported from the West Indies. Between 1840 and 1880, coffee formed the main wealth of the island, and when in 1880 the coffee bushes were attacked by a disease, the cultivation of tea and rubber saved the situation.

Mauritius, which had produced hardly any exports until its conquest by the English in 1810, also rapidly became a sugar colony and soon everything was subordinated to the production of that commodity. In Réunion as well, the sugar industry developed prodigiously. The Dutch, in their East Indies, had resorted to a system of forced agriculture to develop the cultivation of coffee, sugar, and indigo. In all the eastern colonies the sedentary colonist, the planter, began to take precedence over the travelling tradesman. This was especially true in the Mascarenes, Ceylon, and Indonesia, where a real oligarchy of planters was gradually created.

The agricultural development gave rise in no time to a labour crisis in all those countries. Indeed, the settlement of the vast territories conquered by England was still clearly insufficient at the beginning of the nineteenth century. Although the English are commonly thought to have the migrating instinct, the number of colonists they sent to the various countries of the Indian Ocean at that time, and even later, was never very high. This is understandable with regard to Asian countries, where the climate does not lend itself to European immigration, but it should be noted that the settlement of favourable lands, such as South Africa and Australia, was also very slow. In Australia, as we have seen, it was necessary at the beginning to resort to the transportation of criminals.

In the preceding centuries the need for plantation hands had been met by the use of slave labour; but in 1807 England prohibited the slave trade, and in 1835 abolished slavery in all her possessions in the Indian Ocean. The solution then was to turn to those vast reservoirs of cheap labour, India and China. It was thus that in the Indian Ocean, towards the middle of the nineteenth century, a new kind of trade, the 'coolie trade', came into being.

As regards India, this trade has been recently studied by Cumpston, Kondapi, Gangulee, and some others, but we are still far from possessing all the information we should like on the subject. Studies on the emigration of Chinese coolies are still rarer; in fact, there are hardly any except for Purcell's on the Chinese in Malaya.

The Indians had already emigrated in the past. As we have seen, there had been a strong migratory flow towards the Malay Archipelago during the first centuries of the Christian era; but the Indian diaspora throughout most of the countries of the Asian world was a phenomenon peculiar to the nineteenth century, brought about by the rise of industrial capitalism, the needs it created in the plantation colonies, and the impoverishment it brought to the working classes in India.

The first colonies of the Indian Ocean to import coolies were the Mascarenes. At the end of the century Mauritius alone had about 260,000 of them. South Africa, East Africa, Aden, Ceylon, Burma, and Malaya also received a great number of them before the end of the nineteenth century, not to mention the West Indian and Pacific colonies, which also went to India for their labour.

In principle, the coolie trade was duly regulated and controlled; in the main ports of India, at Bombay, Madras, and Calcutta, there were 'emigration agencies', and in the importing countries offices for the aid and protection of immigrants were set up to see that the coolies suffered no wrong. In practice the system gave rise to serious abuses, especially during the first twenty years (1834–54), despite the frequent challenges to it voiced by humanitarian members of the British Parliament.

As long as the coolie trade has not been properly studied, its advantages and disadvantages cannot be satisfactorily evaluated. However, even on the basis of the information at our disposal now, one may question whether the latter did not, on the whole, outweigh the former. In addition to the fact that one of the results of these migrations was to carry deadly diseases, especially cholera, from one end of the Indian Ocean to the other, it also created social and economic problems, serious and still unresolved, in the importing countries.

It must be pointed out as well that many banians (Indian traders) emigrated along with the coolies, and in the countries in which they settled, they gradually took over several branches of the retail and even the wholesale trade. On this aspect of the Indian diaspora in the Indian Ocean during the nineteenth century we are even less well informed, and it needs a thorough

investigation. It should be noted that the Indonesian archipelago did not receive many Indian coolies at that time,
although formerly it had been in frequent touch with India;
on the other hand, it received many Chinese, as well as Arabs
from the region of Aden.

5. COLONIES FOR SETTLEMENT

Only two countries in the Indian Ocean, apart from the tiny
Mascarenes, offered interesting prospects for European immigration: the Cape of Good Hope and Australia. But both were
very backward at the beginning of the nineteenth century, and
their economic situation was not flourishing enough to incite
England to dispatch men and capital there in sufficient
quantity.

Both territories produced wool, and that was a commodity
with which England herself was well provided. On the other
hand, the fact that the Cape had been originally peopled by
the Boers (peasants) and Australia by convicts was not likely
to attract the better elements of the English population. The
general opinion in England at the time was that neither
country was suitable for gentlemen. As settlements, they were
lacking in the very thing that was needed for them to reach
their full development and to play their part in the oceanic
world: a large enough immigration.

In 1802 the Abbé de Pradt, whom we have already cited,
advocated a very interesting plan for the Cape of Good Hope.
This was, to make it the centre of an independent state stretching as far as 22° south latitude, taking in, therefore, Portuguese
Mozambique, and including also Madagascar and the Mascarenes. If the Cape were a free port, affirmed de Pradt, it
would not be long before it became a central market for the
four quarters of the globe. His plan was not badly conceived,
though there would have been great difficulties in its execution.
The development of the vast territory which stretched to the
north of the Cape and that of the semi-continent of Madagascar
would, in fact, have required resources that the colonists of the
Cape, Mozambique, and the Mascarenes did not then have at
their disposal.

The English viewed the colonisation of the Cape in a very

different perspective. The way in which they went about it belongs to the realm of colonial history, and is not our concern here. Suffice it to say that as a result of their approach, the Dutch colonists were forced to turn their backs on the sea and to penetrate into the *veldt* in the interior, where they founded two provinces, the Transvaal and the Orange Free State. When they tried to make contact with the ocean again by going down the coast of Natal, so named by da Gama, because he had discovered it on the day of the Nativity, it was too late. By 1843, Sir Benjamin d'Urban had occupied the main harbour of that coast, which today bears his name (Durban), and when the prospect arose of developing agriculture in the region of Natal, which lent itself to the cultivation of the sugar-cane, it was not the Boers whom the British government called upon, but the Indian coolies (1860).

In Australia progress was even slower. For the average Englishman, leaving for Australia at the beginning of the nineteenth century meant going into exile. The English painter Ford Madox Brown (1821–93) conveyed this feeling very well in a famous picture ('The Last of England'), now in the Tate Gallery, London.

Deportation to New South Wales, in the south-eastern region of Australia, was abolished in 1840, but the system was continued in the western region, which looks out on the Indian Ocean, until 1868. Western and South Australia were not colonised until 1829 and 1836 respectively, in other words, half a century after the settlement of Botany Bay, and their beginnings were very precarious. For several years the colonists of Western Australia were not self-sufficient; they depended for their subsistence on the Dutch East Indies and Tasmania. In 1849 there were still no more than 5250 inhabitants in the region.

An unexpected event changed everything and began a new era in Australian colonisation. In 1851, Hargraves, a colonist in New South Wales, found nuggets of gold in the river bed of Lewis Ponds (Victoria), which he there and then rechristened Ophir. In the twinkling of an eye the prospectors flocked in. The gold rush had begun. From England and America, vessel after vessel arrived bringing in either prospectors or people who came to trade with the prospectors, an enterprise almost as profitable as to dig for gold oneself. The great southern land, dried up and almost desert, which until then had been considered a place of exile, suddenly exerted a magic charm and became the Ophir of the nineteenth century.

The discovery of gold gave an enormous impetus to the development of Australia and greatly stimulated maritime activity in the Indian Ocean in the direction of that country, but it was mainly the provinces of the south-east and the east, facing the Pacific, that profited from it. Western Australia, or Westralia, as it was then sometimes called, where there was no gold, and which was separated from Victoria and New South Wales by vast expanses of desert, continued to vegetate.

Even more than the discovery of gold, it was finally, about 1870, the application of modern techniques (the introduction of steam engines, railways, and electric equipment) that ensured the prosperity of Australia and made it possible for the inhabitants of that country really to control its vast expanse.

6. THE CLIPPER SHIP ERA

During the first decades of the nineteenth century, shipbuilding in the Indian Ocean underwent a marked expansion for various reasons: the necessity of making up the shortage of tonnage, resulting from the wars of the Revolution and the Napoleonic wars; the necessity of satisfying a growing demand for 'country' ships, resulting from the increase of trade with China; and finally, the lower cost of ships built in the Indian and Burmese ports.

This matter has not yet been properly investigated, but we know from the few studies that have been devoted to it, those of Kirk in particular, that shipbuilding was fairly active in the following ports: Bombay, Daman, Cochin, Coringa (Madras), Calcutta, Chittagong, Beypore, Rangoon, and Penang. What they produced were mostly 'country' ships, of not over 1000 tons burden, but we find that there were a few larger ones, such as the *Warren Hastings* of 1700 tons launched at Calcutta in 1818. The figures quoted by Kirk show, besides, that the ship of heavy tonnage was relatively less costly.

The shipyards of the Indian Ocean did not, however, manage to fill the needs of navigation, and it was the ports of the Atlantic that continued to furnish the largest units of the merchant fleets of that water. These ports on the Atlantic were not limited to the English and European, but included those of the maritime regions of the United States, especially Massachusetts and Maine.

Slowed down by Jefferson's embargo of 1807 and then by the war with England (1812–15), the movement of trade between the American ports and the Indian Ocean began to pick up shortly after 1815. In 1819 Saigon, in Cochin China, was added to the Eastern ports already frequented by American ships, which included the main harbours of India and Indonesia as well as Canton and Macao in China, not to mention the intermediate ports of call at the Cape and in the Mascarenes. New York, Boston, Salem, Baltimore, and Philadelphia were regularly sending vessels into the Indian Ocean.

As the ginseng trade with China no longer paid, the Americans then used opium from Smyrna to assure themselves of profits. After England, it was the United States which sent the greatest number of ships to China. Morison notes that in 1833–34 there were in Canton 101 American vessels, 37 from Spain, and 45 from other nations.

The fluctuations of Eastern trade never caught the Americans by surprise, as the following proves. In 1833 an enterprising tradesman from Boston named Frederick Tudor had the idea of dispatching a cargo of ice to Calcutta to cool off the Indians. In 1841 he had made enough money by this original trade to pay outstanding debts amounting to $250,000.

Between 1820 and 1850 the builders of the American Indiamen at Medford and Merrimac looked with contempt on the English Indiamen built on the banks of the Thames, which, as a matter of fact, disappeared almost completely from the Indian Ocean when the East India Company lost its last commercial privileges in 1833. To command an Indiaman was a much sought-after occupation in England; in America it was almost the equivalent of having a title. Then came the famous tea clippers, whose great period began about 1845.

The tea clippers, also called China clippers because they were primarily intended for trade with China, were vessels specially designed for high speed. They represented the last word in the technology of sailing ships. Their predecessors were the Baltimore clippers of the end of the eighteenth century and the opium clippers of the beginning of the nineteenth, of which we have already spoken; but although they were derived from those prototypes, they were in a class quite by themselves and have never been surpassed.

The appearance of the tea clippers followed closely on the opening of Chinese ports to foreign trade in 1842. One of the first American tea clippers was the *Honqua* launched at New York in 1844. It was only of 706 tons burden, but those that were built after it, between 1850 and 1860, were of from 1300 to 2000 tons. The main shipyards were in Boston and New York.

The best works to consult on the clipper ships are those of Clark, Lubbock, and Lacroix. Innumerable articles have likewise been devoted to them in the principle maritime journals. It should be noted that the advent of the clippers was greatly encouraged by the hydrographic work of the Englishman Rennell (1830) and the American Maury (1850), who put at the disposal of sailors very precise data on the winds and currents in the Indian Ocean.

At the beginning, these ships made their way to China via the Cape of Good Hope, crossing the Indian Ocean. After the discovery of gold in California (1848), they took, by preference, the Pacific route via Cape Horn and San Francisco; but they did not disappear from the Indian Ocean, for several were bought by English shipowners for trade with China and also to transport emigrants to Australia at the time of her gold rush.

The superiority of the American ships over the British can be explained in this way; first of all, the English law on tonnage, which dated back to 1773 and was not radically changed until 1854, considerably hindered the development of shipbuilding in England; secondly, the navigation acts while protecting the English shipowners, at the same time deprived them of the stimulus caused by competition; and finally, the American ships cost less.

In France shipbuilding was still more expensive than in England. However, from the mid nineteenth century until 1886, the shipyards of Bordeaux, Nantes, and Le Havre managed to build excellent ships, several of which sailed the

Indian Ocean. But French production was not maintained, and in 1893, after circumstances which are described in the excellent book by Captain Lacroix, France had fallen to ninth place, below Greece, in its ownership of sailing-ship fleets.

In 1851 the Americans were so certain of their maritime supremacy that the American Navigation Club challenged the English shipowners to a race from England to China and back. The English did not take up the challenge, but they were not long in reacting. In the course of the same year Richard Green, of the Blackwall Line, proved that with a clipper of his own design he could do as well as the Americans. The ship in question, called the *Challenger*, became the prototype of a series of British tea clippers called Blackwall frigates, since frigates are what they looked like. They were smaller than their American rivals but just as fast. In addition, they were suitable for trade with Australia as well as with China, whereas the American clippers were suitable only for transporting tea and delicate cargoes, so they gradually caused the disappearance of the latter in the Indian Ocean.

The use of iron (1853) and steel (1864) for hulls also made it possible for the English to catch up with the Americans, for the United States was richer in wood than in iron and steel. At almost the same time, the Civil War dealt a fatal blow to the American merchant marine.

Between 1865 and 1885, the average tonnage of iron vessels was from 1500 to 2000 tons; after 1882, when only steel was used, the figure went up to 3000–4000 tons. This applies, of course, only to sailing ships, which still cut a fine figure in the Indian Ocean, where neither the use of steamships nor the opening of the Suez Canal managed to eliminate them completely.

7. THE FIRST STEAMSHIPS

Contrary to what we might think, the first crossing of the Indian Ocean made by a steamship, in 1825, aroused no special interest. Indeed, the *Enterprise* took 113 days to go from Falmouth to Calcutta via the Cape route, and could use its engines only for 62 days. Another attempt made shortly after by a French ship (the *Betsy*) took even longer. And at that time a good sailing ship easily made the same trip in less than three months.

Because of the use of clippers, which made it possible to complete the still longer trip between England and Australia in the record time of 65 days (around 1850), and the very high cost of steamships, not to mention the many other inconveniences then inherent in steam navigation, it was a long time before the engine-powered vessels took the lead on the Cape route.

It seems that the first vessel propelled by steam to be built in the Indian Ocean was a small steamboat launched at Port-Louis, in Mauritius, in 1827 and named the *Lowry Cole*. It was intended for coastal traffic between that island and Madagascar, but its trial runs did not give satisfaction, and its engines were then transformed into motors for sugar-cane mills. A second trial run, at Mauritius in 1829, of a ship equipped with an engine sent over from England, ended in its shipwreck off the island of Bourbon on its very first voyage.

In 1830 another attempt, made on the India–Egypt run with a small steamship built in Bombay and named the *Hugh Lindsay*, gave better results. It took a month to go from Bombay to Suez, and the letters it carried reached England by way of the Mediterranean in record time. This achievement induced the East India Company to initiate a regular steamship service between Bombay and Suez, from which point both mail and passengers took the overland route to get to the Mediterranean and from there to Europe. The connection was made by coach to Cairo and thence by river to Alexandria. This combined route was not new; it had been used by sailing ships from 1773 to 1798 and given up at the time of the French attack on Egypt. It was greatly facilitated in 1859 by the building of a railway across the Isthmus of Suez.

In 1842 the first steam navigation company, the Peninsular and Oriental, made its appearance in the Indian Ocean. Its ships worked the line Calcutta–Madras–Ceylon–Suez, while the East India Company continued to ensure the Bombay–Suez service. In 1845 the P. and O. extended its service to Singapore and China, and in 1854 to Australia. In 1854 also, the East India Company transferred the Bombay–Suez line to it.

The P. and O. was soon followed by other English companies

(the Austrian Lloyd Co., the British India Steam Navigation Co., the General Steam Navigation Co., and the Ocean Steamship Co., to name only the most important) and in 1862 by the French *Compagnie des Messageries Impériales* (today the *Messageries Maritimes*), which began its operations with a regular line between Suez and Hong Kong. The first Portuguese and Dutch steam navigation companies were not formed until after the opening of the Suez Canal.

The appearance of the great navigation companies in the mid nineteenth century is an event that to a certain extent can be compared to that of the great trading companies in the seventeenth. One result was that a familiar figure disappeared from the Indian Ocean; the 'country' captain, navigating on his own, found he was no longer able to fight the competition of the companies. Another result was to stimulate the development of Cape Colony and to assure it a life of its own, independent of the movement of shipping over the ocean. In 1851, Cape Town became the terminus of a regular line with England.[6] The navigation companies also prepared the way for submarine telegraph cable companies, which were to begin to operate about 1870.

The steamship, however, did not manage completely to replace the sailing ship on the main routes, those of China and Australia, along which the bulk of passenger and goods traffic continued to be carried by clipper, even after the opening of the Suez Canal. The last important voyages of clippers recorded by Lubbock were made in the year 1881.

The situation in the Atlantic was very different. There the steamship took precedence over the sailing ship much earlier, first of all, because the distances to be covered were shorter, and secondly, because the steamship had come into being simultaneously on both shores of the Atlantic, and it was as much in the United States' interest as in that of England and France to develop this kind of navigation, especially for strategic reasons. The Atlantic was really the cradle of steam navigation, while the Indian Ocean long remained the favourite domain of the sailing ship.

[6] On the maritime history of the Cape, see M. Murray's excellent work, *Ships and South Africa*, Oxford, 1933, for which an equivalent dealing with the other ports of the Indian Ocean may be hoped for.

It was not until the end of the nineteenth century that the steamship really triumphed, but even after the great American, English, and European sailing ships had disappeared from the Indian Ocean, the Indian *kotias* and the Arab dhows and *baggalas* continued to be just as much in evidence in its waters as in ancient times.

In the region of the Mascarenes the coastal trade carried on by sailing ships also endured for a very long time. One of the last clippers, the *Sir Lancelot*, was still sailing between Mauritius and Bombay in 1895, under the command of a Creole captain by the name of Brebner, to whom, incidentally, we owe an excellent study on the cyclones of the Indian Ocean, which was published in Mauritius in 1912. Until World War II, a regular coastal trade with the Seychelles and the Chagos was carried on by several sailing ships belonging to Mauritian ship-owners.

XIV. The Suez Canal

I. AN OLD DREAM COME TRUE

THE proposal to link the Indian Ocean with the Mediterranean is an old one; it dates back even to remotest antiquity. As we recall, it was queen Hatshepsut of Egypt (1480–1475 B.C.) who had been the first to attempt to carry it out by connecting the Nile with the Red Sea by means of a 'Suez Canal' that almost paralleled the present one up to Lake Timsah, whence it forked off to the west, joining the Nile at Bubastis.

After the death of that extraordinary woman, the canal became sanded up. Several of the Pharaohs, the Median king Darius, and the Roman emperor Hadrian each in turn put it back into service for some time.

In the great period of the Moslems, the Caliphs Omar and Harun al-Rashid also took an interest in it during the seventh and eighth centuries A.D. In the sixteenth century the Republic of Venice drew up plans for cutting through the Isthmus, but went no further. In the seventeenth century Leibniz brought up the idea once more in a report to Louis XIV. At the end of the eighteenth, Bonaparte had precise calculations made for the first time, by the engineers who accompanied him to Egypt. In 1847 the Saint-Simonian Prosper Enfantin set up an international committee of engineers to study the question once more. They were still discussing it when de Lesseps, who was not an engineer, came along.

'A man's man and a woman's man too,' he was called by one

209

of his biographers, the Englishman Charles Beatty. He did indeed marry a second wife at the age of 64 and went on to produce twelve children. This fact alone would perhaps not be worth mentioning, rare as it may be, even for Frenchmen, had it not, in de Lesseps' case, gone along with an even more remarkable show of exceptional creative power: the Suez Canal, conceived in its present form in 1854, begun in 1859, and finished in 1869.

We shall not go into that magnificent accomplishment here, for its story has been told repeatedly in several works, the best of which are probably those of Edgar-Bonnet and Beatty, and the thesis of Ali Ardehali, not to mention the five volumes of letters and documents on the history of the canal left by de Lesseps himself.

Next to da Gama's discovery of the Cape route, the opening of the Suez Canal was the most notable event in the history of the Indian Ocean. With the canal, Western Asia came back into prominence in the ocean's history. That region, now known as the Middle East, actually a most unsuitable term, was to take on increasing importance as oil replaced coal and became the most sought-after fuel in the entire world.

England was not the last to realise this. Palmerston had described de Lesseps' undertaking as chimerical, but the canal was no sooner finished than his country secured control of it by skilful speculation. From the canal zone that control spread in 1882 to the whole of Egypt, and in 1898 to the Sudan. In 1884 England also established herself in Somaliland so as to be in a position to keep an eye on the small French settlement at Obock.

The Suez Canal unquestionably served England's interests in the Indian Ocean, but at the same time it somewhat weakened her maritime hegemony. Indeed, it prompted France and Holland to build up an appropriate merchant marine for trade with Asia and thus to free themselves from their dependence on England. Ten years after the opening of the canal, almost 40 per cent of India's foreign trade was carried on with European countries which, before 1869, had had to procure Indian products on the English market. Another result of the canal was to turn the attention of certain European peoples to the Indian Ocean, those, that is, who had played almost no part in it before, and to awaken in them imperialist ambitions.

Although Venice had formerly carried on a large trade in the East, Italy had not followed Portugal into the Indian Ocean at the time of the great discoveries. But the Suez Canal, by putting the world of the Indian Ocean within her reach, so to speak, prompted Italy into making her way there and establishing herself along its shores during the second half of the nineteenth century. Beginning in 1882, Italy set about transforming a small settlement acquired in the bay of Assab, on the Red Sea, into an authentic colony, with the object of conquering Ethiopia. The resounding defeat at Aduwa in 1896 put an end to such imperialistic ventures for some time, but Italy did not consider herself beaten and was to return to the charge in the twentieth century.

Germany had not been able to benefit from the discovery of the Cape route in the fifteenth century either, for at that time she was not yet a unified power. Hamburg, as we have seen, had joined in the clandestine trade in the Indian Ocean during the eighteenth century, but the Germans did not really begin to take an interest in that part of the world until after the exploration of East Africa by Krapf, Rebmann, and a few others. We shall see later how Germany gained a foothold in Africa at the end of the nineteenth century and what were the results.

2. THE TRIUMPH OF THE STEAMSHIP

Contrary to what has been assumed, the opening of the Suez Canal, far from leading to the disappearance of the sailing-ship from the Indian Ocean, had the direct result of bringing it new prosperity, for the necessity of competing with the steamship caused the traditional vessel to be continually improved.

Quite recently, Professor Graham, of London University, emphasised this fact, that the opening of the Suez Canal did not mark the end of an era for the sailing ship. On the contrary, the 'ascendancy of the sailing ship', as he calls it, continued until 1885. According to Lacroix, the determining cause of its decline was not the Suez Canal but an overabundance of available tonnage, provoking in 1884 a world crisis, from which the sailing ship was never completely to recover.

There is no doubt, however, that although the Suez Canal encouraged the development of sailing ships, it also encouraged that of steamships, which had far greater possibilities. The tonnage of sailing ships, even those with steel hulls, could not exceed certain limits, whereas that of the steamship was much less limited. The use of metal hulls, the substitution of the propeller for the paddle wheel, increased engine power, and thousands of other improvements, all together made it possible for steamships to attain very large dimensions and great speeds even before fuel oil replaced coal in the early years of the twentieth century.

The decisive moment came not, as is often believed, with the invention of the propeller (1832), but rather with the use of steel boilers, which made it possible to obtain high pressures and consequently greater power. In 1881 the *Aberdeen*, a steamship of 4000 tons, belonging to the Aberdeen White Star Line, covered the distance separating Plymouth from Melbourne via the Cape in only 42 days, at an average pressure of 125 pounds. This record established, once and for all, the triumph of the steamship.

New navigation companies were added to those already operating in the Indian Ocean, but this time the English had to reckon with foreign competition. Of the particularly notable European companies then in the Indian Ocean were the *Navigazione Generale Italiana*, the *Deutsche Ost Afrika Linie*, the *Koninklijke Stoomvaart Maatschappij Nederland*, the *Koninklijke Rotterdamsche Lloyd*, the *Koninklijke Paketvaart Maatschappij* and the *Messageries maritimes* which had increased the services it had begun before 1869. All those lines had achieved great prosperity by the beginning of the present century.

The bulk of the traffic was carried on through the Suez Canal, mainly in the direction of India and the Far East. The steamships serving the coast of Africa took both routes: the Cape route and that of Suez, but those going to Australia preferred the latter. At the end of the nineteenth century they also began to take the Pacific route. As a result of all these changes, the south of the Indian Ocean was frequented far less than in the time of the clippers. The regions of the Mascarenes and Madagascar were thus somewhat isolated. Moreover, with the opening of the Suez Canal, the Mascarenes soon lost their importance as stepping stones to the Orient.

The progress of steam navigation had a marked influence on the life of the ports, whose development was also conditioned by the importance of their position and that of the hinterlands they served. The railways, another manifestation of the triumph of steam in the world of the Indian Ocean, played a prominent part in that respect. It was thanks to the railways that the vast African territories were developed for the first time and those of Australia opened up for settlement.

At the end of the nineteenth century the face of the oceanic world was completely transformed by modern technology. The classical image of Eastern ports, which calls to mind slender sailing ships silhouetted against an exotic background, with slaves busily loading bales of spices and other tropical commodities, that image, so popular during the eighteenth century and still valid for the first half of the nineteenth, no longer retained any reality by 1900.

At that time the engine reigned supreme in the main ports of Asia and Africa, ports which themselves grew to such an extent that they in no way resembled what they had been in the eighteenth century. Cape Town, Bombay, Madras, Calcutta, and Batavia were utterly transformed. Elsewhere, important commercial ports sprang up which had not existed at all or had been merely secondary ports of call: East London, Port Elizabeth, Durban, Lourenço Marques, Beira, Dar es Salaam, Mombasa, and Djibouti, on the coast of Africa; Majunga, Diégo-Suarez, and Tamatave, on the coasts of Madagascar; Steamer Point on the Arabian coast; Karachi on the coast of Gujarat; Singapore in Malaya; Surabaja in Indonesia; and Perth on the west coast of Australia, to cite only the main ones. Mention should also be made of the extraordinary development of the port of Shanghai, in China.

There is still no comprehensive work on the ports of the Indian Ocean. Kirk has been investigating this question for several years, and the articles he has written for periodicals are the beginnings of a long work he hopes to devote to it; this is sure of a welcome from all those who are interested in oceanic history.

3. MAGIC ELECTRICITY

In his classical work on commerce in the Roman Empire, Charlesworth makes certain very judicious remarks on the difference between ancient and modern commerce, and they deserve to be quoted here in their entirety:

> Comparisons are often instituted between ancient and modern commerce, not always with justice to the former. The first difference that occurs to anyone is of course the vastly increased speed with which articles of commerce can be conveyed between country and country. Yet to concentrate attention upon such a point is wrong. It is true that we may congratulate ourselves that where an ancient sailing-vessel with a favourable wind might keep up a steady average of five knots, a modern tramp can maintain twelve to fifteen, but the difference is only one of degree, not of kind. The real alteration has been brought about by the use of electricity; it is not in the transport of goods but in the transmission of news that a change has occurred. The early nineteenth century was little better off than the Roman world as regards the time taken by letters and news, which had always to be brought by a courier or letter-carrier of some sort; but now we have eliminated the personal element (that is the carrying of documents). . . .[1]

The real alteration was indeed brought about by the use of electricity. This was a major occurrence, and one that was as important in the history of the Indian Ocean as the opening of the Suez Canal, for it marks man's definitive conquest of oceanic space.

The details of the invention and advent of electricity belong to the history of technology. All we shall mention here are a few dates. The first experiments in oceanic telegraph communication by means of submarine electric cables date back to 1840, but it was not until 1865 that communication was definitively established between America and England.

India was at first linked to Europe, in 1865, by two overland telegraph lines, one of which went through Persia and the other through Turkey, but these overland lines gave little

[1] M. P. Charlesworth, *Trade-Routes and Commerce of the Roman Empire*, Cambridge, 1924, pp. 224–5.

satisfaction and, for England, had the drawback of belonging to foreign companies. She therefore soon set about having her own submarine lines. The first was laid in 1870, between Bombay, Aden, and Alexandria, by the Eastern Telegraph Company. The network rapidly spread to Australia, Africa, and most of the countries of the ocean. In 1901 the setup was completed with the laying of a cable which connected South Africa with Australia, passing through Mauritius.

From the military point of view, the submarine telegraph tightened England's control over her possessions in the Indian Ocean, which, it should be recalled, formed the largest part of her overseas empire. From the commercial point of view, the results were quite simply sensational.

The considerable difference between the time it took to transmit news and the time entailed in the transport of cargoes had a profound influence on commercial transactions by making it possible to speculate in advance on goods still en route. To a certain extent, it lessened the importance of the middleman by putting the European industrialist in direct relation, as it were, with the raw materials he needed. Thus, after the steamship, along came electricity and transformed commercial operations even more radically.

4. THE DISCOVERY OF BLACK GOLD

After the steamship and electricity came oil. The three formed a triad which has dominated all oceanic history until today. They can be compared to those deities with several arms which are found in Hindu temples. Oil might appear as a kind of terrifying Shiva, frenetically dancing in a circle of fire, principle at once of creation and destruction, yet more often engaged in destroying than in creating, like the Shiva of Hinduism.

There is no doubt that although petroleum did much for modern technology, it was a seed of discord in the oceanic world, and that the wars once fought over gold and spices were as nothing compared to those fought over 'black gold'.

Petroleum was well known to the ancients. Herodotus and other classical writers spoke of it. Yet it would seem never to have been used in antiquity. During the Middle Ages it perhaps served in the preparation of Greek fire, although the actual composition of that substance is unknown. At the beginning of the nineteenth century it was still used only to make oil for lamps.

The main countries of the Indian Ocean where it is found today are Arabia, Iraq, Iran, India, Burma, and Indonesia. Indications of it have also been discovered recently in Tanganyika, Madagascar, and Australia. It was apparently in Burma that petroleum was first commercially exploited as 'Rangoon oil' for lighting needs. Its first exploitation took place around 1830, but remained on a small scale until 1890. The first exploitations in America, Russia, Galicia, and Rumania, where there are also important fields, date back to 1860–80. The fields of Indonesia (Java and Sumatra) did not begin to be worked until 1883.

At first petroleum was used only for domestic needs. For example, one of the largest oil companies of the Indian Ocean, the Shell Company, started its operations in India about 1890 by selling oil for lamps. Its earliest beginnings were even more modest, for originally the object of that enterprise was to sell Oriental curiosities and shells, whence its name. The rise from bazaar items to the distribution of the black gold of modern times is noteworthy.

Petroleum did not really become important until it, and its derivatives could be used as fuels for various kinds of engines, including ship engines, that is, around 1890, and its advent was definitively consecrated by the first World War of 1914, which, in the Indian Ocean was above all a petroleum war, as we shall see.

Petroleum contributed quite as much as the Suez Canal to the comeback of Western Asia in the oceanic world. After having long been the country of aromatics and incense, and later that of coffee, Arabia became in the twentieth century the country of oil, or perhaps we should say the inferno of oil, for that new source of wealth brought her many misfortunes. At the present time, Arabia accounts for about a quarter of the world's production of petroleum, and the transport of that precious product is an important element of the traffic that uses the Suez Canal.

We get a good idea of the part oil plays in the Indian Ocean today when we consider that some 70 million tons of it a year flow through the Suez Canal and some 20 million tons in the direction of the various countries of the oceanic world, whereas in world trade the figure for rice, the largest food product of the oceanic world, is only three million tons.[2]

5. THE LATE-COMERS

On the political level, the first major occurrence which needs to be singled out in the period extending from the opening of the Suez Canal to the beginning of World War II is the appearance of the Italians and the Germans in the Indian Ocean, as well as very distinct pressure from the Russians in the Near East and a revival of French, Portuguese, and Dutch activity.

As there was nothing particularly remarkable about Italy's attempt to create a colonial empire on the Somali coast, it can be disregarded. Germany's penetration in Africa was far more important. A good historical account of it can be found in the works of Schramm and Brunschwig on German overseas expansion.

Briefly, the German penetration began with the explorations of Krapf and Rebmann in East Africa in 1848–49. Those pioneers were soon followed by other explorers who made known to Europe the hidden possibilities of that whole region of Africa. The result was a real race to annex it, and the Germans contrived to be the very first to get there.

In 1884 Peters signed a series of treaties with the kinglets of the coast facing Zanzibar, placing their territories under the protection of a German association for colonisation launched by himself. The Sultan of Zanzibar, who considered himself the legitimate suzerain of these kinglets, at once loudly protested. The Germans retorted, not without justification, that the exercise of his authority was limited to a coastal fringe and did not extend to the interior of the territories concerned; and when he protested even more loudly, the threat of a German fleet anchored in the waters of Zanzibar was not long in sobering him down. The Germans would probably not even have let him keep his throne had not England, intervening as arbitrator, allowed him to save face by retaining Zanzibar,

[2] Figures cited by Auber in 1954.

Pemba, and a few other small strongholds, while she and Germany divided between themselves the territories that today make up Kenya and Tanganyika.

The German possessions in East Africa did not carry much weight, of course, in ocean strategy, but owing to the fact that Germany was then a great power in Europe and that the fate of the countries of the Indian Ocean was always decided, in time of war, in the European theatre, these possessions were susceptible of being increased in case of conflict. This is what Karl Rodenberg pointed out in a study published in the great German maritime journal *Marine Rundschau* in 1904. His study, incidentally, which is entitled 'Der Indische Ozean in der Geschichte des Mittelalters und der Neuzeit', is the first essay on the history of the Indian Ocean.

The revival of French activity was evident in two notable events: the consolidation of the conquest of Indo-China in 1887, and the conquest of Madagascar in 1895, not to mention the occupation of Djibouti in 1888, which ensured France a strategic position at the entrance to the Red Sea. Useless conquests, said the defeatists, since France was not strong enough to contest England's command of the Indian Ocean. This was true in the days of the sailing fleets and as long as her only naval bases were Pondichéry and the island of Réunion. But it was no longer true once she had acquired bases in Madagascar, Indo-China, and Djibouti, and at a time when the navies had substituted steamships for sailing ships and had thus singularly changed the balance of naval forces. Although the occupation of Madagascar and Indo-China was open to criticism from other points of view, it certainly was not from that of naval strategy. Indeed, her presence in these areas in the event of war, allowed France to bring units directly into the Indian Ocean, units that she would otherwise have had to dispatch from very far away and at great risk.

As for Portugal, she experienced a real colonial renaissance in the last decades of the nineteenth century. In 1878–79 the well-known Serpa Pinto considered connecting Angola to Mozambique, thus thwarting the plans of Cecil Rhodes, who dreamt, on the contrary, of extending the English possessions in Africa in the longitudinal direction, from the Cape to Cairo. Little Portugal had finally to yield to powerful England, but in definitively separating Angola from Mozambique by the interposition of Rhodesia, the clever Rhodes reaped only half a victory. Rhodesia had no access to the sea, and was later to depend on the Portuguese port of Beira for her maritime communication, thus making Beira's fortune. In the meanwhile, the Portuguese actively encouraged the development of Lourenço Marques, which in 1897 replaced Mozambique as the capital of Portuguese East Africa. Located on Delagoa Bay, it is the best port on the entire African coast, and today holds its own with Durban.

In Indonesia the Dutch made a serious effort at the beginning of the twentieth century to stimulate agricultural production, with very satisfying results. From 1900 to 1914 the archipelago's production of sugar rose from 700,000 tons to 1,400,000, and of petroleum from 360,000 tons to 1,540,000. The rubber industry also made giant strides.

In another respect, with the creation of the *Koninklijke Paketvaart Maatschappij* in 1891 the Dutch gained prominence in the south-east Asian movement of shipping. In our view, Rodenberg was mistaken when in 1904 he wrote, in the above-mentioned study, that the Dutch East Indies were 'a jewel in the hands of a puny proprietor' and that a colonial empire possessed by a European state which was not numbered among the great powers constituted 'a problem for the Indian Ocean'.

The activities of her European rivals in the Indian Ocean at the end of the nineteenth century might well have been a source of worry to England, but what alarmed her even more and beyond everything else was to see Russia, at the same time, throwing her gigantic shadow across the ocean.

Since her assault on Persia in the eighteenth century, Russia had never ceased looking in the direction of that country, the only one that could provide an outlet to the sea for the vast colonial empire the Tsars had meanwhile carved out for themselves in Asia. At the end of the nineteenth century, Russia had a predominant influence at the court of Teheran, but as soon as her plans took shape, the British government gave her a peremptory warning, in 1902, that any attempt at gaining a fothold in the Persian Gulf would meet with armed resistance. It is probable, however, that if the Russo-Japanese War (1904), instead of ending in a Russian defeat, had turned out differently, Russia would not have drawn back. The question was finally settled in 1907 by an agreement which divided Persia into two spheres of influence, Russian in the north and English in the south.

6. THE BOER REBELLION

After the activities of those whom we have called the 'latecomers', in the Indian Ocean, the other major occurrence during the period 1870–1914 was the Boer rebellion in South Africa. Since the wars at the end of the eighteenth century, this was the first conflict that set Europeans to fight one another in that theatre. It was a limited conflict, but one which nevertheless had repercussions over the entire Indian Ocean.

The discovery of diamond mines in South Africa in 1871 had brought about far-reaching changes in that country, which until then had lived somewhat remote from the stream of history. Among those who then arrived to seek their fortune was a man of extraordinary ambition and dynamism, Cecil Rhodes, who was to have both a salutary and a disastrous influence; salutary, because he gave a remarkable impetus to the development of South Africa; disastrous, because at the same time he sowed the seeds of civil war.

After having acquired wealth and power, and at a time when everything he did seemed to succeed, he came up against a sizeable obstacle in the person of Paul Kruger, the leader of the Boers, a man as fiercely separatist as he himself was federalist. A conflict was inevitable. By 1880 the Boers had to resort to force in their effort to safeguard their group identity and their independence, both of which were threatened by Rhodes' great plan for federation. Taken by surprise, the British government yielded. Rhodes lost the first round, but he did not give up the struggle.

In 1886 the discovery of gold mines in the Transvaal attracted a great number of English to the province. Their presence caused friction with the Boers, who called them *uitlanders* (foreigners) and subjected them to many vexations. Rhodes, of course, championed the newcomers and tried his adversaries to such a degree that he literally forced them to take up arms again in 1899, this time for a far more serious conflict.

The precise cause of the conflict, however, was not the treatment that the Boers inflicted upon the *uitlanders* but rather the construction, in 1894, of a railway connecting Johannesburg, the capital of the Transvaal, to the port of Lourenço Marques, in Portuguese territory. This railway gave the Boers effective access to the ocean and upset all Rhodes' plans.

The war, during which the Transvaal and Orange Free State fought against Cape Colony and the province of Natal, lasted almost four years. The English had to use forces amounting to nearly 450,000 men to defeat 50,000 Boers. The war might have had calamitous effects on the development of South Africa if the British government, anxious to prepare a permanent understanding, had not then adopted a conciliatory and liberal attitude, which was to result in the creation, in 1910, of a South African dominion, grouping the four provinces and corresponding, for the most part, to the Boers' aspirations.

Ten years earlier, while the war was raging in Africa, Australia had attained the status of a dominion. At the beginning of the period 1870–1915 the country had undergone a serious economic crisis due to both domestic and foreign causes. The price of wool dropped considerably at the same time the number of sheep was reduced by half, following prolonged periods of drought. The popularisation of frozen meat, which Australia could furnish in large quantities, and the discovery of new gold mines at Coolgardie in the western province (1892) saved the country just in time. The Coolgardie mines opened an era of unprecedented development for Western Australia. Between 1891 and 1911, its population rose from 49,000 to 282,000 inhabitants; its yearly export figure from £800,000 to £5,400,000; and its cultivated area from 89,000 to 840,000 acres.

On the eve of World War I, Australia, although still numbering no more than five million inhabitants, was already the brightest jewel in Britain's crown in the Indian Ocean. In 1911 she contributed to her own naval defence by maintaining a unit of the imperial fleet, including one battle cruiser, three light cruisers, and several smaller warships, all built at Australian expense, placed under the control of the Australian government, and manned by Australian crews.

7. THE RISE OF AFRICA

Until about the middle of the nineteenth century, Asia had been, for Europeans, the main centre of attraction in the Indian Ocean. In the second part of the century their attention was drawn chiefly toward East and South-east Africa. It was the only continent bordering on the Indian Ocean in which the Europeans had hardly yet gained a foothold; little was still known about it, whereas the other countries of that ocean had all been explored.

About 1850 a whole collection of explorers, several of whom were also missionaries, set out with extraordinary fervour to discover the vast territories stretching along the east coast of Africa. We have already mentioned in this regard the Germans Krapf and Rebmann, but the prize unquestionably goes to the Scotsman David Livingstone, who in a way was for Africa what Francis Xavier had once been for India, and whose heroic work contributed more than anything else to throwing light on the past after so many centuries of indifference of the Dark Continent.

By giving easy access to that whole coast, the Suez Canal crowned the work of the explorers and missionaries. But at the same time it opened up a huge field of action in that region to economic imperialism, a force which soon relegated to the background the goal of evangelisation which was the chief motivating factor for men like Livingstone.

The struggle to divide the spoils of Africa after 1870 is given an important place in all textbooks of modern history, and there is no need to go into it again here. Suffice it to say that, under the influence of industrial capitalism, and despite the protests of the missionaries who had innocently opened the way to the explorers, the partition of the continent was tainted with much corruption.

At the time when the last of the great trading companies in India was dying out, several so-called colonisation companies (the British East Africa Company, the *Deutsche Kolonialverein,* etc.) came into being in Africa for the development, that is, the organised exploitation, of vast territories bought from native chiefs at ridiculously low prices. The detailed history of the activity of these companies has still to be written, but what we already know of them is enough to show that little attention indeed was paid to morality.

It was not until the governments concerned replaced the colonisation companies in the administration of the territories in question that the situation changed and that there was an awareness of what Kipling called 'the white man's burden'. This occurred with regard to the British territories in East Africa in 1895, and with regard to the German in 1890.

'The administration of African territories by legitimate governments,' writes Julien, 'showed considerable progress. It gradually became evident that the protection and education of the peoples were not incompatible with a cautious and forbearing economy. Eloquent voices were raised to affirm that colonial administration had, above all, a social part to play.'[3]

On the economic level the change of system also showed definite progress. Indeed, it was primarily after the arrival of the actual colonial administrators that the construction of railways, indispensable for economic development, was actively pursued. In the years 1870–90 the only railways built in Africa were in Egypt and the Cape Colony. In the last decade of the century, East Africa was rapidly provided with a large network connecting the main ports of the coast with the interior. 'The effects of these African railways', according to Williamson,

> rudimentary as they still are in relation to the vastness of the continent, have been revolutionary. They have been the enabling factor in the planting of capitalistic enterprise at a distance from the coast, and that statement implies enormous economic, political, and social consequences. Without them the employment of white men in the healthy uplands of the Transvaal, Rhodesia and Kenya would be limited to subsistence-farming, a mode of life that has small attraction for the civilized man of today. The Sudan and Uganda would be still a chaos of warring savages, or would be governed from altruistic or military motives by a power which could not recoup the cost.

[3] C.-A. Julien, *Histoire de l'Afrique,* Paris, 1946, p. 104.

In the moist tropical regions trade on the modern scale could not exist, for the tsetse fly kills all draught animals, and transport by human porterage, which virtually implied slavery, was the only available method before the railway era. Slavery being abolished, the cost was prohibitive, and stagnation was unavoidable.[4]

With few exceptions, these comments could apply just as well to the large island of Madagascar, where the introduction of railways shortly after the conquest of the island played a major part. Although Madagascar does not really belong to Africa, her history in the second half of the nineteenth century went through approximately the same stages as did that of the neighbouring African territories: the discovery of the country by the explorers, especially the indefatigable Grandidier, and the missionaries; private enterprise; state intervention; and the construction of railways.

Another fact which played an important part in the development of the African territories was the discovery made by the Englishman Sir Ronald Ross, in 1895, of the malaria parasite and the way it is carried by mosquitoes. True, that discovery did not make it possible to do away with malaria immediately, but it did make it possible at least to lessen its ravages. Now along with the tsetse fly, which as we know is the carrier of sleeping sickness, the malaria mosquito was man's worst enemy in the tropical regions of the African coast.

Despite the efforts of intelligent administrators and devoted missionaries, and despite the introduction of railways and the progress of hygiene, the inadequacy of settlement in the region greatly retarded Africa's development. In 1914, whereas Asia was already overpopulated, the whole of this area still offered vast empty spaces. These have not been filled even today, for lack of men whom neither Africa itself nor Europe can provide.

8. THE EAST–WEST ANTITHESIS

The East–West antithesis which, as we have seen, began to take shape during the first decades of the nineteenth century with the advent of industrial capitalism, became more and more sharply defined at the end of the century with the development

[4] J. A. Williamson, *A Short History of British Expansion*, London, 1950, II, 172.

of technology and the decline of China, the only great Asian state not yet really dominated by Europe.

The treaty of Nanking (1842) had been followed rather closely in China by the Taiping rebellion, which took a xenophobic turn and resulted in a number of casualties among the Europeans established in the country. England, this time with the help of France, took advantage of it to intervene once more. The Chinese were defeated by Anglo-French forces, which moved into Peking and devastated the Summer Palace, the residence of the Manchu emperors (1860). By the convention that put an end to the hostilities, China had to open her ports more freely to European commerce.

Had China then imitated Japan and taken the road to Westernisation, it is probable that she would have avoided the worst; but the Empress Tzu-hsi was hostile to any reforms prompted by European ideas. When the young emperor Kwang-hsü showed an inclination in that direction, she had him confined (1898). Shortly after, she started another xenophobic movement which spread throughout the entire country, the Boxer Rebellion, 'Boxers' being the name of a politico-religious sect transformed by Tzu-hsi into a tool for her own vengeance.

In June 1900 the Boxers began an attack on the foreign legations in Peking and a massacre of the Christian natives. At the same time, Tzu-hsi declared war on the European powers, Japan and the United States. She was clearly heading for disaster. In a few months international forces invaded China. Peking was beleaguered once again. China had to pay a high indemnity, and Tzu-hsi herself would not have kept her throne had it not been for the intervention of Russia, which, in payment for her protection, was permitted to occupy the whole of Manchuria. The final decline of the Manchu dynasty was not long in coming. In 1911 it was swept away by a revolution that resulted in the establishment of a democratic republic.

Europe took over other regions of the Far East in a still more clear-cut way at the end of the nineteenth century. In Burma and Malaya, England continued the conquests she had begun early in the century. France, as we have seen, occupied Cochin China and established her protectorate over Annam and Cambodia.

In Japan—which had long remained inaccessible to Europeans, except the Dutch—the Americans and Russians had forced the shoguns to open their doors to international trade in 1854. This measure might well have become the prelude to a European conquest if Japan, unlike China, had not quickly set out to learn Western ways when the emperor Matsuhito (1867–1912) took over authority from the shoguns and himself directed the Japanese *risorgimento*.

Encouraged by England, which had no base in the Pacific and saw Japan as a possible ally against Russian expansion in the East, the Europeanisation of that country was carried out at a singularly rapid pace. By 1894, Japan had a navy at her disposal, organised on the English model, and strong enough to enable her to launch out into a war of annexation against Korea. Forced to fall back by the intervention of Russia, supported by Germany and France, Japan took her revenge ten years later. She crushed the Russians first at Port Arthur and then at Tsuchima, where Admiral Togo in a few hours destroyed the Russian Baltic fleet sent to the Far East, under the command of Admiral Rozhdzhestvensky, via the Cape of Good Hope and the Indian Ocean.

It was a significant victory, and one that was later to have far-reaching repercussions in the Indian Ocean. The nineteenth century came to an end with a very clear affirmation of the Europeans' will to power, directed towards an Asia and an Africa that were passive and apparently resigned to their fate. The twentieth century, on the other hand, began with the victory of an Asiatic state over a European state and gave an unexpected perspective on the East–West antithesis.

'Japan's victory over Russia', wrote Grousset, 'radically transformed the traditional elements of the Eastern Question. Since the end of the 18th century the question was stated as *the problem of the partition and colonisation of Asia by European powers*. After the Russo–Japanese War, the Eastern Question was *the problem of Asia's revolt against her European masters*.'[5]

At the time, however, it would seem that the Europeans, especially the English, saw the Japanese victory rather as the triumph of Western modernism, with which Japan was so permeated, over a semi-Asian feudalism represented by

5 R. Grousset, *Le Réveil de l'Asie*, Paris, 1924, p. 190.

Russia, and there is no doubt that the issue can be considered in that perspective: of the two belligerents Japan did, in fact, personify Western dynamism, and Russia, Eastern inertia. That is why England, confident in her Japanese alliance and satisfied that Russia had been defeated, seemed readily to agree to share her naval hegemony in the Far East with Japan by a treaty signed in 1911. Or was it because she realised that the agreement, which entrusted the naval defence of South-east Asia to Japan in case of conflict, would secure her rear in the Indian Ocean, thus allowing her to concentrate all her forces in Europe for the imminent struggle with Germany?

Be that as it may, in the light of subsequent events the battle of Tsushima (8 April 1905) can perhaps be considered the real beginning of the current history of the Indian Ocean.[6]

[6] According to Tibor Mende, this event was not, however, the decisive shock that allowed Asia to recover her self-confidence. That shock, he considers, did not come until 1928, with the launching of the Soviet Union's first Five-Year Plan. See Mende, *La Révolte de l'Asie*, Paris, 1951, p. 10.

XV. Cancer and Capricorn

AFTER a century of uninterrupted peace, the Indian Ocean had, twice in less than fifty years, to suffer the consequences of the two great World Wars of the twentieth century.

When the first broke out, the oceanic world was in a period of growth, leading its own life far from the quarrels of the European world, quarrels in which it had had almost no part. Since the weapons then in use had still a very limited radius of action, the conflict never quite reached the Eastern seas, which, moreover, were well protected in the west by England and in the east by Japan, in accordance with the 1911 Convention. From 1914 to 1918, therefore, the Indian Ocean was merely a secondary theatre of operations with two areas of very localised hostilities: the Middle East and East Africa.

At first no more than an operation to protect the British oil concessions in Iran, the Middle East campaign gradually developed into a large-scale movement against Turkey. This country had entered the war on the side of Germany in the hope of recovering Egypt from the English and reconstituting the former Ottoman Empire which had disintegrated at the end of the nineteenth century.

British and Indian effectives detached from the imperial forces in India managed to occupy Basra, on the Persian Gulf (April 1915). But when General Townshend, who commanded them, tried to reach Baghdad, he was stopped by the Turks and forced to capitulate at Kut-al-Amara (April 1916), a bitter defeat, but only a temporary one, for the following year the British resumed the campaign with larger forces under the command of General Maude. In March 1917 he entered Baghdad, the old capital of the Abbassid Empire, and occupied all Mesopotamia.

In the course of the same year, 1917, the British found themselves forced to embark on a campaign in Iran to oust the Turks, who had moved in after Russia's collapse. In 1918 two British expeditionary forces drove the Turks back to the shores of the Caspian Sea and occupied all the Iranian territory.

For its part, the British army in Egypt, under the command of Allenby, moved into Palestine (November 1917) and from there pushed on to Syria. Beaten at the same time in the Balkans, Turkey, driven to the wall from all sides, capitulated on 30 October, 1918 a few days before the Allies' victory over Germany. Far from resulting in the reconstruction of the Ottoman Empire, the venture on which Turkey had embarked did just the opposite and dealt that empire its deathblow.

In East Africa it seemed at the beginning that the Germans' position would be singularly strengthened by the neutrality and even the support of the Boers of the Union of South Africa. But in spite of a small uprising, one, moreover, that was soon quelled, the Boer leaders, Botha and Smuts, flatly adopted a position in favour of England and furnished a large contingent for a campaign against the Germans of Tanganyika, who found themselves at the same time attacked by forces from the Congo, Kenya, and India.

Under the command of a bold, capable leader, Colonel von Lettow-Vorbeck, the Germans put up a magnificent and fierce resistance to the combined forces. By September 1916 they were driven out of the port of Dar-es-Salaam, but they then made their retreat towards the borders of Tanganyika in orderly fashion and did not lay down their arms until after the armistice in Europe was signed.

On the sea hostilities were limited to raids carried out by a few bold privateers, in particular the *Wolf*, the *Emden*, and the *Königsberg*. They did not succeed, however, in seriously disorganising the Allies' lines of communication, although the *Emden* itself captured or destroyed some twenty ships. The *Emden* was finally destroyed at the Cocos Islands by the

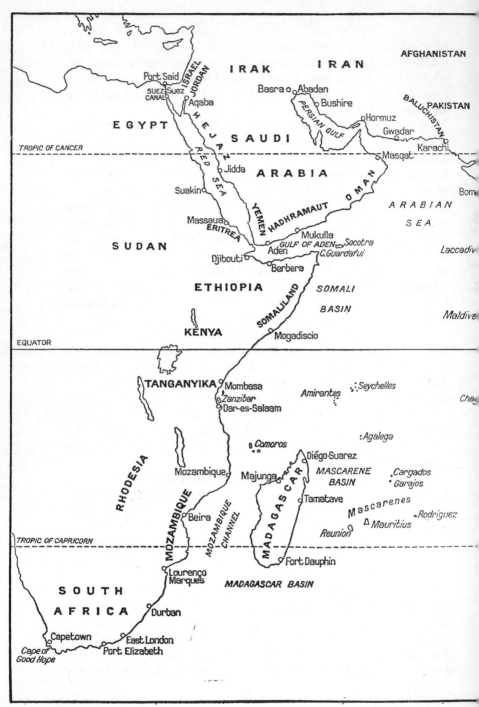

THE INDIAN OCEA

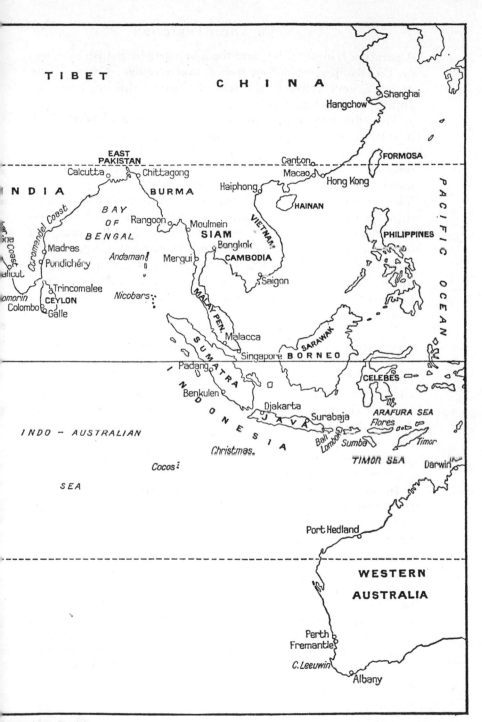

MODERN TIMES

Australian cruiser *Sydney*, and the *Königsberg* by British monitors on the Rufiji river where it had taken refuge. German submarines, very active in the seas of Europe, did not enter the Indian Ocean during this war.

Thus the war of 1914–18 was superficially a rather insignificant episode in the history of that ocean. Yet it was actually the cause of important changes. In the first place, it was responsible for the control of the Middle East passing from the hands of the Turks into those of the British. By 1904, as we have already seen, oil had begun to replace coal as fuel for ships. It was therefore essential for England, which had no oil of its own, to secure the upper hand in the Middle East, then on its way to becoming the most important oil-producing region in the Indian Ocean. The riches of India no longer meant very much compared to that vital product petroleum. However, controlling the Middle East was no easy task, as we shall soon see.

Nor was it easy for the British to replace the Germans in East Africa after the war. What sort of policy was suitable to those vast territories still inadequately peopled by Europeans? How could the aspirations of the Europeans colonists be reconciled with those of the Africans and the Indians? Indeed, alleging the part they had played in the colonisation of East Africa, the latter went so far as to ask the League of Nations, in 1919, to place the region under a mandate of the Indian protectorate. India itself, after the war, was a prey to great political agitation, of which we shall speak later.

In South Africa, and Australia as well, the situation was far from brilliant. After the war, both countries went through a rather marked economic depression. Moreover, although South Africa had agreed to take part in the war on the side of England, it appeared that the animosity between the Boers and the English had not been completely obliterated. A secessionist movement even began to take shape. Meanwhile, in Australia, but for different reasons, Western Australia wanted to separate from the eastern provinces and to form an autonomous dominion. Such dissensions within the two large countries of the Indian Ocean where European influence prevailed were hardly conducive to consolidating the Europeans' position in that part of the world.

From the economic point of view, the effects of World War I on the Indian Ocean can be briefly summarised, according to Carrington and Kahn, as follows. There was first of all a development of industrial production in certain countries of Asia, especially India and Japan, with, as a result, a considerable decrease in England's exports to those markets. For example, whereas in 1918 India received 43 per cent of the products of Lancashire, that percentage dropped by half in 1937. At the same time, the Indian textile industry had developed to the point where it could supply three-quarters of the country's domestic needs. As for Japan, her total exports, thanks to the temporary disappearance of her European and American competitors during the war, rose from a value of 33 million yen in 1913 to 280 million in 1919. Although the end of hostilities allowed the English to reconquer some of the markets they had lost, they nevertheless had seriously to reckon with Japanese competition.

On the international level they also saw a decrease both in their total exports, which from 1913 to 1937 showed a drop of 28 per cent, and in their tonnage in merchant ships, which represented 40 per cent of world tonnage in 1913 and only 26 per cent in 1937. The war also showed up many other weaknesses in the British Commonwealth's economic structure, but it would take too long to go into them here. A good analysis of them can be found in the work of Carrington who concludes that British imperial expansion stopped at 1931.

On the strategic level as well, World War I had two very serious consequences for England. The first was that she was forced to give up her naval ascendancy through treaties concluded at Washington in 1921–22, which put the American navy on a footing of equality with the British; the second was the creation of tremendous competition for the English overseas cable companies by the American companies.

In the Indian Ocean itself, it is true that England kept her predominance as much from the viewpoint of lines of communication as from that of naval forces. In 1934 an English trust, Cables and Wireless Ltd., secured control of all the telegraphic communications in the Indian Ocean; at the same time, the English strengthened their naval bases everywhere, especially at Simonstown (South Africa), Trincomalee (Ceylon), and Singapore (Malaya).

However, just as they had had in 1911 to share naval hegemony in the Far East with the Japanese, they had now to share it with the Americans, Japan having been thrust aside by the Washington treaties, which, in addition, put her in a position of inferiority *vis-à-vis* the Anglo-American coalition. The agreement authorised 20 capital ships amounting to 580,000 tons for England, 18 amounting to 525,000 tons for the United States, and 10 amounting to 315,000 tons for Japan.

By thus changing the balance of naval forces in the Far East, the Washington treaties marked a decisive stage in the history of the Indian Ocean. Forsaken by her former allies and disappointed at having been treated as an inferior, Japan, the most 'European' of all the Asian states, was led to become the champion of Asia's awakening and to seek other alliances, while biding her time, which was not long in coming.

2. THE REAWAKENING OF ASIA

In his book *Le Réveil de l'Asie*, René Grousset made an excellent study, directly after World War I, of the war's political repercussions in the countries of Asia. We can do no better here than summarise his conclusions on what he then called 'the Eastern question' which he formulated in this way: 'Will the Europeans, who now dominate, control, or keep in check 870 million Asians and African Moslems retain their hegemony for long?'[1]

In 1924, at the time Grousset was writing, the situation was briefly as follows. The East–West antithesis had reached an extremely critical phase in each of the large countries of the Near, Middle, and Far East, owing mainly to the errors in judgement of certain British statesmen, Lloyd George, Curzon, and a few others.

Egypt, occupied by the British in 1882, remained in theory a dependency of Turkey until 1914. The war put an end to that situation and transformed Egypt into a British protectorate. Proclaimed in order to cope with the necessities of war,

[1] Grousset, *Le Réveil de l'Asie*, p. 1.

the protectorate was to have terminated at the end of hostilities. The British government's refusal to give Egypt back her independence after the war provoked serious uprisings. Finally, in 1923, England made up her mind to recognize Egypt's independence, yet keeping the Sudan under her own control, and retaining the right to maintain armed forces in the Suez Canal zone. From Egypt's point of view, the question was thus only half settled.

Western Arabia had also been a part of the Ottoman Empire since the sixteenth century. In the course of the war, the British had called upon the Arab leaders to help fight the Turks. The celebrated Lawrence of Arabia had succeeded, perhaps even beyond his greatest hopes, in rekindling an Arab nationalism, whose aspirations, once hostilities were over, came up against British designs on Arabia's oil wells. The new Arab states that sprang up after the war, Saudi Arabia, Jordan, and Iraq, also looked askance at England's attempts to give Palestine back to the Jews as their homeland. Thus to the problems of the Near East were added those, perhaps even thornier, of the Middle East.

In Iran, which, as we know, had been occupied by British forces during the war, the existence of oil wells even more important than those of Mesopotamia prompted England to keep that country under her protection. She also quite sincerely believed that in so doing she was protecting it from another possible Russian assault. But she had finally to yield and evacuate Iran in 1921, allowing a former soldier by the name of Riza Khan to establish a dictatorial regime perhaps even more unbearable than the British one.

On the frontiers of India, Afghanistan, which the British had held in a state of semi-dependency since 1897, rebelled in 1919 and by force of arms regained complete independence. Afghanistan then united with Iran and Turkey to form a kind of Moslem Triple Alliance, one of whose avowed objectives was to free India from the British yoke.

India herself had taken part in the war on the side of the Allies only because she had hoped to gain her independence in return, but England could not resign herself to losing her empire in the Indies and did her best after the war to put it off, merely making matters worse. When on 13 April 1919, at

Amritsar, General Dyer ordered his troops to fire on a crowd that was making a public demonstration in favour of independence, a wave of indignation swept the country. Gandhi's arrest in 1922 finally alienated the Hindus. From that time on, the position of the British in India became precarious. Morally, the great sub-continent no longer belonged to the British Empire.

Thus, despite the victories she had gained in the Middle East during the war, England found herself incapable of consolidating her positions in that section of the Indian Ocean and realised that the nationalism she had contributed to arousing was turning against her. Of course, the same thing was happening to the French and the Dutch in Indo-China and Indonesia. In less than a century, the Europeanisation of the Indian Ocean countries by capitalist-colonialist methods led to this apparently paradoxical but basically very logical result: Asia's revolt against Europe.

In the Far East, outside the Indian Ocean, to be sure, but at the very gateway to it, Japan, voluntarily westernised but remaining nonetheless deeply attached to her traditions, also drew away from Europe, after having made common cause with the Allies during the war. However, and this is of great importance, it was with the help of European methods and thanks to the support of a European nation (Germany) that Japan was to be able to take her revenge and free a part of Asia from the Western yoke.

Moreover, in the Near East, on the Western confines of the Indian Ocean, it was also owing to out-and-out Westernisation that Turkey, under the forceful leadership of Mustafa Kemal Pasha, succeeded in recovering rapidly from the frightful effects of the war and even in defeating, on more than one issue, those who had brought her to heel in 1918.

Asia's awakening! But after all, was Asia really re-awakening or was she, on the contrary, waking up for the first time in her long history to ideas which had virtually nothing Asian about them? And that revolt against the European yoke, was it not at the same time a revolt against Asia itself, against outdated social and economic concepts, against everything that had for so long been the weakness of the Orientals and that to a great extent had given rise to the East–West antithesis? And without wanting to palliate in any way the mistakes of colonial capitalism, should not one fact be stressed, a fact that Eastern writers are perfectly willing to admit, namely, that it was the Europeans who actually formed a national consciousness in so many countries of Asia?

3. THE END OF A HEGEMONY

Certain events in the Indian Ocean were premonitory symptoms of World War II and should be briefly recalled, for they were not unrelated to the causes that set it off.

In that part of the world the only country to have benefited from the previous war had been England, to whom the Treaty of Versailles had granted a mandate over the former German colonies in East Africa. Italy, hoping to receive at least one mandate, obtained no more than a rectification of frontiers on the Somali coast. Consequently, the Italians were to be sadly disappointed, while in Germany the recovery of Tanganyika as a colony became one of the leitmotifs of Nazi propaganda.

The only territory of East Africa that had escaped the 'partition of Africa' at the end of the nineteenth century was Ethiopia or Abyssinia, where an Italian attempt to seize the country had been put down at Aduwa in 1896. Italy had not forgotten that defeat, and came back to the charge in 1935, although Ethiopia then belonged to the League of Nations. After an eight-month campaign, Ethiopia was conquered. Together with Eritrea and Somaliland, she constituted a veritable Italian empire in East Africa which was solemnly proclaimed by Mussolini on 9 May 1936.

The hostilities in the theatre of the Indian Ocean during World War II consequently began in that region. In August 1940 the Italian forces in Eritrea moved into British Somaliland. England was quick to react. In January 1941, troops from the Anglo-Egyptian Sudan and Kenya attacked the Italians in Ethiopia, and Somaliland capitulated. In March, Addis Ababa, the capital of Ethiopia, surrendered in turn. In June the Italian resistance in Eritrea collapsed, and before the year was over the Italian empire in eastern Africa no longer existed.

At the same time, the North African campaign followed its course, and we know the results. After initial triumphs which led Rommel's troops to the gates of Egypt, the *Afrika Korps* had to retreat. In January 1943 the British had the situation well in hand and the danger of a push towards the Suez Canal was averted for good.

Because of Turkey's neutrality, the war did not spread to the Middle East as that of 1914–18 had done. The British and the Russians intervened in time to keep Riza Shah, the dictator of Iran, from coming into the war on the side of the Rome-Berlin axis. In 1941 they occupied the country and deposed Riza Shah. Until the end of the war, the occupation of Iran made it possible for the Allies to send large reinforcements to Russia via the Persian Gulf.

On the other hand, in the eastern region of the Indian Ocean, the Allies found themselves in a very bad position when Japan entered the war against them in December 1941. We know how the surprise attack on Pearl Harbour managed to neutralise the American advanced bases in the Pacific and enabled Japan to beleaguer in no time all the countries of South-east Asia: Indo-China, Malaya, Burma, Indonesia, and the Philippines, make raids as far as India and Ceylon, and even threaten northern Australia.

What we are less aware of, for on the history of World War II there is still much to be written, is that the Japanese push might quite well not have stopped at South-east Asia, but have continued through the whole of the Indian Ocean, without meeting any real opposition, for the British forces were almost wiped out after the battle of the Java sea (February 1942), during which the Japanese crushed the combined British and Dutch forces.

After the fall of Singapore, the main British naval base in the region, the other bases in India and Ceylon became untenable. What was left of the British units had to withdraw across the Indian Ocean to the African port of Mombasa, which was hastily transformed into a naval base. Why the Japanese warships did not pursue them is still a mystery to the Admiralty. In fact they merely attacked Trincomalee and made air raids on Colombo, Calcutta, and Madras.

238

According to Villiers,[2] who took part in the operations in the Indian Ocean during World War II,

> it was a good thing for the allies, firstly, that the main sea-routes now lay in the western waters of the Indian Ocean and, secondly, that the Japanese, for some reason, did not venture into that ocean in strength again. They lost thereby their chance of gaining its overwhelming mastery—a chance which was within their grasp, but did not come their way again.

Indeed, by May 1942, the Allies, having pulled themselves together, inflicted a crushing naval defeat on the Japanese in the Coral Sea and sank over 100,000 tons of their vessels between New Guinea and the Solomon Islands. Then, going on to a large-scale offensive, they harried them unremittingly until Japan's final collapse in August 1945.

All the operations described above took place on the fringe of the Indian Ocean. The only important operation in its very heart was the expedition carried out by troops from South and East Africa against Madagascar in 1942, with the objective of preventing a Japanese push towards that country, which had refused to join the Allies after the fall of France. It was a questionable operation, since, militarily, the only way to have checked the Japanese push was not by holding fortified posts such as Diego-Suarez but rather by holding the sea, for only on the sea could the adversary be neutralised, as can be seen from the battle of the Coral Sea.

Without adequate striking power on the sea, the best bases in the world are worth nothing. The Italians had good bases in Somaliland; yet their intervention in the Indian Ocean during the war was negligible. On the other hand, the Germans, without one base on the ocean, succeeded, by means of submarines and raiders, in doing more harm to the Allies than the Allies had done to them in the previous war. We should note in passing that the German raiders took their revenge on the Australian navy by sinking one of its best ships in the region of the Cocos Islands, where the *Sydney* had destroyed the *Emden* in November 1914. An account of the activity of the German submarines and raiders in the Indian Ocean from

[2] A. J. Villiers, *The Indian Ocean*, London, 1952, p. 229.

1939 to 1945 would in itself constitute an important chapter in the ocean's naval history.

Actually, the 1939 war was merely a repetition of what had happened in the seventeenth century with regard to the Portuguese. The fact of holding all the key positions of the Indian Ocean had not kept the latter from being beaten on the sea and losing their maritime hegemony. In the same way, the fact of holding the best bases of South-east Asia did not prevent the Allies from being beaten on the sea in that region. A thalassocracy can be maintained only with ships, and it is useless to hold the land if one does not at the same time hold the sea.

4. THE WORLD OF CANCER

We know only too well the direct consequences of the war of 1939 in the Indian Ocean: in Asia, a real explosion of nationalism, leading to the eviction of the Europeans from India, Ceylon, and all the countries of South-east Asia; in Madagascar and in eastern Africa, two rebellions that were put down with difficulty; in the Middle East, the advent of a dictatorship which, after having freed Egypt from British protection, is now trying to impose its own protectorate in that region to lay down the law in the Suez Canal.

Auber sees the Indian Ocean today as divided into two worlds. To the north of the equator, all the countries that are freed from European domination make up what he calls the world of Cancer. To the south of the equator, those in which the European element and Christian civilisation have maintained their positions make up the world of Capricorn, consisting of South Africa, East Africa, Madagascar, the Mascarenes, and Australia. But that division is a simplification of the present situation, which is not nearly so clear-cut as Auber affirms. In point of fact, neither the world of Cancer nor the world of Capricorn is in itself a unified and distinct whole.

Let us first consider the former. Even a superficial observer could not fail to notice that the old religious divisions, to begin with those, continue to prevail. Moslems, Hindus, and Buddhists still live in separate worlds, and within each of those worlds how many compartments can still be found? Despite

Nasser's efforts at reviving Pan-Islamism, the Moslem world from Egypt to Pakistan remains very divided, and the new Arab states, as well as Iran and Pakistan, do not seem much inclined to line up under the banner of the Egyptian dictator. Besides, the 'holy war' is a bad expedient, as the events of 1914–18 proved; and it would seem very doubtful whether the Egyptians can succeed where the Turks failed. Moreover, the aspirations of Pan-Islamism conflict with other aspirations in Africa and Asia which Nasser cannot overlook. We must not forget that with regard to the entire east coast of Africa, Islam's past is infinitely more tainted with 'colonialism' than that of the European imperialists, and that the natives are not particularly fond of the Arabs.

As for India, the differences between the Hindus of the north, of Aryan extraction, and those of the south, Dravidian by race, are very marked. The departure of the British cut India off from all her former Moslem provinces, which together now form Pakistan. The states that today go to make up India proper continue to show such diversity that it could well endanger the future of Indian unity, which, as we recall, did not come into being until fairly recently and because of a foreign influence, that of the British administrators. Not very long ago, André Siegfried noted that the expression 'the Indies' was still valid.

On the other hand, the presence of a large Hindu population in several countries of Asia and Africa as a result of the Indian 'diaspora' in the nineteenth century did not fail to cause friction with the native elements as soon as nationalism appeared both in India and in those countries. As a matter of fact, that friction has recently taken something of a turn for the worse in Ceylon, where the problem of peaceful coexistence between Indians and Sinhalese is far from being resolved. Moreover, in Indonesia, despite the civilising influence India once had in the archipelago, Indonesian nationalism refuses to make any concession to Indian nationalism, and the Hindu today can hardly claim a privileged situation in what was once 'greater India'.

In the Far East the nationalist aspirations of Burma, Malaya, and Indo-China have also been in conflict with those of Communist China since 1949, and China's recent intervention in

Indo-China and Malaya might well worry the countries of South-east Asia. Even India looks upon the communist renaissance in China with some anxiety.

In an interesting study published in 1954, on India's present strategic situation, an Indian writer, P. R. Ramachandra Rao, stressed the point that a resuscitated China, with ancient maritime traditions, might perfectly well launch out into a naval career, and that the possibility of a Chinese push by sea in the direction of India must not be excluded. Recent events in Tibet show that the push could just as well be carried out by land, without even waiting for China to rebuild her navy.

The Afro-Asian Bandung Conference (1955), a kind of Eastern Holy Alliance, whose specific objective was to unite the world of Cancer so that the principles of *Panch Shila*[3] could triumph and the last vestiges of European imperialism be eliminated, was, as we know, only half successful. Nothing very constructive has yet come out of it, and Pandit Nehru himself did not hide his disappointment. Actually, the dominant factor in the present situation appears to be rather what Ramachandra Rao calls 'Balkanisation', that is, a complete absence of unity. Besides, the phenomenon is not peculiar to modern times, and the facts we have given in this book show quite clearly that lack of unity has always been an old ailment of the Eastern world. At no time have we seen the Orientals, whether before or after da Gama, working together for any common objectives. On the contrary, we have seen that their lack of unity was precisely the main cause of their misfortunes. How is it possible to imagine that a state of things that has existed for so long can be radically changed between one day and the next?

And even if tomorrow the peoples of the East from Egypt to China, manage to form a common and solidly united front, to what would that common front now be opposed? The ghost of European imperialism, or the very real designs of the Russians and Americans, who have become, so to speak, the heirs and successors of the West? Whether they want to or not, the only way the Eastern peoples can recover their strength is not by opposing Europe but, on the contrary, by becoming more and more Europeanised, without, in so doing, giving up

[3] *Panch Shila* designates the five 'sacred' principles of peaceful coexistence.

their individuality. Even in Russia the keynote still is to catch up with Europe and with America, that 'greater Europe'.

Shortly before his death, Grousset had started on a synthesis of the present situation in Asia, a kind of sequel to his *Réveil de l'Asie*. The work was published in 1958, unfortunately in an incomplete form,[4] still, it gives a good enough idea of what Asia owes to Europe; how India owes the recovery of her unity, through the suppression of the Islamic dynasties, to England; how close the Iranians are, in fact, to Europeans; how Moslem patriotism can be compared with the Christian patriotism of the Middle Ages; and how the 'European' reformer Mustafa Kemal restored Turkey's national self.

5. THE WORLD OF CAPRICORN

What do we now see in what Auber calls the world of Capricorn? In South Africa, since the death of Smuts (1950), Boer irredentism, which the old leader had succeeded in checking, is gaining in intensity and thus deepening the rift between the South African nationalists and liberals. The nationalists' intransigence in racial matters has at the same time started South Africa on a road which apparently can lead only to an impasse.

Indeed, in a world that is moving more and more towards the mixture of races, apartheid would appear to have no future, especially considering that Mozambique, a country bordering on the Union of South Africa, is successfully carrying out a policy diametrically opposed to it: assimilation. When we note, in addition, that in South Africa racial problems are complicated by religious problems, we are forced to admit that the future of that country looks far from brilliant.

In the neighbouring African countries where the British had still until very recently supreme control, their lack of numbers makes their situation rather precarious. It will probably become more and more so as African nationalism, which already has capable and determined leaders in several of these countries, grows stronger, unless, completely breaking

[4] R. Grousset and G. Deniker, *La Face de l'Asie, données permanentes et facteurs de renouvellement*, Paris, 1958. Only half the work is by Grousset.

with the Anglo-Saxon tradition, they decide to follow Mozambique's lead and to encourage assimilation.

In the Mascarenes and Madagascar, the situation presents itself in a different light. Although not all the islands are free from prejudice, it can hardly be said that racism is rampant. The Europeans, of French extraction for the most part, live on fairly good terms with the Africans and Asians. Moreover, the native population of the Mascarenes is very small, and in Madagascar the autochthonous primitive element has long since disappeared or has mingled with the mass of immigrants from Indonesia. The recently proclaimed Malagasy Republic would not seem to have affected seriously the situation of the French in that country, a country which can make no headway toward progress unless it becomes thoroughly westernised, the only alternative being a rapid return to anarchy.

As for Australia, she is still the most homogeneous country of the world of Capricorn, with her nine million Europeans, mainly of Anglo-Saxon extraction. The aboriginal population, which represents only a small minority, poses no real problem. But the striking fact is that the population of Australia remains well below the figure it should reach if that vast country is to develop to the maximum. Australia today is in a dilemma; should she count on European immigration only and run the risk of becoming an under-developed country, or should she open her doors to Asian immigration and thus procure the man-power which is indispensable if she wants to make full use of her resources, but cease thereby to be a 'white Australia'?

We must realise that in the African territories of Capricorn and in Madagascar, the problem of shortage of manpower is just as real and no less acute. All these countries, with the exception of the already overpopulated little Mascarenes, are, in fact, capable of receiving several million more inhabitants. In this respect the situation in Madagascar is similar to that in Australia. Madagascar contains only six million inhabitants, whereas it could feed ten million.

It would thus seem that the opposition, if opposition there is, between the worlds of Cancer and Capricorn should be considered as much from the point of view of the East versus Africa as from that of the East versus the West; for, in fact, the East has already begun to besiege an Africa it had often

244

swarmed to in the past, and we may well wonder what the result will soon be. The geographer E. F. Gautier's reflection becomes more valid every day: 'On a planet where all the large continents are at present on the road to rapid overpopulation, *Africa is the empty continent*.'

René Servoise, from whom we have taken the quotation, writes on the subject:

> In this vacuum created by the departure of the Westerners, in that of the Indian Ocean and the Middle East, high pressure zones are building up against Africa. The Asians are likely to start out again on their old roads of invasion toward a thinly populated Africa. The European peace had stabilised the frontiers and stopped the migratory flow; migrating Asia, as the Indian R. Mukerji wrote, would willingly set out again to conquer empty spaces such as these, and the Indian Ocean is perhaps more a call to expansion than a geographical expression.[5]

But why stick to antitheses? Why not, like the English geographer Kirk, envisage complementary relations between the worlds of Cancer and Capricorn, and consider the future from the aspect of interpenetration leading to the realisation of a true community of the oceanic world?

6. TOWARDS A NEW BALANCE

From many points of view, World War II was a blessing for the Indian Ocean. This statement may seem surprising, but if we think about it for a moment we shall see that it is justified.

On 8 April 1905, the battle of Tsushima completely changed the Eastern question, but it did not resolve it. Far from hastening the solution, World War I had, on the contrary, done no more than delay it by giving new life to British imperialism and even urging it to undertake a gigantic and impossible task, that of 'carrying by itself the weight of the Asiatic continent', as Grousset put it. This resulted in a state of affairs that might have lasted a very long time and perpetuated the East–West antithesis had not World War II come along and burst the abscess, putting a sudden end to a hegemony that for some time had lost its reason for existence. The operation was brutal, but it was necessary.

[1] R. Servoise, 'Perspectives eurafricaines et afro-asiatiques,' *Comptes rendus des séances de l'Académie des Sciences d'Outre-mer*, XVIII, p. 228.

But at the same time that it put an end to British thalassocracy in the Indian Ocean, the second war led to a period of unstable balance and to an interregnum rather similar to that which followed the end of the Portuguese thalassocracy in the seventeenth century. Since the withdrawal of the British, who, with Singapore's independence, have now lost their last base in the eastern part of the ocean and retain only a few fortified posts in its western region, the Indian Ocean has become a real naval vacuum which can be filled, in case of war, only by the Americans or the Russians.

The United States, securely established in the Pacific and South-east Asia, and having learned from the lessons of World War II, is in a position to take over military control of the Indian Ocean at any moment. Moreover, many signs would seem to indicate that the Americans are trying to take the place of the European 'colonialists' in that region. As for the Russians, although they have not yet appeared in the ocean, their activities in the Middle East are clearly aimed at fulfilling that old dream of the Tsars: the possession of an outlet on the Persian Gulf.

It would thus seem that a dual threat weighs on the Indian Ocean, and perhaps a third as well: that of Chinese expansionism. Back in 1924 Grousset foresaw 'the powerful economic organisation, the formidable business democracy, that China will be tomorrow.' He himself anticipated an Americanised China. In fact, China, instead of becoming Americanised, has become communised and to a certain extent Russianised, but the result is the same.

This situation seems most conducive to the formation of an Indian Ocean community and an understanding among the peoples of the oceanic world without further dealy; but it does not *necessarily* follow that this entente will come about. The surest way of preparing for it is not to flaunt, in turn, the American bugbear, the Russian bugbear, and the Chinese bugbear, but rather to intensify the contacts between the various countries of the Indian Ocean, which, in spite of technological progress, are still too isolated, as much on the economic as on the cultural level.

The 'country' trade which, as we have seen, played such an important part in the ocean's history, is almost non-existent today. As Auber has noted:

Although the economic similarity of the ocean lands, despite the seasonal opposition of Cancer and Capricorn, spares them sterile rivalries, it tends, on the other hand, to isolate them dangerously. The interocean traffic is negligible compared to the traffic towards foreign countries. Apart from the rice trade in the zone of Cancer and that of oil in the regions of Cancer and Capricorn, the interzone trade is limited to very little: sodium carbonate, eucalyptus wood, leguminous plants, and cashew nuts. Ceylon has a small trade in peppers and dried vegetables with Kenya via Mombasa, and Indonesia received some canned goods from Madagascar and peas from the Cape, a small and unimportant trade.[6]

Besides this lack of interocean trade, however, the same writer notes the steady industrialisation of the Indian Ocean countries and sees it as an encouraging phenomenon. It shows, indeed, that the oceanic world is gradually freeing itself from the industrial yoke of Europe, and that it will produce more and more of its own consumer goods, which hitherto have had to be imported from very far away.

Kirk, who firmly believes in the possibility of an Indian Ocean community, thinks that economic factors will play a major part in the formation of such a community, but unless European or American capital continues to pour into that part of the world, a prospect eminently displeasing to Eastern nationalism, it is not clear how the influence of those factors could be brought to bear.[7]

On the cultural level everything has still to be done, but there is no doubt that the first steps have already been taken. Proof of this is the Pan-Indian Ocean Science Association, formed in 1951, which has brought together most of the Indian Ocean countries with a view to studying various scientific questions of common interest and which has already held three congresses, in India, Australia, and Madagascar. Other similar institutions are to be hoped for, institutions on the same pattern and devoted to a study of the Indian Ocean's history, sociology, linguistics and so on.[8]

Orientalism, of course, is a rather recent field and has

[6] J. Auber, *Histoire de l'Océan Indien*, Tananarive, 1954, p. 401.
[7] On this point see also Tibor Mende's essay *La Révolte de l'Asie*.
[8] An international association for the study of the history of the Indian Ocean is now being organised. A first meeting of historians and archivists was held in Madagascar in April 1960.

247

progressed far more slowly than geography or cartography. The École des Langues Orientales in Paris dates back only to 1795. The School of Oriental and African Studies in London was formed even more recently (1911). However, thanks to Unesco, very real progress has been made in promoting closer cultural ties between East and West. There is no doubt that Europe has been taking more and more of an interest in the East and that orientalist bookshops in the large European cities find no lack of either books or customers. On the other hand, it would seem that in most of the countries of Asia and Africa there has been a dearth of serious works showing Europe in its true light.

Is there hope, then, that the oceanic world, instead of being divided up into isolated or hostile elements, will in the future evolve towards unity, a condition essential to the complete development of all the regions that go to make it up, whether they be in the zone of Cancer or in the zone of Capricorn? Why not, indeed? It is interesting to note in this connection that it was on the very shores of the Indian Ocean, in that curious little 'colonial' town of Pondichéry where Dupleix formerly invented 'nabobism', that one of the great thinkers of modern India, Sri Aurobindo, the founder of an *ashram* where East and West live in perfect symbiosis, wrote a masterpiece during the interwar years: *The Ideal of Human Unity*, a book which may be counted among the classics of the Indian Ocean.

To the pessimists who think that the answer to the above question is No, we shall repeat what Sri Aurobindo himself said of his ideas in a postscript added to his book shortly before his death in 1950:

This view of the future may under present circumstances be stigmatised as a too facile optimism, but this turn of things is quite as possible as the more disastrous turn expected by the pessimists, since the cataclysm and crash of civilisation sometimes predicted by them need not at all be the result of a new war. Mankind has a habit of surviving the worse catastrophes created by its own errors or by the violent turns of Nature, and it must be so if there is any meaning in its existence, if its long history and continuous survival is not the accident of a fortuitously self-organising Chance. . . .[9]

[9] Sri Aurobindo, *The Ideal of Human Unity*, Pondichéry, 1950, p. 388.

Appendix: The Southern Sea

At the very beginning of this book, I pointed out the fact that geographers are not in agreement on the question as to whether the Indian Ocean should include the southern sea or be considered as separate from it.

To my mind, the southern sea, at least from a historical point of view, is clearly different in character from the Indian Ocean. Moreover, there is a whole literature devoted to the polar oceans which considers them as separate oceans and not as extensions of the other three.

However, since the Pan-Indian Ocean Science Association has recently decided to extend the southern limits of the Indian Ocean to Antarctica and to include in it islands located below 35° south latitude, it may be useful to give here, in the form of an appendix, a few brief indications about man's activities in that region since the Portuguese discovery of the islands of Saint Paul and Amsterdam in the sixteenth century.

That discovery was not followed up for some time, and it was not until the eighteenth century that three French navigators, Marion Dufresne, Crozet, and Kerguelen, explored most of the other islands in that region of the southern sea.

The islands comprise, in all, five groups spread out between 38° and 78° east longitude and between 38° and 50° south latitude. Of those five groups, three (the largest) today belong to France, and the two others are British possessions.

The three French groups are: (1) the group formed by the islands of Saint Paul and Amsterdam; (2) the Kerguelen archipelago; and (3) the Crozet Islands. All these islands as well as the part of Antarctica named Adélie Land have been established, by a law of 6 August 1955, as an autonomous territory of the French Union called the French Southern and Antarctic Lands.

First discovered by the Portuguese in the sixteenth century, and then explored in the seventeenth by the Dutchman Vlaming (1696) and in the eighteenth by the Frenchman d'Entrecasteaux (1792), Saint Paul and Amsterdam were fishing sites familiar to the colonists of the Mascarenes by the end of the eighteenth century. Two attempts at occupying them from the island of Réunion at the end of the nineteenth century ended in failure. The attempt was made again, successfully, in 1950.

The Kerguelen archipelago was discovered by Kerguelen in 1774 and visited again in 1776 by Cook, who called the archipelago Desolation Island, because it looked so uninviting. It is the largest of France's southern lands. Beginning from 1873, it was visited by several scientific missions, but not until 1950 was it also permanently occupied.

The Crozet archipelago was named after the French navigator Crozet, who discovered it in 1772. The climate is even more severe than that of the Kerguelen islands, and there is still no permanent settlement there.

The two British groups are: (1) the Marion–Prince Edward group about 450 nautical miles west of the Crozets; and (2) the Heard–Macdonald group, about 200 miles south-east of the Kerguelens.

Marion Island and Prince Edward Island were both discovered by Marion Dufresne in 1772 and explored once again by Cook in 1776. Subsequently, they were often visited by sealers and whalers. The South African government annexed them in 1948.[1] Heard Island and Macdonald Island were discovered in 1853 and 1854 respectively, by two captains of whalers, from whom they took their names. Today they belong to Australia.

It would seem that none of the British southern islands, with the possible exception of Prince Edward Island, is fit for human habitation. On the other hand, the islands of Amsterdam and Saint Paul as well as the Kerguelen archipelago are perfectly habitable. Since 1950, France has been carrying out a most interesting experiment there in human, animal, and vegetal acclimatisation, the stages of which can be followed in the journal *T.A.A.F.* (*Terres australes et antarctiques françaises*), published regularly by the French Overseas Ministry since October 1957.

The settlements that have been created on New Amsterdam and the Kerguelen Islands are neither simple antarctic stations nor

---

[1] See the account of that annexation in J. H. Marsh, *No Pathway Here*, Cape Town, 1948.

centres for purely scientific studies. In addition to radio-telegraphic, meteorological and medical stations, they include horticultural and stock farming services, which have already produced encouraging results, and public works sections, whose accomplishments are worthy of praise.[2]

At this point it is possible to affirm that the wind conditions of the Kerguelen archipelago do not present insuperable difficulties for maritime and aerial navigation. Although winds of about 120 or 125 miles per hour have been recorded, it must be recalled that the cyclones which periodically pass over the Mascarenes and Madagascar reach much higher velocities. After the Mascarenes, the Kerguelens would thus seem to be marked out for an important role in the air connections of the future in the southernmost regions of the Indian Ocean.

As for Antarctica itself, the assault on that vast continent began in 1821, the year the American captain John Davis reached it for the first time.[3] Carried on thereafter at a very slow pace, it was remarkably accelerated in the years following World War II.

Exploration of the region reached its highest point during the International Geophysical Year, which lasted eighteen months, from 1 July 1957 to 31 December 1958. During those eighteen months much work was accomplished, a fascinating account of which can be found in a recent book by Paul-Émile Victor, the director of the French Polar Expeditions.[4]

It would seem that the Antarctic continent possesses unsuspected resources and that modern technology can cope with the severity of the elements with good results. On the condition, of course, that twentieth-century man contrives to live on his own planet before going out to colonise others, Paul-Émile Victor even foresees the possibility of human settlement in the very heart of Antarctica in a fairly near future. When that is accomplished, the Southern Sea will, with good reason, occupy its place, after the Erythraean Sea and the *Mare Prasodum*, in the history of the Indian Ocean. For the time being, we can but hope that events will confirm the expectations of science.

[2] *T.A.A.F.*, October 1957, I, 7.

[3] The whole question of priority of sighting and discovery of the Antarctic Continent has been clouded by controversy. It seems that the Russian navigator Bellingshausen was the first person actually to sight part of the continent on 27 January 1820 and that the American John Davis probably made the first landing in the Hughes Bay area of Graham Land on 7 February 1821. (Information kindly supplied by the Scott Polar Research Institute of Cambridge.)

[4] P.-É. Victor, *Pôle Sud*, Paris, 1959.

Bibliography

There is still no comprehensive bibliography on the Indian Ocean, and the following list is not meant to constitute one. Only the main works consulted in the preparation of this book are here mentioned.

GENERAL

1. Comprehensive Works and Textbooks

BAGROW, L., *Die Geschichte der Kartographie*, Berlin, 1951.

BARTHOLD, V. V., *La Découverte de l'Asie: Histoire de l'orientalisme en Europe et en Russie*, trans. from the Russian by B. Nitikine, Paris, 1947.

COX, E. G., *A Reference Guide to the Literature of Travel*, 2 vols., Washington, 1935.

LACOUR-GAYET, J. (ed.), *Histoire du commerce*, 6 vols., Paris, 1950–55.

LAIRD CLOWES, C. S. L., *Sailing Ships: Their History and Development, as illustrated by the Collection of Ship-models in the Science Museum*, 2 vols., 4th edn., London, 1952.

PARIAS, L. H. (ed.), *Histoire universelle des explorations*, 3 vols., Paris, 1955.

PHILIPS, C. H. (ed.), *Handbook of Oriental History*, London, 1950.

PIRENNE, J., *Les Grands courants de l'histoire universelle*, 7 vols., Paris, 1950–56.

RUSSO, F., *Histoire des sciences et des techniques*, Paris, 1954.

TOYNBEE, A., *A Study of History*, 10 vols., London, 1934–54.

WRIGHT, J. K. and PLATT, E. T., *Aids to Geographical Research*, New York, 1947.

ZECHLIN, E., *Maritime Weltgeschichte*, Hamburg, 1947.

253

2. Periodicals

American Neptune (quarterly), Salem, Mass., 1941.
Annales, économies, sociétés, civilisations (quarterly), Paris, 1929.
Bulletin de L'Ecole Française d'Extrême-Orient (quarterly), Hanoi, 1901.
Economic History Review (monthly), London, 1927.
Geographical Journal (monthly), London, 1893.
Imago Mundi (published irregularly), Berlin, 1935.
Journal of Modern History (quarterly), Chicago, 1929.
Journal of the Royal Asiatic Society (quarterly), London, 1835.
Marine Rundschau (monthly), Berlin, 1890.
Mariner's Mirror (monthly), London, 1911.
Revue de L'Histoire des Colonies (quarterly), Paris, 1913.
Revue Historique, Paris, 1876.
T'Oung Pao (published irregularly), Leiden, 1890.

CHAPTER I: A NEGLECTED OCEAN

ALBION, R. G., *Maritime and Naval History: an Annotated Bibliography*, Mystic, Conn., 1955.
AUBER, J., *Histoire de l'océan indien*, Tananarive, 1954.
BRAUDEL, F., *La Méditerranée et le monde méditerranéen à l'époque de Philippe II*, Paris, 1949.
CODINE, J., *Mémoire géographique sur la mer des Indes*, Paris, 1868.
DRYGALSKI, E. VON, *Das Indische Ozeanreich*, Munich, 1935.
FAIRBRIDGE, R. W., 'Report on Limits of the Indian Ocean', *Proceedings of the Pan-Indian Ocean Science Association*, Perth (W. Australia), 1954.
FREEMAN, O. W., *Geography of the Pacific*, London, 1951.
GARDINER, J. S., 'The Indian Ocean', *Geographical Journal* (Oct. and Nov. 1906), pp. 313–32, 454–71.
KRUMMEL, O., *Handbuch der Ozeanographie*, 2 vols., 2nd edn., Stuttgart, 1907.
PANIKKAR, L. M., *India and the Indian Ocean*, London, 1945.
PEDELABORDE, P., *Les Moussons*, Paris, 1958.
POUJADE, J., *La Route des Indes et ses navires*, Paris, 1946.
RODENBERG, K., 'Der Indische Ozean in der Geschichte des Mittelalters und der Neuzeit', *Marine Rundschau*, 1904, pp. 763–92.
ROGERS, H., *The Indian Ocean*, London, 1932.
SCHOTT, G., *Geographie des Indischen und Stillen Ozeans*, Hamburg, 1935.
VALLAUX, C., *Geographie générale des mers*, Paris, 1933.
VILLIERS, A. J., *The Indian Ocean*, London, 1952.
WEULERSSE, J., *L'Afrique noire*, Paris, 1934.

BIBLIOGRAPHY

CHAPTER II: PUNT AND OPHIR

BEAZLEY, J. H., *The Dawn of Modern Geography to 1420*, 3 vols., 2nd edn., New York, 1949.
BREASTED, J. H., *A History of Egypt from the Earliest Times to the Persian Conquest*, London, 1920.
CARY, M. and WARMINGTON, E., *The Ancient Explorers*, London, 1929.
CATON-THOMPSON, G., *The Zimbabwe Culture*, Oxford, 1931.
CONTENAU, G., *La Civilisation phénicienne*, Paris, 1939.
GHIRSHMAN, R., *L'Iran, des origines à l'Islam*, Paris, 1951.
HERAS, H., *Studies in Proto-Indo-Mediterranean Culture*, Bombay, 1953.
HERMANN, J., *Les Révélations du Grand Océan*, 2 vols., Paris, 1927.
HERRMANN, P., *Conquest by Man. The Saga of Early Exploration and Discovery*, London, 1954.
HOURANI, E., *Arab Seafaring in the Indian Ocean*, Princeton, 1951.
KEANE, A. H., *The Gold of Ophir, Whence Brought and by Whom?*, London, 1901.
KENNEDY, J., 'Early Commerce between India and Babylon', *Journal of the Royal Asiatic Society*, 1898.
KOSTER, A., *Antike Seewesen*, Berlin, 1923.
MACIVER, D. R., *Mediaeval Rhodesia*, London, 1906.
MASPERO, G., 'De Quelques Navigations des Égyptiens sur les côtes de la mer Erythrée', *Revue historique*, 1878.
MOOKERJI, R. K., *A History of Indian Shipping*, 2nd edn., Bombay, 1957.
PAVER, B. G., *Zimbabwe Cavalcade*, 2nd edn., London, 1957.
WAGRET, P., 'Vers La Solution d'un mystère: les ruines de Zimbabwe et le test radio carbone', *Annales, économies, sociétés, civilisations*, X, 1955, 363–86.
WILSON, A. T., *The Persian Gulf: An Historical Sketch from Earliest Times to the Beginning of the 20th Cent.*, London, 1954.

CHAPTER III: THE ERYTHRAEAN SEA

BERTHELOT, A., *L'Asie ancienne centrale et sud-orientale, d'après Ptolémée*, Paris, 1930.
BOWEN, R. L., 'Origin and Diffusion of *Oculi*', *American Neptune*, XVII (1957), 262–91.
CHARLESWORTH, M. P., *Trade Routes and Commerce of the Roman Empire*, Cambridge, 1926.
FILLIOZAT, J., 'Les Echanges de l'Inde et de l'Empire romain aux premiers siècles de l'ère chrétienne', *Revue historique*, CCI (1949), 1–29.

GERINI, G. E., *Researches on Ptolemy's Geography of Eastern Asia*, London, 1909.

GIBBON, E., *History of the Decline and Fall of the Roman Empire*, 7 vols., London, 1900.

JOUVEAU-DUBREUIL, G., 'Articles sur l'antiquité de Pondichéry', *Revue historique de l'Inde française*, VIII, 1952.

MCCRINDLE, J. W., *Ancient India as Described in Classical Literature, Being a Collection of Greek and Latin Texts*, 2nd edn., Calcutta, 1927.

MALLERET, L., *L'Archéologie du delta du Mékong*, Paris, 1959.

RAWLINSON, A. G., *India and the Western World, from the Earliest Times to the Fall of Rome*, 2nd end., Cambridge, 1926.

RENAULT, J., *Jouveau-Dubreuil à Pondichéry*, Pondichéry, 1953.

SCHOFF, W. H. (ed.), *The Periplus of the Erythraean Sea*, New York, 1912.

VAN LEUR, J. C., *Indonesian Trade and Society*, The Hague, 1955.

WARMINGTON, E., *The Commerce between the Roman Empire and India*, Cambridge, 1928.

WHEELER, M., *Rome beyond the Imperial Frontiers*, London, 1954.

QUIGLEY, C., 'The Origin and Diffusion of *Oculi*: a Rejoinder', *American Neptune*, XVIII (1958), 25–58.

CHAPTER IV: FROM THE SASSANIDS
TO THE CALIPHS

CHRISTENSEN, A., *L'Iran sous les Sassanides*, Copenhagen, 1944.

COUPLAND, E., *East Africa and Its Invaders*, London, 1938.

DEVIC, M., *Le Pays des Zenjs ou la côte orientale d'Afrique au Moyen Age*, Paris, 1883.

FERRAND, G., *Voyage du marchand arabe Sulayman*, Paris, 1922.

FERRAND, G. (ed.), *Bibliothèque des géographes arabes*, 7 vols., Paris, 1928.

GRANDIDIER, H., *Histoire de la géographie de Madagascar*, 2 vols., Paris, 1885.

GUILLAIN, N., *Documents sur l'histoire, la geographie et le commerce de l'Afrique orientale*, 3 vols., Paris, 1856.

HITTI, P. K., *History of the Arabs from the Earliest Times to the Present*, 5th edn., London, 1953.

HOLLINGSWORTH, L. W., *A Short History of the East Coast of Africa*, London, 1929.

KIRKMAN, J., *The Arab City of Gedi*, London, 1954.

NAINAR, S. M. H., *Arab Geographers' Knowledge of Southern India*, Madras, 1942.

REINAUD, J. T., *Voyages faits par les Arabes et les Persans dans l'Inde et la Chine*, 2 vols., Paris, 1845.

SAUVAGET, J., *Introduction à l'histoire de l'Orient musulman*, Paris, 1943.
SAUVAGET, J. (ed.), *Relation de la Chine et de l'Inde (Voyage de Sulayman)*, Paris, 1948.
STRONG, S. A. (ed.), 'Chronicles of Kilwa', *Journal of the Royal Asiatic Society*, 1895.

CHAPTER V: GREATER INDIA

BASHAM, A. L., *The Wonder that was India*, London, 1954.
CODRINGTON, L. W., *A Short History of Ceylon*, London, 1939.
COEDÈS, G., *Les États hindouisés d'Indochine et d'Indonésie*, Paris, 1948.
HALL, D. G. E., *A History of South-East Asia*, London, 1955.
HARRISON, B., *South-East Asia: A Short History*, London, 1956.
LÉVI, S., *L'Inde civilisatrice*, Paris, 1938.
MAHALINGAM, T. V., *South Indian Polity*, Madras, 1955.
MAJUMDAR, R. C., *Ancient Indian Colonisation in South-East Asia*, Baroda, 1955.
MAJUMDAR, R. C. (ed.), *An Advanced History of India*, 2nd edn., London, 1956.
MORELAND, W. H., and CHATTERJEE, A. C., *A Short History of India*, 4th edn., London, 1957.
NILAKANTA SASTRI, *History of Sri Vijaya*, Madras, 1949.
NILAKANTA SASTRI, *History of South India*, Madras, 1956.
VAN OORDT, J. F., *Who Were the Builders of the Great Zimbabwe?*, Cape Town, 1909.
WALES, H. G. Q., *The Making of Greater India*, London, 1951.
WALES, H. G. Q., *Prehistory and Religion in South-East Asia*, London, 1957.

CHAPTER VI: THE ROLE OF THE CHINESE

BAPAT, P. V. (ed.), *2,500 Years of Buddhism*, New Delhi, 1956.
CHAU-JU-KUA, *Chu-Fan-Chi*, trans. F. Hirth and W. Rockhill, St. Petersburg, 1911.
CORDIER, H., *Histoire générale de la Chine et de ses relations avec les pays étrangers*, 4 vols., Paris, 1920–21.
DONNELLY, I. A., 'Early Chinese Ships and Trade', *Mariner's Mirror*, 11 (1925), 344–54.
DUYVENDAK, J. J. L., *China's Discovery of Africa*, London, 1949.
FA-HSIEN, *Foe-Koue-Ki*, trans. A. Rémusat, Paris, 1836.
GROUSSET, R., *Histoire de la Chine*, Paris, 1942.
HIRTH, F., *China and the Roman Orient*, Leipzig, 1885.
HIUEN-TSANG, *Si-yu-ki*, trans. S. Beal, London, 1906.

BIBLIOGRAPHY

I-TSING, *Voyages*, trans. E. Chavannes, Paris, 1894.

LATOURETTE, K. S., *The Chinese, Their History and Culture*, 2 vols., New York and London, 1934.

MILLS, J. V., 'Notes on Early Chinese Voyages,' *Journal of the Royal Asiatic Society*, April 1951.

PARIS, P., 'Quelques Dates pour une histoire de la jonque chinoise,' *Bulletin de l'Ecole Française d'Extrême-Orient*, XLI, No. 1. (1952), 267–78.

PELLIOT, P., 'Les Grands Voyages maritimes chinois au début du XV*e* siècle,' *T'oung Pao* (1933).

PELLIOT, P., *A Short History of the Far East*, New York, 1951.

YULE, H., *Cathay and the Way Thither*, London, 1866.

YULE, H. (ed.), *The Book of Marco Polo*, London, 1875.

CHAPTER VII: QUEST FOR THE ORIENT

BRAGADIN, M., *Histoire des républiques maritimes italiennes*, Paris, 1956.

COOLEY, W. D., *History of Maritime and Inland Discoveries*, 3 vols., London, 1830–31.

DIEHL, C., *Une Republique patricienne: Venise*, Paris, 1915.

ESTANCELIN, L., *Recherches sur les voyages et découvertes des navigateurs normands en Afrique, dans les Indes orientales et en Amérique*, Paris, 1832.

HART, H. H., *Sea Road to the Indies*, New York, 1950.

HEYD, W., *Histoire du commerce du Levant au Moyen Age*, Paris, 1885–1886.

JULIEN, C. A., *Les Voyages de découvertes et les premiers établissements (XVe–XVIe siècles)*, Paris, 1948.

LA RONCIÈRE, C. DE, *La Découverte de l'Afrique au Moyen Age*, 3 vols., Cairo, 1935.

LA VARENDE, J. DE, *La Navigation sentimentale*, Paris, 1954.

LEMERLE, P., 'Sur le Moyen Age oriental', *Annales, économies, sociétés, civilisations*, XII (1957), 639–41.

PENROSE, B., *Travel and Discovery in the Renaissance, 1420–1620*, Harvard, 1952.

REEVE, S. A., *The Evolution of Social Crises*, New York, 1933.

CHAPTER VIII: THE CONQUISTADORES

AXELSON, E., *South-East Africa, 1488–1530*, 2nd edn., London.

BOTELHO DE SOUSA, A., *Subsidios para a historia militar maritima de India*, 4 vols., Lisbon, 1947.

BOXER, C. R., *Fidalgos in the Far East*, The Hague, 1948.

BIBLIOGRAPHY

CORTESÃO, A., *Cartografia e cartografos portugueses dos seculos XV e XVI*, 2 vols., Lisbon, 1935.

CORTESÃO, A. (ed.), *The Suma Oriental of Tome Pirés*, London, 1944.

CORTESÃO, J., *L'Expansion des Portugais dans l'histoire de la civilisation*, Antwerp, 1930.

DANVERS, F. C., *The Portuguese in India*, London, 1894.

HAMILTON, G., *In the Wake of da Gama. The Story of Portuguese Pioneers in East Africa, 1497–1729*, London, 1951.

KAMMERER, A., *La Mer Rouge, l'Abyssinie et l'Arabie aux XVIe et XVIIe siècles et la cartographie des portulans*, 3 vols., Cairo, 1937–52.

PRESTAGE, E., *The Portuguese Pioneers*, London, 1933.

UHDEN, R., 'The Oldest Portuguese Original Chart of the Indian Ocean', *Imago mundi*, III (1939), 7–11.

VISDELOU-GUIMBEAU, G. DE, *La Découverte des îles Mascareignes*, Port Louis, Mauritius, 1948.

WHITEWAY, S., *The Rise of Portuguese Power in India (1497–1550)*, London, 1899.

CHAPTER IX: THE GENTLEMEN MERCHANTS

BHATTACHARYA, S., *The East India Company and the Economy of Bengal*, London, 1954.

BONNASSIEUX, P., *Les Grandes Compagnies de commerce*, Paris, 1892.

CASTONNET DES FOSSES, H. L., *L'Inde française avant Dupleix*, Paris, 1883.

CHARLIAT, P. J., *Trois siècles d'économie maritime française*, Paris, 1931.

DALGARD, S., *Danish Enterprise and Mauritius Ebony, 1621–1624*, Copenhagen, 1956.

ELDRIDGE, F. B., *The Background of Eastern Sea Power*, 2nd edn., New York, 1948.

FURBER, H., *John Company at Work*, Cambridge (Mass.), 1948; reprinted 1952.

GLAMANN, K., *Dutch Asiatic Trade, 1620–1740*, The Hague, 1958.

HECKSHER, E. F., *Mercantilism*, 2 vols., 2nd edn., London, 1956.

KRABBE, J. T., *Histoire du Denmark, des origines jusqu'à 1945*, Paris, 1950.

MUKERJI, R., *The Rise and Fall of the East India Company*, 2nd edn., London, 1955.

PHILIPS, C. H., *The East India Company, 1784–1834*, Manchester, 1940.

VAN DER LINDEN, H., *Histoire de l'expansion coloniale du Danemark XVIIe et XVIIIe siècles*, Brussels, 1911.

VILLEY, D., *Petite Histoire des grandes doctrines économiques*, Paris, 1944.

WEBER, H., *La Compagnie française des Indes (1604–1875)*, Paris, 1904.

CHAPTER X: THE INTERREGNUM

BALLARD, G. A., *Rulers of the Indian Ocean*, New York, 1928.
BIDDULPH, J., *The Pirates of Malabar*, London, 1907.
DELORT, T., *La Première Escadre de la France dans les Indes*, Paris, 1876.
DESCHAMPS, H., *Les Pirates à Madagascar aux XVIIe et XVIIIe siècles*, Paris, 1949.
GODECHOT, J., *Histoire de l'Atlantique*, Paris, 1947.
GOSSE, P., *The Pirates' Who's Who*, London, 1924.
GOSSE, P., *The History of Piracy*, London, 1934.
GROTIUS, H., *The Freedom of the Seas or the Right which Belongs to the Dutch to Take Part in the East Indian Trade*, English edn., New York, 1916.
LOUGNON, A., *L'Ile Bourbon sous la Régence*, Paris, 1956.
PRINGLE, P., *Jolly Roger. The Story of the Great Age of Piracy*, London, 1953.
VALENTIJN, F., *Oud en Nieuw Oost Indien*, 8 vols., Amsterdam, 1724–1726.
VLEKKE, B. H. M., *Nusantara: A History of the East Indian Archipelago*, Cambridge (Mass.), 1943.
WOOD, G. A., *The Discovery of Australia*, London, 1922.

CHAPTER XI: THE ANGLO-FRENCH CONFLICT

BAMFORD, P. W., *Forests and French Sea-Power, 1660–1789*, Toronto, 1956.
BOURDE DE LA ROGERIE, H., *Les Bretons aux îles de France et de Bourbon au XVIIe et au XVIIIe siècle*, Rennes, 1934.
CALMON-MAISON, M., *L'Amiral d'Estaing (1729–1794)*, Paris, 1910.
CRÉPIN, P., *Mahé de Labourdonnais*, Paris, 1922.
CUNAT, C., *Saint-Malo illustré par ses marins*, Rennes, 1857.
GARNERAY, L., *Voyages de Louis Garneray*, 2 vols., Paris, 1853.
JOUVEAU-DUBREUIL, G., *Dupleix*, Pondichéry, 1941.
LE DUC, SAINT-ELME, *Ile de France: documents pour servir à son histoire civile et militaire*, Port Louis, Mauritius, 1925.
MAHÉ DE LABOURDONNAIS, B. F., *Memoire des îles de France et de Bourbon*, ed. A. Lougnon and A. Toussaint, Paris, 1937.
MALLESON, G. B., *Final French Struggles in India and the Indian Seas*, London, 1878.
MARTINEAU, A., *Dupleix et l'Inde française*, Paris, 1920–28.
PARKINSON, C. NORTHCOTE, *War in the Eastern Seas, 1793–1815*, London, 1954.

BIBLIOGRAPHY

PRENTOUT, H., *L'Île de France sous Decaen*, Paris, 1901.
ROBIDOU, F., *Les Derniers Corsaires malouins*, Rennes, 1919.
TRAMOND, J., *Manuel d'histoire maritime de la France des origines à 1815*, Paris, 1948.
WADIA, R. A., *The Bombay Dockyard and the Wadia Master Builders*, Bombay, 1955.

CHAPTER XII: SEARCHING FOR GOLD
AND NEW HORIZONS

APRÈS DE MANNEVILLETTE, N. D. D', *Le Neptune oriental*, Paris, 1745 (2nd edn., 1775).
BLANCARD, P., *Manuel du commerce des Indes orientales et de la Chine*, Paris, 1806.
BROSSES, C. DE, *Histoire des navigations aux Terres australes*, 2 vols., Paris, 1756.
COTTON, EVAN, *East Indiamen: The East India Company's Maritime Service*, London, 1949.
GREENBERG, M., *British Trade and the Opening of China*, Cambridge, 1951.
GREENBIE, S. and M. B., *Gold of Ophir: the China Trade in the Making of America*, New York, 1937.
HEAWOOD, E., *A History of Geographical Discovery in the Seventeenth and Eighteenth Centuries*, Cambridge, 1912.
HICKEY, W., *Memoirs of William Hickey (1749–1809)*, 4 vols., London, 1913.
HOWE, S. E., *In Quest of Spices*, London, 1939.
LATOURETTE, K. S., *Voyages of American Ships to China, 1784–1844*, New Haven, 1927.
LAUDE, N., *La Compagnie d'Ostende et son activité coloniale au Bengale (1725–1730)*, Brussels, 1944.
LY-TIO-FANE, M., *Mauritius and the Spice Trade: the Odyssey of Pierre Poivre*, Port Louis, Mauritius, 1958.
MARGUET, F., *Histoire générale de la navigation du XVe au XXe siècle*, Paris, 1931.
MILBURN, W., *Oriental Commerce*, 2 vols., London, 1813.
PARKINSON, C. NORTHCOTE, *The Trade Winds*, London, 1948.
PHILLIPS, J. D., *Salem and the Indies*, Boston, 1948.
RASCH, A., *Dansk Handel på Isle de France*, Copenhagen, 1953.
SPEAR, T. G. P., *The Nabobs: a Study of the Social Life of the English in Eighteenth Century India*, London, 1932.
TOUSSAINT, A., *Early American Trade with Mauritius*, Port Louis, Mauritius, 1954.

18   HIO

CHAPTER XIII: BRITISH MARITIME SUPREMACY

CLARK, A. H., *The Clipper Ship Era, 1843–1869*, New York, 1911.

COLIN, A., *La Navigation commerciale au XIXe siècle*, Paris, 1901.

CUMPSTON, I. M., *Indians Overseas in British Territories, 1834–1854*, Oxford, 1953.

DOBB, M., *Studies in the Development of Capitalism*, London, 1947.

KIRK, W., 'Shipbuilding in Southern Asia Ports, 1800–1820', *Mariner's Mirror*, 39 (1953), 266–75.

KONDAPI, C., *Indians in the Empire Overseas, 1838–1949*, Bombay, 1951.

LACROIX, A., *Les Derniers Grands Voiliers*, Paris, 1950.

LUBBOCK, B., *The China Clippers*, 2nd edn., Glasgow, 1914.

MORISON, S. E., *The Maritime History of Massachussetts, 1783–1860*, Boston, 1921.

PRADT, M. DE, *Les Trois Âges des colonies*, 2 vols., Paris, 1802.

PURCELL, V., *The Chinese in South-east Asia*, Oxford, 1951.

ROSE, J. H. *et al.* (ed.), *The Cambridge History of the British Empire*, 7 vols., Cambridge, 1929–59.

SÉE, H., *Les Origines du capitalisme moderne*, 5th edn., 1946.

SMITH, A., *The Wealth of Nations*, London, 1776.

VAN DEN BERG, L. W. C., *Le Hadhramaut et les colonies arabes dans l'archipel indien*, Batavia, 1886.

WIENS, H. J., *China's March into the Tropics*, Washington, 1952.

CHAPTER XIV: THE SUEZ CANAL

ANSTEY, V., *The Trade of the Indian Ocean*, London, 1929.

ARDEHALI, A., *The Suez Canal, Its History and Economic Development*, Worcester (Mass.), 1952.

BEATTY, C., *Ferdinand de Lesseps*, London, 1956.

BRUNSCHWIG, H., *L'Expansion allemande outre-mer du XVe siècle à nos jours*, Paris, 1957.

DUFFY, J., *Portuguese Africa*, London, 1959.

EDGAR-BONNET, G., *Ferdinand de Lesseps*, Paris, 1951.

GOLDSMITH, F., *Telegraph and Travel*, London, 1874.

GRAHAM, G. S., 'The Ascendancy of the Sailing Ship, 1850–1885', *Economic History Review*, IX (August 1956), 74–88.

JULIEN, C. A., *Histoire de l'Afrique*, Paris, 1941.

RITT, O., *Histoire de l'isthme de Suez*, Paris, 1869.

RODENBERG, K., 'Der Indische Ozean in der Geschichte des Mittelalters und der Neuzeit', *Marine Rundschau* (July 1904), 763–92.

SCHRAMM, P. E., *Deutschland und Übersee*, Brunswick, 1950.

BIBLIOGRAPHY

VERNEAUX, R., *L'Industrie des transports maritimes au XIXe siècle et au commencement du XXe siècle*, 2 vols., Paris, 1903.

WILLIAMSON, J. A., *A Short History of British Expansion*, 2 vols., London, 1950.

CHAPTER XV: CANCER AND CAPRICORN

AUROBINDO, SRI, *The Ideal of Human Unity*, 2nd edn., Pondichéry, 1950.

BERREBY, J. J., *La Péninsule arabique, Terre Sainte de l'Islam et empire du pétrole*, Paris, 1958.

CARRINGTON, C. E., *The British Overseas. Exploits of a Nation of Shop-keepers*, Cambridge, 1950.

FISHER, W. B., *The Middle East. A Physical, Social and Regional Geography*, London, 1950.

GROUSSET, R., *Le Réveil de l'Asie*, Paris, 1924.

GROUSSET, R. and DENIKER, G., *La Face de l'Asie, données permanentes et facteurs de renouvellement*, Paris, 1958.

KIRK, W., 'Indian Ocean Community', *Scottish Geographical Magazine*, LXVII (1951), 161-77.

LÉGER, F., *Les Influences occidentales dans la Revolution de l'Orient: Inde, Malaisie, Chine (1850-1950)*, 2 vols., Paris, 1955.

MENDE, T., *La Révolte de l'Asie*, Paris, 1951.

PANIKKAR, L., *Asia and Western Dominance*, 2nd edn., London, 1954.

RAMACHANDRA RAO, P. K., *India and Ceylon*, Bombay, 1954.

SERVOISE, R., 'Perspectives eurafricaines et afro-asiatiques', *Comptes rendus des séances de l'Académie des Sciences d'outre-mer*, XVIII (May-July 1958), 222-3.

SIEGFRIED, A., *Voyage aux Indes*, Paris, 1951.

SPANZENBERG, H., *Die Veränderungen des Seeverkehrs im Indischen Ozean seit dem Weltkriege*, Stuttgart, 1930.

RECENT PUBLICATIONS

ALBION, R. G., *Naval and maritime history. An annotated bibliography*, 3rd edn., revised, Connecticut, 1963.

AXELSON, E., *Portuguese in South East Africa, 1600-1700*, Johannesburg, 1960.

BENNETT, N. R., *Studies in East African History*, Boston, 1963.

BEURDELEY, M., *Porcelaine de la Compagnie des Indes*, Fribourg, 1962.

BOXER, C. R., *Four Centuries of Portuguese Expansion, 1415-1825, a Succinct Survey*, Johannesburg, 1961.

BOXER, C. R. and AZEVEDO, C. DE, *Fort Jesus and the Portuguese in Mombasa, 1593–1729*, London, 1960.

COEDÈS, G., *Les États hindouisés d'Indochine et d'Indonésie*, 2nd edn.

COOLHAAS, P. W., *A Critical Survey of Studies on Dutch Colonial History*, Revised edn., The Hague, 1960.

CROWLEY, F. K., *Australia's Western Third: A History of Western Australia from the First Settlements to Modern Times*, London, 1960.

DAVIDSON, B., *Old Africa Rediscovered*, London, 1959.

DAVIES, D. W., *A Primer of Dutch Seventeenth Century Overseas Trade*, The Hague, 1961.

DEFOS DU RAU J., *L'île de la Réunion. Etude de géographie humaine*, Bordeaux, 1960.

DERMIGNY, L., *Cargaisons indiennes, Solier et Cie, 1781–1793*, 2 vols., Paris, 1959–60.

DESCHAMPS, H., *Histoire de Madagascar*, Paris, 1960.

DIVINE, D., *These Splendid Ships. The Story of the Peninsular and Oriental Line*, London, 1960.

FREEMAN-GRENVILLE, G. S. P., *The Medieval History of the Coast of Tanganyika with Special Reference to Recent Archaeological Discoveries*, London, 1962.

GILL, C., *Merchants and Mariners of the 18th Century*, London, 1961.

GRAY, SIR JOHN, *History of Zanzibar from the Middle Ages to 1856*, London, 1962.

LOBATO, A., *A expansão Portugueza em Moçambique de 1498 a 1530*, 3 vols., Lisbon, 1954–60.

LONGRIGG, S. H., *Oil in the Middle East. Its Discovery and Development*, 2nd edition, London, 1961.

MARLOWE, J., *The Persian Gulf in the Twentieth Century*, London, 1963.

MARSTON, E., *Britain's Imperial Role in the Red Sea Area, 1800–1878*, Hamden, 1961.

MEILINK-ROELOFSZ, M. A. P., *Asian Trade and European Influence in the Indonesian Archipelago between 1500 and about 1630*, The Hague, 1962.

MULLER, F., *Deutschland-Zanzibar-Ostafrika: Geschichte einer Deutschen Kolonialeroberung 1884–1890*, Berlin, 1959.

OLIVER, R. and MATHEW, G., *History of East Africa*, Oxford, 1963.

PARRY, J. H., *The Age of Reconnaissance. Discovery, Exploration and Settlement 1450 to 1650*, London, 1963.

PERES, D., *Descobrimentos Portugueses*, Lisbon, 1959.

PHILIPS, C. H., *The East India Company, 1784–1834*, 2nd edn., Manchester, 1961.

RAYCHAUDHURI, T., *Jan Company in Coromandel 1605–1690; a Study in the Interrelations of European Commerce and Traditional Economies*, The Hague, 1962.

SALETORE, A., *India's Diplomatic Relations with the East*, Bombay, 1960.

SERJEANT, R. B., *The Portuguese off the South Arabian Coast: Hadrami Chronicles; with Yemeni and European Accounts of Dutch pirates off Mocha in the Seventeenth Century*, Oxford, 1963.

SPEAR, P., *The Nabobs. A Study of the Social Life of the English in Eighteenth Century India*, 2nd edn., London, 1963.

STRANDES, J., *The Portuguese Period in East Africa*, trans. from the German by J. F. Wallwork, 2nd edn., Nairobi, 1961.

TREGONNING, K. G., *A History of Modern Malaya*, London, 1964.

VAN LOHUIZEN, J., *The Dutch East India Company and Mysore*, The Hague, 1961.

WHEATLEY, P., *The Golden Khersonese: Studies in the Historical Geography of the Malay Peninsula before A.D. 1500*, Kuala Lumpur, 1961.

WRIGHT, H. R. C., *East-Indian Economic Problems of the Age of Cornwallis and Raffles*, London, 1961.

Memorable Dates

1. *The Age of Antiquity* (*c.* 2900–30 B.C.)

c. 2900–2700	First and Second Egyptian dynasties. First Egyptian expeditions to Punt.
2637–2582	Reign of Sargon I. First Sumerian expeditions in the Persian Gulf.
2600–2300	Harappa and Mohenjo-Daro civilisations in India.
1490–1475	Reign of Hatshepsut, queen of Egypt. Frescoes of Deir el-Bahari.
1090	End of Egyptian expeditions to Punt.
973–933	Reign of Solomon (Israel). Phoenician expeditions to Ophir.
704–681	Reign of Sennacherib (Assyria). Phoenicians in the Persian Gulf.
650	Beginnings of the Sabaeans in Southern Arabia.
609–593	Reign of Necho II (Egypt). Phoenician circumnavigation of Africa (*c.* 600).
563–483 (?)	Life of the Buddha.
550	Beginnings of Median ascendancy in Persia.
521–485	Reign of Darius I (Persia).
510	Scylax's sea voyage.

c. 500	Maritime relations between India and Mesopotamia.
c. 450	Herodotus' *History* composed.
337–323	Reign of Alexander the Great.
331	Founding of Alexandria.
325	Nearchus' sea voyage.
305–285	Reign of Ptolemy I. Exploration of the Red Sea.
302	Commercial treaty between Seleucus Nicator and the Indian king Chandragupta.
285–246	Reign of Ptolemy Philadelphus. Founding of Arsinoë and Berenice.
247–221	Reign of Ptolemy Euergetes I. Founding of Adulis.
255	Beginnings of the Parthians.
119–111	Eudoxus of Cyzicus' voyages.
115	Himyarites succeed Sabaeans in Southern Arabia.
57	Height of the Parthian power.

2. *From the Romans to Islam* (30 B.C.–A.D. 622)

30	Roman Conquest of Egypt.
29	Beginning of Augustus' reign.
25	Augustus received an Indian embassy.
c. 20	Utilisation of the Monsoon.
1	Beginning of the Christian era.
25	Death of the geographer Strabo.
c. 78	Arrival of first Indian colonists in Java.
79	Death of Pliny the Elder.
c. 80	*The Periplus of the Erythraean Sea.*
105–06	Roman conquest of Nabataean Arabia.
107	Embassy sent to India by Trajan.
115	Roman conquest of Mesopotamia.
161–80	Reign of Marcus Aurelius.
226	Roman traders in Canton.
228	Beginnings of Sassanid kingdom.
320–55	Reign of Ezanas, King of Axum.
324–37	Reign of Constantine.
324	Founding of Constantinople.
329	Conversion of Axum to Christianity.
340	Decline of the Himyarites in Southern Arabia.
394	Partition of the Roman Empire between Arcadius and Honorius.
399–414	Fa-Hsien's voyages to India.
400	Java converted to Buddhism.
527–65	Reign of the emperor Justinian.

529	Axumite invasion of Yemen.
c. 530	Byzantine commercial deals with the kingdom of Axum.
531–79	Reign of Khosrau I. Climax of Sassanid power.
560	Cosmas Indicopleustes' *Christian Topography*.
570	The Sassanids chase the Axumites out of Yemen.
589–628	Reign of Khosrau II. The Sassanids in trouble.
c. 610	Beginning of Mohammed's preaching at Mecca.

3. *From Islam to the Portuguese* (622–1498)

622	Mohammed's flight to Medina. Birth of Islam.
629–45	Hiuen-Tsang's voyage to India.
632–738	Expansion of Islam.
634	Founding of Basra.
639	Arab conquest of Egypt.
651	Death of the last of the Sassanids. Arab conquest of Persia.
661–749	Omeyyad Dynasty.
671	First Arab voyage to Canton.
671–95	I-Tsing's voyage to India.
c. 675	Beginnings of Sumatran kingdom of Shrivijaya.
711	Penetration of Islam in India.
739	First Moslem migration to the coast of Africa.
750–1258	Abbasid Dynasty.
758	Closing of Canton to foreign merchants (reopened in 792).
762	Baghdad, capital of the Abbassids.
773	First use of Arabic numerals.
786–808	Reign of the Abbasid caliph Harun al-Rashid.
802	Birth of the Khmer kingdom of Angkor.
c. 850	Beginnings of Chola power.
850–900	Temples of Borobudur in Java.
c. 851	Suleiman's *Silsilat-al-Tawarikh* composed.
878	Massacre of foreign merchants at Canton.
917	Second Moslem migration to the coast of Africa.
c. 960	*Ajaib al Hind* composed.
968–1171	Fatimid Dynasty in Egypt.
975	Third Moslem migration to the coast of Africa. Beginnings of the Zenj empire.
1005	Conquest of Ceylon by the Chola.
1025	Chola expeditions against Shrivijaya.
1050	Conquest of Baghdad by the Seljuk Turks.

1070	Decline of the Chola.
c. 1150	Idrisi's *Geography*.
1177	Beginnings of the search for Prester John.
c. 1180	Height of the Sumatran kingdom of Shrivijaya.
1182	Renaud de Chatillon's incursion into the Red Sea.
1222	Beginnings of the Javanese kingdom of Singhasari.
1225	*Chu-Fan-Chi* composed.
1254–69	Polo brothers' first voyage to China.
1258	Conquest of Baghdad by the Mongols.
1271–85	Polo brothers' second voyage to China.
1279–94	Kublai Khan's reign in China.
1293	Beginnings of the Javanese kingdom of Madjapahit.
1298	Publication of Marco Polo's account.
1320	Venetian commercial treaty with Persia.
1330	Founding of the port of Ormuz.
1336	Beginnings of the Dravidian kingdom of Vijayanagar.
1368	Beginnings of the Ming Dynasty in China.
1381	Ottoman push in Asia.
1385–1433	Reign of John I of Portugal.
1389	Decline of the Javanese kingdom of Madjapahit.
1405–31	Cheng-Ho's expeditions to the Indian Ocean.
1423	Height of Venetian commercial expansion.
1453	Conquest of Constantinople by the Ottoman Turks.
1460	Death of Prince Henry the Navigator.
1485	Dias rounds the Cape of Good Hope.
1486	Voyage of Covilham and Payva to the Indian Ocean.

4. *Portuguese Ascendancy* (1498–1641)

1498	Vasco da Gama at Calicut.
1503	Albuquerque in the Indies.
1504	Venice forms an alliance with the Sultan of Egypt and the king of Calicut against the Portuguese.
1507	Defeat of Mir Hussein's fleet.
1509–29	Climax of Portuguese cartography.
1510	Portuguese conquest of Goa.
1511	Portuguese conquest of Malacca.
1512–15	Tome Pirés' *Suma Oriental* composed.
1516	Turkish conquest of Egypt.
1519–21	Magellan's voyage round the world.
1526	Baber founds the Mogul empire in northern India.
1528	First Portuguese expedition against Mombasa.
1529	Hispano-Portuguese compromise on the Moluccas.

1538	Turks occupy Aden.
1542	St. Francis Xavier in the Indies.
1551	Defeat of Piri Reis' fleet.
1553	Defeat of Sidi Ali's fleet.
1557	Portuguese establish themselves in Macao.
1562–1605	Reign of the Mogul emperor Akbar.
1565	Battle of Talikot. Destruction of the Dravidian kingdom of Vijayanagar.
1569	Kunjali's victory over the Portuguese.
1572	Publication of Camoens' *Lusiads*.
1580	Annexation of Portugal by Spain.
1585–89	Ali Bey's cruises along the coast of Africa.
1591	First English expedition to the Indies.
1592	Portuguese finally subjugate Mombasa.
1595	First Dutch expedition to the Indies.
1600–20	Founding of the first East India trading companies.
1607–65	Activities of the *Muggs* and *Feringhis* in the Bay of Bengal.
1609	Grotius states the principle of freedom of the seas.
1611	Brouwer's discovery of a direct route from the Cape to the Indies.
1616	English in Surat.
1619	Founding of Batavia.
1621	Danes in Tranquebar.
1621	Publication of the *Wu Pei Chih*.
1622	Reconquest of Ormuz by the Persians.
1623	'Amboina massacre'.
1638	Dutch occupy Mauritius.
1639	Founding of Madras.
1640	Portugal separated from Spain.

5. *The Interregnum* (1641–1815)

1641	Dutch conquest of Malacca.
1642	Tasman's voyages.
1643	First French settlement in Madagascar.
1645	Beginnings of Dutch cartography.
1648	Reconquest of Masqat by the Arabs.
1650–80	Dutch conquer Java.
1651	Creation of the Society of Foreign Missions.
1652	Dutch at the Cape of Good Hope.
1652–54	First Anglo-Dutch War.
1668	Bombay granted to English East India Company.
1670	Expedition of Admiral de la Haye to the Indies.

1674	Founding of Pondichéry.
1683–1758	Activities of the Maratha pirates.
1685–1726	Activities of the pirates of Madagascar.
1687	French in Siam.
1690	Founding of Calcutta.
1698	Arab reconquest of the coast of Africa.
1702–13	War of the Spanish Succession.
1707	Death of Aurangzeb. Beginning of the decline of the Moguls.
1718	Creation of the Ostend Company.
1735–46	La Bourdonnais in the Mascarenes.
1740	Dupleix becomes 'nabob'.
1740–48	War of the Austrian Succession.
1745	First edition of the *Neptune oriental*.
1751	Abbé de la Caille at the Cape of Good Hope.
1753	Nutmegs introduced in Île de France.
1756–63	Seven Years' War.
1757	Battle of Plassey.
1765–67	Clive, governor of Bengal.
1768–71	Cook's first voyage to the southern seas.
1769	French East Indies Company abolished.
1770	French colonisation of the Seychelles.
c. 1770	Development of route to China.
1771–73	Kerguelen's voyage to the southern seas.
1772–85	Warren Hastings, governor of Bengal.
1778–83	American Revolutionary War spreads to the Indies. Suffren's campaigns.
1784	First American voyage to the East.
1788	British occupation of Australia.
1793–1805	Height of privateering.
1798	Bonaparte's expedition to Egypt.
1803	Decaen in the Mascarenes.
1805	Final conquest of the Cape by the British.
1810–11	Conquest of the Mascarenes and Java by the British.
1812–15	War between the United States and England.

6. *British Ascendancy* (1815–1945)

1815	Vienna treaties.
1819	Raffles at Singapore.
1824	Anglo-Dutch Convention.
1825	First steamship connection Falmouth–Calcutta.
1834	Beginnings of the coolie trade.
1839	British in Aden.

1840–42	First opium war.
1841	British annexation of Natal. The Sultan of Masqat established himself at Zanzibar.
1842	Beginnings of the Peninsular and Oriental Steam Navigation Company.
c. 1845	Height of the tea clippers.
1848–49	Krapf and Rebmann in East Africa.
1850	Maury's hydrographic work.
1851	Discovery of gold in Victoria (Australia).
1853	First railway in India.
1854	Opening of Japanese ports to Europeans.
1854–56	Livingstone explores East Africa.
1057–58	Indian Mutiny. Suppression of East India Company.
1869	Opening of the Suez Canal.
1870	First submarine telegraph cable connecting India to Egypt.
1873	England buys 176,000 shares in the Suez Canal.
1876	Queen Victoria, Empress of India.
1881	Steamship connection Plymouth–Melbourne via the Cape in 42 days.
1882	British intervention in Egypt.
1883	Commercial exploitation of Indonesia's oil fields.
1884	Peters in East Africa.
1884–85	British annexation of Burma.
1885	Decline of the great sailing ships.
1886	Discovery of gold in the Transvaal.
1887	French conquest of Indo-China.
1888	First petrol engine.
1889	Italian protectorate over Somaliland.
1890	Anglo-German Convention on East Africa. British protectorate over Zanzibar.
1892	Discovery of gold at Coolgardie (Australia).
1895	French conquest of Madagascar.
1896	Italian defeat in Ethiopia.
1899–1902	Anglo-Boer War.
1900	Australia becomes a dominion.
c. 1904	First use of fuel oil for ships.
1904–05	Russo-Japanese War. Battle of Tsushima (1905).
1907	Founding of Shell Petroleum Co.
1910	South Africa becomes a dominion.
1911	Anglo-Japanese naval Convention.
1914–18	World War I.
1919	Agitation in India.
1921–22	Washington naval treaties.

1922	End of British protectorate in Egypt.
1930	Beginning of Sino-Japanese War.
1932	England abandons free trade.
1934	Beginnings of Cables and Wireless Co.
1935	Italy attacks Ethiopia.
1936	Creation of the Italian Empire of East Africa. German–Japanese pact.
1939–45	World War II.
1942	Battles of Java and the Coral Sea.

7. *The Present* (1945–   )

1945	Independence of Indonesia.
1947	Independence of India and Pakistan.
1948	Independence of Ceylon and Burma.
1949	Communist victory in China.
1950	Publication of Colombo Plan.
1951	First Congress of the Pan-Indian Ocean Science Association held at Bangalore.
1952	Mau-Mau rising in East Africa.
1954	Independence of Indo-China. Creation of SEATO.
1955	Bandung Conference.
1956	Anglo-French intervention in Suez.
1957	Independence of Malaya.
1959	Independence of Madagascar. Agitation in East Africa.
1960	First congress on the history of the Indian Ocean, held at Antananarivo.
1960	Formation of Somali Republic.
1961	First conference of South-east Asian historians. Annexation of Goa by India.
1962	Independence of Uganda and Tanganyika. Chinese invasion of India. Rebellion in Yemen.
1963	Final organisation of Federation of Arabia. Independence of Kenya and Zanzibar.
1964	Rebellion in Zanzibar. Independence of Nyasaland (Malawi).

Index

Abbasids, 48, 51, 229
Aberdeen, 212
Aberdeen White Star Line, 212
Aboukir, 163
Abyssinia, 14, 41, 90, 96, 187. *See
   also* Ethiopia
Acapulco galleon, 99
Achaeminids, the, 26, 44
Achinese, 111
Acila, 38
Acre, 19
Adam, Guillaume d', 94
Addis Ababa, 237
Adélie Land, 249
Aden, 3, 34, 38, 43, 45, 51, 56,
   71, 79, 90, 92, 94, 96, 108, 164,
   189, 199, 215; attacked by Albu-
   querque, 105, 106
Adriatic Sea, 88
Adulis, 33, 37, 41, 43, 45
Aduwa, 211, 237
Afghanistan, 28, 68, 235; nomads of,
   151
Africa, 20, 21, 22, 79, 186; as source
   of slaves, 58; exploration of,
   222–4; map of, 116; Moslems in,
   51–3; relations with India, 70–
   71
Afrika Korps, 238
Afro-Asian Bandung Conference,
   242
Agalega Island, 110

Agatharchides, the, 34
Ajaib al Hind, 55
Akbar (emperor), 73, 142
Akesines (city), 28
Albion, Robert Greenhalgh, 1
Albuquerque, Affonso de, 105, 106,
   152, 159, 188
Aleppo, 88, 108, 126
Alexander III, Pope, 89
Alexander the Great, 25, 28, 29, 32,
   48
Alexandria, Egypt, 29, 33, 34, 93,
   215; as Moslem seat, 88
Alexandria on the Indus, 28
Alexandria Urachosiorum, 28
Ali Bey, 108–9
Almirante Islands, 110
Amboina, 111, 179
Amboina massacre, 123, 136, 160
American Navigation Club, 205
American Neptune, 1, 35
American Revolutionary War, 157,
   158, 161, 176, 184
Amiens, Peace of, 160
Amirante Islands, 110
Amritsar, 236
Amsterdam, 148, 175; merchants of,
   118, 119
Amsterdam Island, 249, 250
Amoy, 196
Andrianampoinimerina (king), 54
Angkor, 58, 64, 65, 66, 67

275